Psychoanalysis and...

Psychoanalysis and...

edited by

Richard Feldstein and Henry Sussman

ROUTLEDGE · New York and London

Published in 1990 by

Routledge
An imprint of Routledge, Chapman and Hall, Inc.
29 West 35 Street
New York, NY 10001

Published in Great Britain by

Routledge
11 New Fetter Lane
London EC4P 4EE

Library of Congress Cataloging in Publication Data

Feldstein, Richard.
  Psychoanalysis and--.

   1. Psychoanalysis--Miscellanea.   I. Sussman, Henry.
II. Title.
RC506.F4   1989   150.19′5   89-10228
ISBN 0-415-90152-9
ISBN 0-415-90153-7 (pbk.)

British Library Cataloguing in Publication Data

Psychoanalysis and -
   1. Psychoanalysis
   I. Feldstein, Richard, 1947-   II. Sussman, Henry
   150.19′5

   ISBN 0-415-90152-9
        0-415-90153-7 (pb)

For E. Tito Cohen

Contents

Introduction

As the profession rides the jet-stream of a post-structuralist crossing, many of us wonder where psychoanalytic theory will situate itself in relation to the changing critical climate. Now that critics are familiar with Lacan's return to Freud, Derrida's economy of *differance* which is irreducible to a metaphysics of presence, Irigaray's critique of "hom(m)o-sexual" mirroring that objectifies women in a system of scopic exchange, and Jameson's historicization of a "political unconscious," many of us find the prospect remote for recovering a psychoanalysis of positivist persuasion that denies the diverse challenges repeatedly posed to it. Gone are the days in this country when psychoanalytic literary critics could turn unproblematically to the classical clinic for support of their claims; few are the attempts to establish a scientific bias based on the law-like repetition of empirically observable phenomena. Instead, we find that lately psychoanalysis has been appropriated in the United States by literary critics whose ties to the clinic, affective and otherwise, are marginal at best. One only has to examine the numerous parodic accounts of the analyst/analysand encounter to determine that many literary critics today view the clinic with suspicion as a site of analytical mastery masquerading as a privileged place of praxis. Add to this scholarly disaffection the recent influence of interdisciplinary studies in this country, and we have a situation in which a hybrid form of psychoanalysis could become decontextualized from the mirror of clinical relations that has customarily supported its claims.

Questions abound when contemplating the linkage of such a psychoanalytic variant to the clinic. For instance, recent psycho-political critics might wonder what is the conjunction between psychoanalytical theorizing and the delivery of a clinical service? Or to what diminished degree can a set of psychological hypotheses and clinical etiquettes predicate a recognizably "normative" interpersonal behavior? These questions shuttle us toward the observation that, although theoretical models do not fully account for what transpires within the therapeutic space, such a "full account" is neither necessary nor desirable. From within some clinical settings, theorizing all too often becomes supplemental to the enterprise of "delivering" treatment; from within the space of criticism, however, actual treatment occupies the marginal position of the supplement. Today, the blanket requirement that literary practitioners of psychoanalytical theory undergo some form of therapy would be viewed by many as absurd in addition to manipulative and intrusive. A pronounced avoidance of psychoanalytical treatment on the part of scholars who invoke it would, on the other hand, be symptomatic, of something. Of what? Of ambivalence toward the theoretical model that so often appears to furnish coherence to literary artifacts that are inherently slippery and evasive? Of a desire to know but also not to know? Of a wish for the stability that a synchronization between mental and textual space would provide?

Still, it would be an overstatement to say that all psychoanalytic critics have rejected the idea that the clinic can be theorized, and, if challenged on the viability of maintaining a link to it, they might ask the following questions. Have literary applications of psychoanalytic theory accounted for those elements of the psychoanalytical encounter not referable to the theoretical approach? Specifically, have they accounted for the set of psychoanalytical manifestations attributable, say, to the spontaneous rapport between the analyst and the analysand, or to the effect of interior decoration or duration of analysis on both of them? Today, many critics ignore such questions as well as the recognition that patients who suffer (and sometimes suffer immensely) seek help from clinicians who are dedicated to providing relief from diagnosed symptoms they attempt to treat. Concerns like these are minimalized by psychoanalytic critics more interested in language, the page, and the textualization of the mind that lends itself to literary production and analysis. It is this gap between the mind and the page that has fascinated recently, a distance small but significant enough to have generated many absorbing questions: are there analogical parallelisms between the spaces of the mind and of reading and writing; if written language sets off associations in a mental space, to what extent does it effect a transfer of mental associations to the page?

But if the concerns of present-day psychoanalytic critics are textually based, they are also directed along the slope of political engagement to expose the cultural bias of proposed theories of the subject and structure. For instance, in "Why Does Freud Giggle When the Women Leave the Room?" Jane Gallop, quoting Jeffrey Mehlman, explains how Freud's joke theory, though structured as "a mythical scene between a man and woman, never takes place except between two men." Tracing Freud's marginalization of women in *Jokes and their Relation to the Unconscious*, Gallop determines that the founder of psychoanalysis denies unsettling difference by constructing his linguistic joke-theory on an analogy to the dream-work, which provides him with a form of "guilty pleasure in this analogical gratification, homological acquisition." While Gallop demonstrates how such theories perpetuate the exchange of women in the "exchange of dirty jokes," Samuel Weber critiques the recent dispute between Jacques-Alain Miller and *APRES* (*Association pour les Recherche et l'Etablissement des Séminaires*). When considering the legal ruling that left Miller as the "testamentary executor and trustee" of Lacan's writings, Weber links the issue of publishing an "authoritative" version of Lacan's work with that of authorial rights, the status of the author, and the subject of the unconscious in Lacanian discourse. While sketching these issues, Weber calls attention to the ambiguity that attends such a judgment if we consider that Lacan "never thought of himself as an 'author' " yet explicitly bequeathed to Miller the right to publish theories which propose that "any statement of authority has no guarantee other than its very enunciation." Weber's psycho-juridical analysis, then, highlights an area of ambiguity or indefinite divide between theory and praxis.

These present-day critical interventions are very different from those of the 1950s and 1960s, when the spokespersons for New Criticism prompted us to limit our focus to decoding the text. Cary Nelson accuses psychoanalytic critics from that period of making a "Faustian bargain with the close reading of the sacralized literary text" in which "larger philosophical, social, political, and epistemological questions would be repressed or deferred in favor of close readings of individual texts or studies of authorial careers." New Criticism, the insularized discourse which dominated entry into the profession, found psychoanalytical insights threatening because psychoanalysis was bound to a "clinical history" that put it "inherently at risk." The result was that psychoanalysis was marginalized even as it was sanctioned by wary professionals who ensured its banishment as the supplement. But with the decline of New Critical influence and the importation of continental theory to the States, psychoanalytic critics joined feminists, Marxists, and others who wrote from the margins in depicting the previously ineffable relation between meaning-making, the interpretative mode, and the fractured, symptomatic critic who was supposed to know.

While psychoanalytic critics of that period were clinicians or literary critics who based their research on clinical findings, theorists today often delimit psychoanalysis to an optics applicable to interdisciplinary perspectives that cut across the curriculum. In the 1980s many critics view psychoanalysis ambivalently, hold it suspect for its partisanship, accountable for its self-enfranchisement. It is a mark of the contentious nature of the current debate in critical theory that most of the psychoanalytic criticism published in prominent journals and literary presses is written by critics as well-versed in feminism, film theory, Marxism, semiotics, and/or deconstruction as in psychoanalysis itself. Moreover, it is to our advantage to have so many critics rethinking psychoanalysis in relation to other methodologies, adding their criticisms of its phallocentrism to those voiced by the French Freudians who have accused the psychoanalytic establishment of harboring such biases. Accordingly, the title of this volume reflects how contemporary psychoanalytical theory could engender psychoanalysis as critique as well as critiques of psychoanalysis, cross-purposed responses which replicate an interesting ambiguity: the title of this volume retains for psychoanalysis the position of the first term while the second vanishes in indefinite ellipsis even as commentators critique such binary juxtapositions by introducing a third term against which the positioning of the first or second terms is reestablished. Consideration of the third term which defies binary divisions alerts us to a fallacy; even if the volume were entitled . . . *and Psychoanalysis*, another term would be required to mark difference. Otherwise we would remain lost in a struggle of positionality, snared in the compartmentalized logic of first/second, master/slave, analyst/analysand.

Such interdisciplinary linkage, however, built upon sometimes conflicting multiple-identifications, encourages ambivalence by critics whom Cary Nelson describes as "not neutral or disinterested; they have consequences for how power is distributed across the theoretical universe." Refusing the role of disinterested spectator, contemporary feminist critics have redefined psychoanalytic theory so that if foregrounds the issue of woman's agency in the social and textual formulations of gender and sexuality. For example, Ruth Salvaggio pursues this line of inquiry when examining Derridean and Lacanian theories in which she says the "feminine operation . . . functions both as a passive 'subject of' and as a more assertive 'speaking subject'—that is, as both object and subject at once." Salvaggio suggests that the use of Derridean and Lacanian models as critical resources enables women to speak "through the agency of a womanly man . . . to reach her own woman" theorists who give voice to feminist issues. Like Irigaray, however, Salvaggio constructs a speaking subject who seeks ways to avoid discipleship—the objectification and commodification of women in a homosocial system of (theoretical) exchange established for and between men. Another feminist psychoanalytic critic in the volume, Jerry Aline Flieger, both tries to delineate herself from those who would concede too much to "the sacred cow of the castration-complex" or "the privileged place of Phallus as a signifier" even as she resists the tendency to fetishize the body as a "new fiction of unified subjectivity." Flieger wishes instead to recast the question, what does woman want, so that women themselves can pose "the question, from the position of speaking subject" rather than in the muted, hysterical gestures of a voiceless speech which Claire Kahane vividly depicts in her study of hysteria in *The Bostonians*. Flieger finally advocates that women demand a " 'full and equal' subjectivity, without undue squeamishness about the terms, stemming from our habit of defining 'full' as exempt from desire and 'equal' as phallic." Through such diverse strategies, then, feminist critics like Salvaggio, Flieger, and Kahane link the constitution of a non-identical, gendered subject of uncertainty to the issue of voicing oneself into agency so that women will no longer be dispossessed by an unconscious logic that has been revealed as alterable.

In *Psychoanalysis and . . .* critics also use Marxist and/or semiotic methodologies to evaluate the applicability of psychoanalytic theory to the study of classed and gendered subjects in historically specific societies. For instance, Andrew Ross argues that identity is a shifting, incomplete, highly problematical construct "composed of multiple subject-positions, articulated differently from moment to moment," which helps to account for Freud's affixing of "un" to the word conscious, whose prefix designates "the shifting articulation of incomplete psychic process." Connecting Freud's concept of psychical division to Lacan's observation that there is a lack in the disjunct subject which causes compensatory desire, Ross shows how these interrelated theories inform Mouffe and Laclau's description of the social as a *"discourse of impossibility"* which is "open, incomplete, and politically unstable, criss-crossed by a plurality of different social logics." Throughout, Ross analyzes the effects of positivism while examining its influence on Freudian and Marxist theories of identity formation which are based on notions of Enlightenment rationality. Slavoj Zizek also provides a psycho-historical critique that supplements an account of the subject's construction in the semiotic order. In his analysis, the subject-of-symbolization functions as an object as well as a subject, creating a split-subjectivity and unsymbolizable excess related to it. Zizek would supplement the semiotic with what in Lacan's words goes "beyond speech without leaving the very effects of language." Zizek notes that in Lacan's later years "far from endorsing any kind of language reduction . . . [he] articulate[d] the difficult modes of the real kernel (*das Ding, objet petit a*) which presents an irreducible obstacle to the movement of symbolization." Zizek's psycho-historical analysis of post-modernism draws attention to the limitations of "textual" modernism, which is preoccupied with a centralized emptiness withheld from the field of representation except through substitutive variations that demonstrate its effects. Post-modernism is rather a mode of proximity that draws us closer to a supposedly beneficent God long celebrated in capitalized Oneness, now seen as *"das Ding*, the atrocious-obscene thing," not shunned or posited in modernism as unrepresentable, but pictured in post-modern overexposure, a metonymic "automovement" which remains baffling to interpretive endeavors because it reveals the all-too-present, unidealized *objet*.

Such multi-determined analyses attest to a theoretical drift which resists representational coherence and the logic of the same. This weave of psycholinguistic strategies is nowhere more noticeable than in those essays which examine the literary text for the establishment and transgression of boundaries within it. In his study of literary subjectivity effects, Joel Fineman shows how the *O* of *O*thello alters our understanding of the Greek verb "ethelō" and its New Testament antecedent, "thelō," which mean " 'wish,' 'want,' 'will,' 'desire,' " "Thelō" is cast by the sound of *O* into the past tense of " 'I wished' or 'I desired,' " as if in recognition of the temporal disjunction that attends desire's evocation of past-tense lack in relation to which it is predicated. Adeptly, Fineman analogizes Iago as "the motivator of Othello, Othello's first cause" when he posits the Moor as a corollary whose double gives voice to "the opposite of Yahweh's self-denomination, 'I am not what I am,' " a verbal trace signifying the invisible relation of zero to " 'one' inhabited by 'none' " which produces a subjectivity effect Fineman describes as distinctly Shakespearean. In an article that traces the muddled boundary of a problematic designation, Ellie Ragland-Sullivan focuses on the stream-of-consciousness fiction of James Joyce, who changed prose styles after *Ulysses* when creating the vertiginous line of *Finnegan's Wake*, which becomes a sign of its own symptomology. Ragland-Sullivan invokes Lacan's phrase "Joyce the Symptom" when examining the intersection of imaginary and symbolic registers to the "impossible *jouissance* of the Real . . .residing on the side of an inarticulable blockage," an unsymbolized knowledge given symptomatic expression by signifiers of the knotted Joycean textual body.

Whether it be Charles Bernheimer's assertion that Virginia Woolf tried to shock her readers to undermine "the esthetic closure her texts simultaneously strive to achieve," or Fineman's blurring of antecedental borders between the Shakespearean and Lacanian subject, or Ragland-Sullivan's tracing of Joycian boundaries that disregard traditional notions of "grammatical structure," all three analyses demonstrate how distinctions are imposed even as they are overwritten. One interesting example of historical overwriting comes from French-speaking Switzerland where a group recently formed the *Cercle Freudian Roman* which established *une clinique littéraire* [a literary clinic] interested in issues like writing and the phantasm, and writing and psychosis in the text. This clinic has experimented by displacing the application of psychoanalysis with a clinical study of literary writings and their rhetorical effects. *Le Cercle Freudian Roman* presents one direction that psychoanalysis has taken recently, a veering off course that leaves us wondering if we are at the near reaches of an inchoate poetics—a post-psychoanalysis which could arise phoenix-like from its disassociation from psychoanalytic orthodoxy, a coda of the unconscious born of its split from the clinic-as-institution. If a post-psychoanalysis were engendered from such division, would it attempt to succeed its point of departure even as it evokes what it seeks to surpass? Or would post-psychoanalysis become just another form of institutionalized discourse, a repetition with a difference presenting the return of the pre/post dichotomy so overworked recently? These questions are difficult to answer from our historical vantage point since it is not easy to determine the nature of the post-psychoanalytic beast, its hour not having come round at last. Rather, like Donald Barthelme's dead father (a post-modern figure of hyphenated uncertainty), post-psychoanalysis still evades the attempt to determine its ontological status, whether it is present or absent, with us or not.

Yet in the crowded theoretical universe of post-structuralist, post-modernist, post-Marxist, and post-feminist criticism, will it be long before a post-psychoanalytic poetics follows in the tradition of enunciating its (dis)relation to the theoretical tradition that proceeded it? If and when this happens, unless post-psychoanalysis imposes itself as a form of foreclosure, it will have to discover a way of distinguishing itself from its predecessor. Ironically, in initiating such a strategy, it would follow in the Freudian tradition, for Freud repeatedly undercut the scientific claims he accumulated to support a theory of the unconscious which overturned the positivist assumptions upon which he had built his dream of scientificity. Similarly, Lacan's analysis of the unconscious subject of desire has led to a bracketing of the "self" in quotation marks and, ironically, to the Derridean assertion that there is no real or subject of psychoanalysis. Would it not be ironic if Lacan's enigmatic theories inadvertently helped to generate a post-psychoanalytic reformation while they remained a point of resistance to such a movement, and for obvious reasons: Lacan, who considered himself a psychoanalyst, not a post-psychoanalyst, staged seminars that, not being originally produced as a written record, withstand attempts to overtextualize the "talking cure." But while most American analysts have turned a deaf ear to Lacan's formulations, literary critics interested in his theories continue to grapple with his perplexing prose line in hopes of sufficient intellectual yield.

It is a cliché of our times, this coextensivity of theoretical approaches and cross-checking of methodological suppositions in light of other theoretical positions. If in the future a post-psychoanalytic project should follow from this trend, it will have to contend with *"le temps pour comprendre"* Lacan's oeuvre, which has appeared in piecemeal fashion. *Psychoanalysis and . . .* supplies examples of critics grappling with this "time for understanding" as well as their resistance to it. While today it is readily apparent that such polyglot analyses are susceptible yet resistant to what Cary Nelson calls the "centrifugal tendency" which influences their "dissemination and incorporation into other discourses," it is considerably more difficult to predict the possibility of a post-psychoanalytic poetics following from these developments. If such a possibility is to become more than a hypothetical consideration, psychoanalysis will hopefully avoid the rush to a priori methodological assumptions and accord a decisive place to its other(s) by inscribing them fundamentally within its deliberations.

Psychoanalysis and Theoretical Criticism

1

Psychoanalysis as an Intervention in Contemporary Theory
Cary Nelson

> As a method based on truth and the demystification of sub-
> jective camouflages, does psychoanalysis display an excessive
> ambition to apply its principles to its own corporation: that is,
> to psychoanalysts' views of their role in relation to the patient,
> their place in intellectual society, their relations with their peers
> and their educational mission?[1]—Jacques Lacan, "The function
> and field of speech and language in Psychoanalysis"

As a question addressed to psychoanalytic interpreters in the humanities
and social sciences, this passage cannot now easily be answered without a
multi-layered sense of irony. For "the demystification of subjective cam-
ouflages" is exactly what people expect of (and fear from) their psychoanalytically committed colleagues but not at all what they are likely to receive.
Nor do psychoanalytic critics in fields like literary studies, art, history, or
sociology display much interest in applying psychoanalytic principles to
analyses of their own disciplinary incorporation. Writing in 1953, Lacan
might himself have expected psychoanalysis within the academic establishment to show some of the same history of volatile self-scrutiny and aggression that had characterized (and would continue to characterize) its clinical
organizations. But this did not come to pass.

I want to talk here about what did come to pass when psychoanalysis, beginning in the 1950s, began to be highly visible in a number of academic
fields. My emphasis will be on literary studies, but the psychodynamics of
the incorporation of psychoanalysis into literature departments resembles in
many respects its history in other fields as well. I am proceeding in this way
in part because I believe this will help us to understand the structural position and political impact of psychoanalytic theory in the current rather fragmented, multiple, and competitive critical scene—both in terms of psychoanalytic theory's most effective interventions and in terms of the issues it
typically avoids confronting.

To understand the place of psychoanalysis in the humanities and social
sciences it is necessary not only to recall the history of the theory's abstract

contributions and its record of textual rereadings but also to recognize and credit the sometimes awkward and ambivalent subject positions occupied by its practitioners. These subject positions are of necessity only partly constituted by the shifting and contested roles psychoanalysis plays in the written work of the profession; they are also constructed by interpersonal dynamics in individual departments across the country. Theory thus also lives through and grows out of the network of historically driven but variable local social relations in which it is inscribed and altered: psychoanalytic bodies encounter non-psychoanalytic bodies in department hallways. The discursive practices of academic disciplines are not in fact always precisely replicated in individual departments, not only because departments may poorly represent (or even intensely resist) the diversity of the discipline but also because many important features of academic life—including negotiations over appointments and curricula—are rarely given detailed scholarly analysis. In all of these struggles psychoanalytic critics can play distinctive roles, roles that end up not only influencing the way they read and interpret the objects formally studied by the discipline but also helping to establish the structural positions psychoanalytic theory can occupy in the current critical scene. Psychoanalytic critics in particular might be expected to be willing to credit the partly social and interpersonal determination of their theoretical positions. Whether they are so inclined, however, it is still appropriate to insist that there is both an intellectual and a social history behind the contemporary moment in psychoanalytic literary studies, rather a longer one than there is for some other bodies of modern literary theory; that history is worth keeping in mind.

For the story I want to tell, then, the 1950s are a good starting point, for it was then that psychoanalysis began to achieve its partial, encrypted institutionalization in literary studies. Acquiescing in New Criticism's growing dominance of literature departments, psychoanalysis had begun to make the same Faustian bargain with the close reading of the sacralized literary text that every radical theory—from Marxism to psychoanalysis to deconstruction, it seems—would come to make upon arriving in the New World. That psychoanalytic critics made these compromises, of course, does not prove their moral weakness; the historical situation at the time gave them little sense that they had any alternatives. Our dismay at what psychoanalysis lost in the process, while a useful intervention now, does not give us much basis to hold people accountable for how they worked out their professional lives during the height of New Criticism. The range of obvious choices now, however, is much wider, and those who still cling to an earlier set of options are appropriately open to criticism.

From the New Critical perspective, the terms of the bargain are these: that the gaze of psychoanalysis would be cast only on the academic profession's agreed objects of study; that larger philosophical, social, political, and epistemological questions would be repressed or deferred in favor of close readings of individual texts or studies of authorial careers; that those texts would remain distinctly privileged in psychoanalytic readings. In many ways, psychoanalysis is still struggling to keep the terms of this contract; thus psychoanalytic critics are still trying to find ways to valorize authorship, rather than view it as the partly involuntary reflection of psychic life. One current solution to this problem—a particularly paradoxical one for psychoanalysis—is to see major authors as uniquely courageous in giving detailed verbal witness to psychic development. Writers in effect become the culture's symbolic representatives in working through the traumatic material of psychic life. Moreover, though their knowledge may be more metaphoric and symbolic than scientifically discursive, more intuitive than conscious, they are taken to be singularly well informed about these matters.

Curiously enough, despite efforts like these, the bargain didn't entirely take—neither in the case of psychoanalysis nor in the case of the other modern philosophies of determination. Or at least the reactionary forces in the literary establishment were canny enough to know, without ever perhaps being either quite willing or able to articulate the knowledge, that psychoanalysis represented a risk that simply taking up the honorific close reading of literary texts would not really ameliorate. The risk was that psychoanalysis would provoke an uncomfortable series of revelations throughout the structures of the institution of literary studies. Not only was the fiction of a transcendent authorial genius in danger; the motives of faculty members in the classroom, the department meeting, and in scholarship itself were vulnerable before psychoanalytic scrutiny.

Read as having distinct but unacknowledged interests and investments, individual scholars could no longer maintain a front of disinterested inquiry. The idealization of literary texts might come to seem a category of psychic and social economy rather than a transcendent value conferred from above. And the institution of literary studies—devoted to securing and promoting these values both in the discipline and in the culture at large—would itself require psychoanalytic scrutiny. Psychoanalysis, in short, opened up the possibility not only of making the psychodynamics of scholarly authorship visible but also of exposing some of the real interests behind the politics of the profession. Whether such motives, once exposed, would be considered illicit, it was clear both that acknowledging their presence might alter the profession's cultural role and that, once acknowledged, their meaning could not be controlled, since their meaning could be substantially altered by a subsequent psychoanalytic reading. No matter that psychoanalytic critics showed little inclination to break the taboo against psychoanalyzing professional behavior. The potential was always there, and the conservative wing of the profession was not about to take the chance of trusting a theoretical position whose clinical history put them inherently at risk.

Psychoanalysis thus achieved an odd but understandable position within academic culture; it was granted a place but that place was to be contained. It was an arcane, self-contained, uneasily obsessional area of research. One might hire an eighteenth-century specialist or a psychoanalytic critic, but their interests were taken to have no necessary points of contact. Indeed, if it was not quite like other areas in English, it would be guardedly treated like one. Individuals could apply its principles to the profession's approved objects of study—literary texts, historical figures—but psychoanalytic insights would not be permitted to permeate literary studies. It was treated as a form of specialization with no necessary general implications for anyone who chose not to learn and adopt its special vocabulary, a particularly ironic and illogical status for a discourse devoted to studying both individual and universal elements of mental life, a discourse inherently applicable to all of human culture. Psychoanalysis in effect remained encapsulated and unintegrated, specifically institutionalized *as* unacceptable, though in particular ways and for particular reasons that are worth recovering, for they are with us still. Indeed, one could argue that the phenomenon is more widespread now that academia has given so many cultural domains a contained and demarcated institutional status. Even within psychoanalysis, however, there are people still living out the structural implications of this history.

Through the 1950s and 1960s in American literary studies psychoanalysis was, I would argue, the preeminent site of theory as rejected other—excluded, contaminating, destabilizing, foreign, irrational, embarrassing, reductive, programmatic, bodily, desacralizing, anti-hierarchical, and self-reflexive. Some, though not all, of these unacceptable (and sometimes contradictory) characteristics were later projected onto structuralism and later onto feminism. Neither psychoanalysis nor structuralism were by any means always able to embody these qualities. But the potential, whether acknowledged or not, was either recognized or suspected, and for a time psychoanalysis filled the role of that internal exile in the academic body politic—the theory to which we could articulate all the qualities we needed to deny in ourselves.

There were other exclusions at the time, to be sure, both material and theoretical, but none so decisively marked *as theoretical* and no others of which the academy was so consciously aware and uneasy. The exclusion of women and Blacks from the canon, for example, was not yet a matter of debate, if thought about at all by the literary establishment. The wholesale rejection of Marxist theory—indeed its virtual repression barely more than a decade after it was a pervasive influence among American intellectuals—reproducing its hysterical rejection in the world of practical politics, also remained largely unthought in American English departments and thus seemed decisive and uninteresting. Had Marxist theory been able at the time to gain a hearing in American literary studies, the structural function of psychoanalysis might have worked out quite differently. The social implications of a psychoanalytic reading of institutional practices would, for example, be less easy to ignore in a politically reflective and self-critical atmosphere. And, of course, if Marxism had been intricately engaged by American literary critics in the 1950s, it could easily have occupied the site of the overtly rejected other. But that was not to be. Yet psychoanalysis, on the other hand, was regularly evident on the margins of literary studies and to it were articulated many of the discipline's anxieties that required boundaries demarcating unacceptable difference and otherness.

This was a time, moreover, when the intellectual and political coherence, integrity, and vitality available in marginalized positions—positions from which critiques of the dominant culture could be mounted—was not yet clearly recognized, so psychoanalytic literary critics generally worked hard to make themselves acceptable, while the discipline routinely rejected even their most compromising accommodations. Now, of course, a marginalized position may choose to preserve its antagonistic sense of difference—as Black and lesbian separatism have—because its critique of the dominant culture requires it to reject offers of integration. Similarly, theory as a whole is now a strong enough counter-tradition to operate partly as an entire alternative model of literary studies. But in the 1950s psychoanalysis was largely alone in occupying the site of special structural unacceptability. (Frye's archetypal criticism, for example, angered a number of critics but never posed the same level of threat as psychoanalysis, in part because he cannily located it as an external other, as a general theory of literature located in a different cultural space with no necessary implications for or challenges to critical or historical writing.)

In the unsuccessful effort to win acceptance, many psychoanalytic critics came to identify with the profession's superego—convincing themselves, say, that the phenomenon of transference had no bearing on their relations with their students or with the authors they analyzed—convincing themselves, in general, that the professional study of literature, uniquely among human activities, was altogether a phenomenon of the conscious mind. This process of re-education—a process by which psychoanalytic writing was separated from self-reflection and self-analysis, a process, one needs to add, to which people at the time probably saw no alternative—helps explain why some psychoanalytic critics now, ironically, find themselves allied with the conservative counterreaction to theory. Happily, this alliance represents only one amongst several competing tendencies in psychoanalytic criticism. The divisions within psychoanalysis, of course, intensified with the translation of Lacan into English, which foregrounded many of the issues academic psychoanalysis had worked for decades to prove irrelevant in the study of literature. That a significant portion of a generation of psychoanalytic critics should find themselves aligned with a wholesale rejection of theory is clearly one of the notable ironies of the contemporary critical scene. The aim, of course, is to gain acceptance or reposition themselves within the center of the discipline by articulating a boundary with a new rejected other. They would position themselves as a trustworthy form of psychoanalysis, properly respectful of the discipline, by casting out their dark, skeptical, theoretical side. Yet the discipline now has no center. Moreover, anti-theoretical psychoanalytic critics will still not be fully accepted by traditional scholars and thus they have nothing to gain from that alliance, but it is apparently easier than self-reflection. It must be said that this final compromise with traditional English studies leaves psychoanalysis altogether disempowered—alienated from its natural allies among the theorists and with no authentically *psychoanalytic* role to play in literary culture. Although that group is now uneasy at the prospect of being marginalized *within* psychoanalysis, one will nevertheless not reach them by, say, displaying the riches of a poststructuralist psychoanalysis. That portion of the generation of the 1950s and 1960s will need instead to come to terms with their own history if they are to see why accommodation of this sort no longer offers anything that psychoanalysis needs.

The conservative elements of the profession, I would like to think, had it right. There was something the academy had to fear from psychoanalysis, despite all the efforts by its practitioners to normalize it to the habitual self-confidence, disciplinary constraints, hierarchical structures, and social and intellectual identity of the profession. Psychoanalytic literary criticism did not, of course, begin with compromise. Indeed what came to be viewed as the reductive or simplistic element in analyses by, say, Freud or Marie Bonaparte—specifically the tendency to see the artifacts of high culture as determined by unconscious forces, as expressive of infantile fantasy—include some of psychoanalysis's more powerful insights. Even the most notoriously reductive element in psychoanalysis—the inclination to read every concave object in a text as a vagina and every convex object as a penis—has an aggressive, deflating politics that is worth preserving, despite the effort many psychoanalytic critics have made to distance themselves from this kind of "vulgar" project. (Like Marxism, psychoanalysis has something to lose in rejecting the "vulgar" portion of its early history.)

But for a long time some psychoanalytic literary critics tried to deliver a very different message—that art was a controlled, managed manipulation of unconscious material, that psychoanalysis would confirm rather than undermine the assumptions of a rational humanism. In effect, despite its foregrounding of citations from Freud, psychoanalytic literary criticism was often in harmony with American ego psychology. "Fiction," Simon Lesser wrote in 1957, "endeavors to gratify as many of our longings as possible, but the very effort to teach us how they can be reconciled with one another and with reality compels it to take cognizance of the ineluctible limits of the human situation."[2] It is perhaps difficult now, in the wake of poststructuralism, to associate psychoanalytic theory with such reassuring bromides, yet this is representative of the discoure of the psychoanalytic pact with literary humanism. Moreover, under the influence of the same cultural pressures that helped promote the growth of American ego psychology—not necessarily under the influence of ego psychology itself—literary critics in fact sought to reassure the discipline on two rather more crucial fronts. The acknowledged, overt disputation was over the nature of literary meaning and the status of literary creativity and authorship. This was, I would argue, a displacement of the real power struggle—over the status of the literary critic and the integrity of the discipline. Literature was not really the issue at all. The problem was less whether the writer of literature was a coherent, fully integrated, conscious human subject than whether the writer of criticism was.

In its rapprochement with New Criticism, or rather its willing self-denial within the constraints that compromise imposed, psychoanalysis supported a view of critical writing wholly at odds with its own theoretical roots. For psychoanalytic critics were implicitly willing to reassure the profession that a critic is not intersubjectively and phantasmatically implicated in his or her own observations, insights, and conclusions about literary texts; that neither the individual nor the social investment of desire—and certainly not the historically specific cultural organization of those investments—is at issue in critical writing; that, most remarkably, one should, as it were, properly remain *quite unchanged* by anything one learned from the psychoanalytic study of literature. Literary criticism would be an activity able simultaneously to strengthen the critic's ego and the existing structures of socialization. Moreover, the discipline's theoretical, social, and political boundaries, with their self-reinforcing idealizations, would remain secure.

Instinctively, the conservative members of the profession have known that none of this can be guaranteed, that psychoanalysis as a body of theory implicitly undermines the restrictive contract it makes with academic disciplines. Through the early 1970s—despite their cooptation by the widespread academic resistance to overt self-reflection within critical writing—psychoanalytic critics were nonetheless marked by the history of psychoanalytic theory with the contaminating possibility of self-knowledge. Indeed, their symbolic witness to the possibility of self-knowledge rendered them distinctly untrustworthy in the eyes of some of their colleagues. Moreover, the contradictory behaviors displayed by people either anxious about or offended by psychoanalysis perfectly captured its ambiguous social status in the profession. Over and over again I overheard faculty members projecting their own ambivalent views of themselves onto colleagues identified with psychoanalysis. Psychoanalytic critics were at once expected to be sources of embarrassing revelations and at the same time thought to be uniquely likely to be the victims of their impulses. Thus I can remember tenure discussions as recent as a decade ago when psychoanalytic critics were thought particularly susceptible to having their objective professional judgment overcome by investments of desire, an anxiety that reactionary faculty members have now, of course, transferred to feminism. People working with psychoanalysis were felt instinctively to be in touch with the instabilities of the psyche, as if departmental decisions might, with their participation, be overrun with primary process thinking. Psychoanalytic critics were needed in departments, it seemed, to provide positions onto which such anxieties as these could be projected. Similarly, the profession has known collectively, if silently, that its disciplinary integrity was inescapably challenged by the universality of psychoanalytic insights into cultural production, this despite psychoanalysis's own long ambivalent history of privileging literary creativity.

What is, in part, interesting about this history is that psychoanalytic literary criticism may now be in a position to begin to make good on some of its own long-suppressed revolutionary potential. There are a number of features of the current critical scene that make this possible, though, again, in no way guaranteed. First of all, in a way that evokes the development of concepts in Freud, no body of theory can now be sustained as a fixed and immutable network of concepts, for different theoretical positions are now multiply reconstituted, rearticulated, and questioned within each other's domains. Like other bodies of theory, such as Marxism, psychoanalysis can no longer maintain and police a wholly separate discursive subculture. Indeed, one can no longer be certain precisely who is (and is not) a psychoanalytic critic. One is not certain what range of discourses and what commitments psychoanalytic criticism entails. This condition is, of course, not unique to psychoanalysis; it is a general feature of our moment in critical history. Marxism is continually in crisis over what discursive and political commitments constitute Marxist criticism and thus over who does and does not fulfill the minimum requirements for being a Marxist critic. More surprisingly, perhaps, it is now possible to recognize that the moment may not be far off when one will be uncertain who is and is not a feminist critic. Certainly there are feminist critics with relatively little textual corpus and virtually no practical politics in common. In the case of Marxism and psychoanalysis, indeed, one hopes only for a shared commitment to the founding texts of Marx and Freud. But there are many feminist and Marxist literary critics with essentially no active commitments to social change. More broadly still, it is now realistic to think of a psychoanalytic, feminist, or Marxist mode of negotiating the whole range of influential theories on the contemporary scene.

For all bodies of theory, there are losses and gains from this condition. There have clearly been benefits from feminist and Marxist efforts to historicize elements of psychoanalytic theory, especially as these efforts foreground the contemporary political and social impact of the theory's efforts to universalize. Psychoanalysis has everything to gain from efforts to revise, extend, and radically rethink its assumptions. At the same time, the confident rejection of everything in psychoanalysis as a mere local historical product needs itself to be read in terms of its own libidinal investments and resistance to self-knowledge. For we will never fix for all time those elements of Freud's work that are and are not merely products of his moment in time.

In order for us to do so, history would need to be decidable and available to us in a way it never will be. To do so, moreover, our own unconscious processes would need to be decidable and available to us in a way they never will be. Nonetheless, at least for now an aggressive and historicizing interrogation of psychoanalytic concepts will probably be a continuing feature of its discursive extension into other bodies of theory.

Like other theories, however, psychoanalysis must partly resist the centrifugal tendency toward its dissemination and incorporation into other discourses. It is not that such processes are illegitimate but rather that they are not neutral or disinterested; they have consequences for how power is distributed across the theoretical universe. Feminism certainly aims in part to reread the culture of theory in terms of sexual difference. And Marxism is implicitly positioned to read the politics of theoretical controversy as part of its totalizing project. Theoretical interchanges, therefore, are not merely instances of enlightened, pluralistic dialogue. However selfless or liberating their will to power may appear to be, they also represent struggles for a degree of cultural hegemony.

I realize, of course, that many people will be uncomfortable with my claim that a desire for mastery is one determining feature of psychoanalysis's relations with contemporary culture. Certainly psychoanalysis is not alone in exhibiting a certain will to power as one element of its articulation in the contemporary scene. Other bodies of theory—from Marxism to feminism to reactionary humanism—hide an impulse to dominate in their explanatory projects. It is also true that the desire for mastery within most of these theories is complicated by other more generous aims—therapeutic, pedagogical, revolutionary, redemptive. Only reactionary humanism, because of its articulation to state power in the United States in the 1980s, has let its will to power take over its cultural interventions. Psychoanalysis, feminism, and Marxism have retained their compensatory investments in promoting self-knowledge. It is also true that no theory, for now, is likely to be able to dominate the contemporary scene. The tendency of psychoanalysis, feminism, and Marxism to challenge and correct one another—while not producing simple liberal diversity—does to some degree operate like an unstable system of checks and balances. But the relative power of these bodies of theory keeps shifting and, in any case, varies considerably across the social field. My argument, then, is that psychoanalysis is in partial retreat and needs to reclaim some of its impulse to mastery. I would not make this argument in every historical context, but it seems pertinent at this historical conjuncture. It is, in effect, the only way psychoanalysis can gain some freedom from its long history of accommodation with American academic institutions, a historical burden Marxism and feminism do not yet have. It may also be the only way psychoanalysis can begin to realize its full potential within contemporary debates.

It is appropriate, therefore, that psychoanalysis more broadly recover what now seems largely lost, except within its Lacanian and post-Lacanian wings—its own will to be the master discourse of theory. This is not an achievable aim, but the will to be the master discourse of theory could empower a kind of future contribution we have not yet seen from psychoanalysis—a psychoanalysis of the politics and rhetoric of theory, of its alliances and disputations, its claims and counter-claims, its marking of differences and similarities. I have in mind that psychoanalytic critics might in turn begin to ask what libidinal investments are at stake when we negotiate the contemporary theoretical terrain. What are the psychodynamics of theoretical debate?

Such analyses would follow an important (though hardly universal) impulse in contemporary theory in not unthinkingly respecting the separation between academic disciplines. It has been clear for many years that the problematics of interpretation cut across disciplinary boundaries, not obliterating them but providing a basis for marking similarities and differences and a ground for cross-disciplinary critique. As psychoanalysis undertakes the comparative study of interpretive practice in various disciplines, however, it is likely to work toward more general theories of the psychodynamics of culture. We will be able to see how successful psychoanalysis is in this project by tracking its influence within the emerging discourses and institutional structures devoted to cultural studies in the United States. Thus the contemporary theoretical scene may empower psychoanalysis to recover its own historic connections with the impulse toward general theories of culture. Particularly in America psychoanalysis has betrayed its deeply and irrevocably metadisciplinary assumptions by rearticulating itself within disciplinary boundaries. Psychoanalysis should properly be the interrogator of the disciplines, not their sycophant.

Yet we need to be clear about what psychoanalysis has gained and lost by way of its idealization of the discplines. One assumes the bargain was for respectability, which psychoanalysis never received, and for institutionalization, which to a degree it did. But these were not the only issues at stake in these negotiations. A deeper issue still is what psychoanalysis actually gave up in the process of accommodating itself to academic specialization in the humanities and social sciences. It is at least worth asking whether these partly unconscious contracts employed disciplinary idealization as a mechanism to aid the repression of psychoanalysis's historic burden of self-reflection and self-critique. To the extent that the Lacanian revolution has helped restore our sense that Freud's texts are exemplary in their practice of problematizing their own claims and interrogating Freud's own place in his inquiry, it is indeed a return to the roots of psychoanalysis. Of course applied Lacanian psychoanalysis can be as unreflective as any other faith. But it can help point to where the challenge of psychoanalysis for the future lies as it intervenes in contemporary theory—in promoting a vertiginous self-knowledge within theoretical debate.[3]

2

Psychoanalysis, Literary Criticism, and the Problem of Authority

Samuel Weber

A few weeks before Christmas, a brief article appeared on the last page of the Parisian daily, *Le Monde*, under the head-line:

JACQUES LACAN
"BELONGS" TO HIS SON-IN-LAW

The text of the story reads as follows:

> On the 11th of December, 1985, the First Chamber of the Paris Civil Court recognized the rights of Jacques-Alain Miller, as the testamentary executor and trustee, [. . .] over the work of Jacques Lacan. J.-A. Miller, Lacan's son-in-law, and the Editions du Seuil, had brought several charges against the association, *APRES*, for publishing a transcribed version of the seminar of Jacques Lacan, on "Transference," in its internal bulletin, *Stécriture*. [. . .]
>
> The Association, *APRES*, is found guilty of copyright violation; the court orders distribution of the bulletin to be stopped, existing copies to be destroyed, and damages to be paid.
>
> It should be noted, however, that the individual members of the association are exonerated of any further responsibility. Moreover, the only part of the sentence to be executed, for the time being, concerns the ban upon distribution: the court leaves it up to the parties involved to decide whether or not to publicize the verdict ["signifier . . . le jugement"]. This decision, therefore, may perhaps not constitute the epilogue of this "murky affair" [cette ténébreuse affaire].

The Balzacian allusion with which the article concludes could hardly have been more pertinent: the "case" of the purloined papers of Jacques Lacan raises the very issue around which the writings of Balzac—but also those of

21

contemporary literary theory in general—incessantly turn: the question of the "rights" of an author and correlatively, that of the status of a "work."[1] It is the importance of this question that makes the Paris case more than merely a "fait divers," more, that is, than what we in English call a "human interest" story. Allow me, therefore, to dwell upon this incident for a moment.

The association APRES: acronym signifying "Association for the Research and Establishment of the Seminars" [Association pour la Recherche et l'Etablissement des Séminaires], was constituted in 1983, two years after the death of Lacan, by researchers and analysts, including many former members of the Ecole Freudienne de Paris, the institution first founded by Lacan, and later dissolved by him, amid general confusion and much protest. The group, as it describes itself, strives "to elaborate a theory of the transition from the spoken to the written work of Lacan." The results of this effort are published in a bulletin which takes its name from a word-play of Lacan: "Stécriture." The group sees the "originality" of its "method" reflected in the production of a "critical apparatus" and of a text, which, unlike the authorized edition of Miller, does not efface the multiplicity of sources that is at its origin. This multiple origin includes: the stenographic record of Lacan's lectures, the notes of his listeners, the many tape recordings that were made, and, last but not least, the various interpretive interventions of the editorial collective itself.

By thus retaining a certain textual plurality, or, if you prefer, a certain intertextuality, in which not merely the speaker, Lacan, is inscribed, but also his listeners and even certain of his readers, *Stécriture* endeavors to produce "a collective version" of the Seminar that is "as close as possible to Lacan."

The question, of coure, here is: just how close is close? Or rather, given thé nature of this particular *case*, just how close is *just* or at least legal? How close can one get to Lacan, without violating French copyright law?—this is the question that the editors, and lawyer, of Stécriture seek to confound, if not to resolve. "Stécriture does not pretend (prétend) 'to publish' Lacan and thus to compete with the Editions du Seuil."[2] But if Stécriture is not publishing "Lacan," what is it publishing under the title, "Transference in its Subjective Disparity, Its putative Situation, its Technical Excursions" [Le Transfert dans sa Disparité Subjective, Sa prétendue situation, ses excursions Techniques]? How, in short, can one publish a text that comes as "close as possible to Lacan" without infringing upon the "droits d'auteur," firmly in the hands of Miller? There is only one possible way: by contesting that there is any "author" at all, at least in this particular case. This is precisely the way taken by Stécriture.

The text from which I have been quoting, entitled "Who is the Author of 'Lacan's' Seminar?," begins by raising precisely this question: "The spoken work constituted by the 'Seminar' of Jacques Lacan poses, in a very particular manner, the question of the 'right of the author.' " Lacan, Stécriture argues, like Foucault, never thought of himself as an "author," once even going so far as to assert that, "contrary to my friend, Lévi-Strauss, I will not leave behind a work." Where there is no work, however, there can be no author, the latter always being defined as the originator or creator of the former. And if there is one issue upon which both Miller and Stécriture agree, it is that "the spoken work constituted by" Lacan's Seminar is not really a work at all, or at least, not the work of an author. Stécriture supports this assertion by referring to the peculiar nature of Lacan's *enseignement*, his "teaching," which, it argues, did nothing less than "put into practice the theory he developed."

One of the decisive tenets of this theory is that the subject receives its message in a more or less distorted (Lacan says: "inverted") form, on the rebound, as it were, from the Other that is constituted by its interlocutors. Given the constitutive importance of such interaction, the oral teaching of Lacan cannot be considered to be the sole of exclusive product or property of an author. (In view of this argument, it is hardly surprising, that the seminar chosen to serve as a test-case of this approach, would be that dealing with the topic of "transference." We will return to this topic later.)

Stécriture might have strengthened this argument, theoretically if not legally, had it cited a passage from the essay entitled, "The Subversion of the Subject and the Dialectics of Desire," which indicates just how complex the issue of authorial rights becomes in a Lacanian perspective. Lacan has been elaborating the significance of what he calls "the paternal function" in the light—or rather, in the chiaroscuro of his "conception of the Other as place of the signifier." He then goes on to describe the kind of legality that derives from this "place":

> Let us set out from the conception of the Other as the place of the signifier. Any statement of authority has no guarantee other than its very enunciation [son énonciation même], and it is vain for it to look for such in another signifier, which in no way would be able to appear outside of this place. This is what we formulate in stating that there is no metalanguage which might be spoken, or, more aphoristically, that there is no Other of the Other. It can only be as an imposter, in order to compensate (pour y suppléer), when the Legislator presents himself in that place, as the one who claims to erect the law.
>
> But not the Law itself, nor whoever assumes its authority (celui qui *s'en autorise*).[3]

Although Alan Sheridan's translation, which I have modified here and there, renders the final phrase of this passage admirably as "whoever assumes its authority," the formulation still requires at least a gloss. For what does it mean to "assume" the authority of a law that necessarily remains without an author? Can we be sure that such a "law" is itself legitimate? What if it were "only" *powerful*, based on a more or less opaque force? Would it still be "legally" binding?

Having thus established the importance, in reading Lacan, of the supposition of an all-knowing subject, Miller goes on to point out that this subject should not be confused with an author:

> Lacan undoes the position of the author as someone who knows what he is saying, such that the dimension of supposition persists, and that in place of truth—to refer to his discourse—there is precisely this supposed knowledge, not the author identical to himself. (64-65)

Although the accent here is placed on the *supposition* of knowledge, rather than on the knowledge itself, it is clear that such a supposition cannot impose itself in a void. If knowledge is to be supposed, and if this supposition is to *impose* itself upon readers, it will have to respect the forms of cognition, even if its contents will prove to be elusive. Miller seeks to describe this by emphasizing the *systematic* character of Lacan's thought. The subject-supposed-to-know articulates itself in Lacan's work not through a refusal or an absence of systematization, but through the tireless transformation of each successive system, in a thought that constantly calls itself into question (44). "I believe that Lacan continually thought against Lacan" (44), Miller remarks, while also acknowledging that such questioning is obscured by the often apodictic, formulaic character of Lacan's affirmations: "The cutting edge of his formulas does not alter the fact that their exact theoretical value depends upon the moment of their enunciation" (46).

Once again, then, we find ourselves back at the problem of "enunciation," the enigma of which is hardly resolved by introducing, as Miller does, the Hegelian notion of "moment." For the movement of the Signifier, unlike that of the Concept, is not circular, its "chain" is no daisy-chain, nor does it spiral towards totality. How "exact" therefore "theoretical value" can be, insofar as it depends upon determinations which in turn are part of an ongoing movement of signification, is a question to which Miller does not reply.

In the meanwhile, to be sure, one reply has been furnished, provisionally, at least, by the First Chamber of the Paris *Tribunal de Grande Instance*. It should be noted that the name of this court is difficult, and perhaps impossible to render adequately in English, first of all, because of the incommensurability of the two legal systems: we have a Small Claims Court, but no Large Claims Court. What is more interesting, however, is the fact that the French appellation contains a term in which precisely the problems we have been discussing are articulated in a highly condensed manner. That term is, of course: *Instance*. The current legal meaning of "jurisdiction" is, etymologically, a "metonymic" or perhaps "metaleptic" product of the more literal notion, derived from *in-stare*, being present, but in the sense of *insisting* and *persisting*. The same word is used by Freud to designate the different and conflicting tendencies of the subject. Although in the English translations of Freud, the term is generally rendered as "agency," this obscures one of its most important aspects, both in psychoanalysis and in its etymological history: the sense of *urgency* that the word once denoted, and that, in some languages, at least, still connotes. In any case, this relation of *Instanz* to the driving forces with which Freud was concerned is conserved in the title of one of Lacan's most seminal texts, *L'instance de la lettre dans l'inconscient ou la raison depuis Freud.* Initially, this text was translated into English as "The Insistence of the Letter," before being reissued, in Sheridan's collection, under the title, *The Agency of the Letter.*[6]

What is suggestive in such speculation, is the possibility that the very judicial "instance," "agency," or institution which decides and pronounces sentence, which applies the law and defends the right of property, might itself turn out to be part and parcel of the insistent pleading that it pretends to resolve. In short: the Court has power, but does it have authority over the Signifier? And if it does, whence does that authority derive its legitimacy? In democratic societies, we are prone to point to the People as the source of such authority: but it remains to be seen in what sense the People, as a collective subject, can claim to dictate the law to language, if all subjectivity only comes to be in and through the movement of signifiers.

The *Tribunal de Grande Instance* delivers its verdict, recognizes rights, and prohibits all reproduction, distribution, exchange, and circulation by Stécriture of its version of the Seminar on "Transference." It also "stays" the execution of its verdict, except for the ban on distribution, pending appeal. "Transference" is thus stopped, provisionally, until an authorized version can be produced. The "law" of language, however, as elaborated by Lacan, and before him by Freud, "knows" no such stoppage. The "overdetermination" of unconscious inscription, as in the dream, both requires interpretation, and at the same time can never be exhausted or rendered fully by any interpretation.

Interpretation thus is construed, and practiced less as a faithful rendition than as a struggle for power, or rather—in the Nietzschean sense of the phrase, as a Wille *zur* Macht, a "will *towards* power." This power is not something that can be "reached," situated in a place that one might hope to occupy (besetzen: "cathect"), once and for all. Rather, it entails a constant struggle which Freud, in the *Interpretation of Dreams* describes as "Selbstüberwindung," *overcoming of Self*, and not, as the Standard Edition would have it, "self-discipline."[7]

To be sure, to the extent to which all interpretive practice necessarily attempts to establish its authority, the distinction between self-discipline and the overcoming of self inevitably becomes blurred; nevertheless, the fact remains that today, psychoanalysis, where it is informed not only by Lacan, but by the more general movement of thought of which Lacan is an eminent participant, but by no means the only one, and which we can call "poststructuralist," for the sake of convenience, to be sure, but also in order to stress a certain filiation, is one of the areas in which the illicit Law of Language struggles to articulate the problematic Right of the Author. Another such area is the study of literature.

This has, of course, been the case ever since the beginnings of Western thought. It is the case that has been made against literature ever since Socrates—or was it Plato?—excluded the poets from his ideal state. They were banished for "forgetting themselves," for allowing themselves to be carried away by their mimetic impulses. In so doing, Plato—or was it Socrates?—argued that they forgot their diegetical obligations, abdicated their authorial responsibilities, and thereby forfeited their palce in the polis.

> "Do you know the first lines of the *Iliad*, in which the poet says that Chryses, implores Agamemnon to release his daughter, and that the king was angry and that Chryses, failing of his request, heaped curses on the Achaean in his prayers to the god?" "I do." "You know then, that [. . .] the poet himself is the speaker [there], and does not even attempt to suggest to us that anyone but himself is speaking. But what follows he delivers as if he himself were Chryses and tries as far as may be to make us feel that not Homer is the speaker, but the priest, an old man. And in this manner he has carried on nearly all the rest of his narration about affairs in Ilion, all that happened in Ithaca, and the entire *Odyssey*." (393a-b)

As the possibility of such "mimetic" narration, poetry poses a danger to the statesmen, the "guardians" who, if they must imitate, "should from childhood on imitate what is appropriate to them" (395c). By "likening himself to another," by speaking with the voice of another, the poet undermines the authority of his discourse. The verdict is ironic, but without appeal:

> If a man [. . .] who by his cunning were capable of assuming every kind of shape and imitating all things should arrive in our city, bringing with himself the poems which he wished to exhibit, we should fall down and worship him as a holy and wondrous and delightful creature, but should say to him that there is no man of that kind among us in our city, nor is it lawful for such a man to arise among us, and we should send him away to another city, after pouring myrrh down over his head and crowning him with fillets of wool . . . (397a-398b)

Reading this passage today, we are liable to react with a certain condescension, as though the irresponsibility of language is no longer a problem for us, schooled as we are on Bakhtin and Barthes, and protected by International Copyright Conventions. Were we to react in this manner, however, we would be pulling the wool over our eyes: the issues that preoccupied Socrates (or was it Plato, who was really speaking?), are still very much with us. To confirm this, we need only reflect for a moment on the importance, in our own writing, on the one hand of quotation marks, and on the other, of proper names, in particular those of authors or of titles. Without the latter, how could we identify "works"; without the former, their meaning? Imagine what would become of our jobs, and of our practice as teachers, scholars, and critics, were we no longer able to rely upon quotation marks to distinguish direct from indirect discourse, or to demarcate the writing of others from that we claim as our own?

For almost a century, reflection upon literature has been occupied, indeed increasingly occupied, with the problem of authoritative discourse: from Henry James and Percy Bullock's thematization of "point of view," to Wimsatt and Beardsley's critique of the "intentional fallacy"; from Bakhtin's polyphonic-dialogic theory of the novel, to Barthes's obituary of the Author and the more cautious, more historical investigation of Foucault,[8] literary practice and theory has grown increasingly suspicious of authorial positions and discourse. Until fairly recently, however, such criticism almost always stopped short of reflecting upon the implications of such suspicions for its own "position" and project, and with good reason. For if the "omniscient narrator" is at best unreliable, and at worst, an illusion, what of the Critic? To what kind of authority can the discourse of criticism legitimately lay claim?

The response most recently in vogue, in this country, of certain "neopragmatist" critics, such as Stanley Fish: is that it is the "community of interpreters" alone which authorizes interpretation. But such an answer merely begs the question it seems to be addressing. Constructing a collective subject to serve as the authoritative instance accomplishes little, if that subject is construed to have the same, self-identical, undivided structure as the individual critic it is meant to supplant. For the divisions with which we are confronted, today no less than in the past, affect "communities" no less than "individuals." The question therefore to be addressed is not just: how does a community constitute itself, but also: what does the notion of community entail? Indeed, if we feel impelled to recur to this notion today, it is because our interpretive practice calls into question the establishment of precisely such "communality." What is involved in interpretation, is not so much the analysis of works, perhaps, as the imposition of meanings, always more or less at the expense of other, competing schemes. Interpretation would therefore address neither the meaning of works, nor even the condition under which such meanings take place, but the very process of "taking place itself," that is: of taking place away from others. The real object of interpretation would be division and conflict, and this would determine its practice as negotiation and strategy.

It is in allowing us to explore the nature of such division and conflict, in its structural, and structuring effects, that psychoanalysis has an important, and probably indispensable contribution to make to current theoretical discussions. In conclusion, then, I will try to indicate briefly wherein one such contribution might consist, and also how it refers us to another kind of text, this time not psychoanalytical, but one situated on the margins of philosophy.

Let us return, then, for a moment, to the problem of *transference*. One of the key terms of psychoanalysis, it is also one of the most enigmatic. The history of its use by Freud is illuminating. In *The Interpretation of Dreams*, the German word, *Übertragung*, is employed by Freud to describe the distortions of the dream-work, which "shifts" from one representation to another in order to accomplish its goal: that of producing a distorted, self-dissimulating fulfillment of a conflictual wish. *Übertragung*, the German word that literally corresponds to the Greek, meta-phore, thus designates both the particular dream-device of "displacement" (Verschiebung), and the more general instability of psychic energy that characterizes the "primary process" and the unconscious. Freud describes this "primary process" in terms of the volatility and mobility of its "cathexes," i.e. the manner in which energy is associated with representations. This he contrasts with the "secondary process," to which he attributes a greater stability: in it, energy is bound up in a more enduring manner to representations, to "intellectual identities," as he calls them, in contrast to the "perceptual identities," which are epitomized in the equivocal imagery of the manifest dream-content.

What is striking, however, is that this opposition of primary and secondary process, of volatile and stable cathexis, does not suffice to account for the phenomenon of transference, which exhibits traits of both processes: as distorted representation, *Übertragung* presupposes the volatile movement, the "carrying over" from one place or thought to another; but at the same time, like "metaphor" itself, it also entails an element of fixity, indeed, of fixation. What is perhaps most significant of all, however, is that these two elements—movement and fixation—do not simply *oppose* one another, as one might expect, but rather converge: the movement of representations is "fixed," and the fixation is in movement. The movement is fixed, arrested, inasmuch as the process of symbolization has come to "rest" in the "manifest" dream-content; but it is also in movement, insofar as that apparently stable content leads us inevitably in multiple directions: "forward," into the future, through the fact that the dream depends upon its belated narration in order to function; it only comes to be the morning after, as it were, in its distorted reproduction; and "backward," towards the infantile complexes that are always more or less at the "origin" of the dream. In this sense, then, the dream does not simply make use of *Übertragung*: it has the structure of an *Übertragung*.

This curious conflict of fixation and mobility, which also entails a form of *repetition*, is what emerges with increasing emphasis in Freud's later use of the term to designate the pivotal mechanism in the analytic situation itself. The analysand, instead of remembering—that is, instead of *representing the past as past*, and hence, as representation, *repeats the past as though it were the present*. The past, instead of being remembered, is reenacted. Again, we are confronted with a movement of repetition that is simultaneously submitted to the constraints of a certain fixation. The differences of the present are ignored and thereby reduced to sameness.

What, however, gives this latter usage of the term "transference" its specific quality, is that its fixation is bound up with the figure of the analyst, who becomes the object of love, hate, or both at once. Freud stresses that transference becomes increasingly intense as the analysis progresses, that is, as the analysand begins to approach, to articulate, and to assume the conflicts of desire involved in neurosis. The projective mechanism of transference is a way of both acknowledging and resisting that development: the split in the subject is bridged, as it were, by an amorous (or antagonistc) relation to the Other, whose rôle in the analysis is played by the analyst. By being treated as the object of erotic passion, this Other is thus made into an Object of love, the reality of which is no longer to be questioned. The Other is no longer analyst, but beloved, no longer agent of the signifier, but quintessential signified. The conflict is no longer *within* the subject, but *between* subjects construed as self-identical egos.

Such transference, Freud emphasizes, poses the greatest dangers to the analytic process, but at the same time is its only chance of success. For only by means of such transferential projection can analyst and analysand hope to "work through" the resistant and conflictual reality of the signifieds of desire in order to reach its signifying passion.

There is every reason to think that something very similar is at work in our dealings with texts, generally, and literary texts in particular. If, at least, by "literary" we mean something akin to what Kant had in mind—and here I come to my second text, on the margins of philosophy—when, in the Preface to the *Critique of Judgment* he noted that it is "primarily in those forms of evaluation, which are called aesthetic" that we find that "embarrassment concerning principles" in which judgment has no universals to fall back on, in its confrontation with the particular case at hand, except perhaps a certain pleasure. Faced with the inexhaustible multiplicity of experience, with an alterity which cannot be subsumed under existing knowledge, what the judging subject does is something not so very different from the analysand, or for that matter from the literary critic: in order to judge, the subject considers the particular thing that confronts it as though it were the product of an "understanding," different from ours, and yet strangely reminiscent of it. Faced with the unknown, what the subject does is to suppose a subject that knows, that comprehends what we do not, because it has produced it according to its knowledge. Through this "assumption" the judging subject seeks to assure itself that the unknown is, at least potentially, knowable.

This, for Kant, is the a priori, transcendental principle of what he calls "reflective judgment": it is "reflective" because, properly understood, it tells us nothing about the object, nothing about the other to be judged, but is only a "law" that the judging subject "gives" to itself, in the process of judging the unknown (that for which no general law or rule is "given"). And it is this that Kant finds at work in that most exemplary case of reflective judgment: aesthetic judgments of taste. Thus, the entire Kantian conception of beauty as "form," as "purposiveness without purpose," depends upon this initial, initiating *assumption*: that of an Author, having produced a Work. However, the fact that this judgment is defined by Kant as "reflexive," also renders that assumption of authority fictional: it applies not to the object, but to the judging subject; it is an "as if." And yet, the status of this as-if, of this assumption, proves difficult to determine in any univocal manner. For what does it entail to assume such an Author, while at the same time "knowing" that it is "only" an analogy, a projection of the knowledge we desire? Can such an assumption, which does not or should not constitute a statement about reality, be "really" assumed, as a pure fiction? Were it recognized to be a pure product of the subject, would it still operate to enable investigation and thus prepare us to discover the missing "universal" law, rule, or concept?

What the psychoanalytic theory of transference suggests, is that such assumptions, or projections, can never be made innocently, or as mere "heuristic devices," for the simple, or rather, for the complex reason that the reason to suspect that it will take more than exposures of the Intentional Fallacy to rid us of its literary correlative, the Authorial assumption. Perhaps what we should try to think about are ways, not so much of escaping from it, as of putting it into play; in this case, however, criticism itself might turn out to have a leading rôle.

3
The Sound of *O* in *Othello*: The Real of the Tragedy of Desire
Joel Fineman

> Thus it follows that in love, it is not the meaning that counts, but rather the sign, as in everything else. In fact, therein lies the whole catastrophe.—Jacques Lacan, *Television*
>
> The sexual impasse exudes the fictions that rationalize the impossible within which it originates. I don't say they are imagined; like Freud, I read in them the invitation to the real that underwrites them.—Jacques Lacan, *Television*
>
> Iago: I must show out a flag and sign of love, Which is indeed but sign. *Othello*, 1.1.156-157
>
> Othello: O, Desdemon dead, Desdemon dead, O, O! *Othello*, 5.2.282

I have two preliminary remarks.[1] First, this paper adapts material from a chapter on *Othello* in a book I am writing called *Shakespeare's Will*.[2] This book builds upon an argument I develop elsewhere, in a different book on Shakespeare's sonnets, whose claim is that in his sonnets Shakespeare introduces into literature an altogether novel, lyric, first-person poetic subject or subjectivity effect, which subsequently becomes, for more or less formal, even formalist, reasons having to do with the history of literary history, the governing and paradigmatic model of subjectivity in literature successive to Shakespeare.[3] In the book I am writing now, I am initially concerned, as a matter of practical literary criticism, with understanding how the lyric, first-person poetic subject of Shakespeare's sonnets informs both the authorial third person of Shakespeare's narrative poems and the formally zero-authorial person immanent in Shakespeare's plays. I am also concerned, however, in this new book, with understanding why the literary formalism to which I have referred possesses its historically documentable power. In my current project, therefore, I am concerned, on the one hand, with formal constraints governing the formation and reception of Shakespearean literary character-ology, on the other, with the connection of the historical, singular, authorial Shakespeare—the one who writes "by me, *William Shakespeare*" when he signs his will—to these more general formal literary exigencies. In short, I am concerned with what relates Shakespeare, the person, a particular and idiosyncratic historical subject, to the literary invention of Shakespearean subjectivity effects; in particular, with how the contingency of the former informs and is informed by what I understand to be the necessity of the latter. This accounts for my interest in what I call, very literally, Shakespeare's "Will," or what I will be calling "The Real of the Tragedy of Desire."

Because this discussion is set within the context of a colloquium on the psychoanalytic work and thought of Jacques Lacan, I will be concerned here mostly with the way language, as theme and performed action, generates in *Othello*, the play, a specifically Shakespearean psychologistic formation marked by what I want to identify as a characteristically Shakesperean signature. I must say in advance, however, that, given the constraints of the context, I will be obliged to do this only perfunctorily and to presuppose almost completely the full-scale reading of *Othello* on which much of my argument depends. Perfunctory, therefore, as my account will be, I nevertheless think it is relevant to the concerns of this colloquium because, insofar as it suggests an explanation for the way, at the level of subjectivity, the particularity of Shakespeare's person is related to Shakespeare's literary personae, it also helps to explain how the uniquely individual and individuated Shakespeare speaks to and founds an institution, the Shakespearean in general. In several respects this is relevant to a colloquium on Lacan, not only because, as I will try to show, there are striking thematic homologies between, on the one hand, the psychoanalytic subject as described by Lacan and, on the other, the characteristically Shakespearean (most especially with regard to a real that can be neither specularized nor represented), but also because these homologies raise the historical question of the relation of psychoanalysis to the institution of literature as such. This allows us to ask whether we should understand Shakespeare as corroborating evidence of Lacanian psychoanalysis or, instead, whether we should understand Lacanian psychoanalysis as epiphenomenal, institutional, and literary consequence of what is characteristically Shakespearean.

Second, still preliminary, I want, before beginning, to note that it was Angus Fletcher who first drew my attention to the sound of *O* in *Othello*, in a graduate seminar in which he remarked the haunting quality of the sound in the play. While it is altogether likely Angus Fletcher will not be altogether persuaded by the explanation I propose to offer of the force of the sound of *O* in *Othello*, I want to acknowledge this particular debt, and, more generally, a larger debt, since the work of Angus Fletcher has very much influenced my thinking about psychoanalysis, literature, and the relation of each of these to the other.

If Shakespeare knew even a little of the little Greek Ben Jonson begrudgingly allowed him ("small Latine & lesse Greeke," says Jonson in his prefatory verse to the *First Folio*), he would most likely have known the Greek verb *ethelō*, which means "wish," "want," "will," "desire," though Shakespeare would more probably have known the word in its *New Testament* form, *thelō*, where the initial epsilon has dropped out.[4] Since Shakespeare appears to have chosen or invented Othello as proper or appropriate proper ◦◦ name for the more or less anonymous "The Moor," whom he reads about in Cinthio's source-story, we are actively entitled to think the semantic field attaching to *ethelō*—"wish," "want," "will," "desire"—identifies the specifically Greek resonance—appropriate to Cyprus, birthplace of Aphrodite, and also the locus of the central action of the play—that *The Tragedy of Othello* calls forth for or from Shakespeare, a nominal speculation further warranted by the fact that Cinthio, at the end of his version of the story, explicitly explains the destiny of Desdemona by reference to the meaning of ◦◦ her name in Greek: *dusdaimon, "the unfortunate."*[5] Accordingly, assuming Shakespeare read a little Greek and also read a little Cinthio—and scholarship speaks for both assumptions—we can say *The Tragedy of Othello*, as it is called in both the Quarto and Folio versions of the play, would have been for Shakespeare, at least in one summary, etymological register, a tragedy of wishing and wanting or, quite literally, *The Tragedy of Will* or *The Tragedy of Desire.*[6] Yet more precisely, if we hear the first *O* of O-thello as some ◦◦ reflection of the Greek augmenting and inflecting prefix, either aorist or imperfect—again assuming Shakespeare would have known the *New Testament*, not the classical, form of the word, i.e., *thelō*, not *ethelō*—we can still translate *The Tragedy of Othello* as *The Tragedy of Will* or *The Tragedy of Desire*, but with the understanding now that both *Will* and *Desire* are here denominated as something in or of the past, "I wish" or "I desire" becoming "I wished" or "I desired" when one adds to its beginning the *e* (ε) or *ē* (η) to *thelō.*[7]

Taking, therefore, this name, Othello, as it is given, at its word, a series of interrelated questions almost immediately arises. First, why is this, for Shakespeare, the proper proper name for the unhappy Moor? Initially, this is a question about Shakespeare, the person, not about the Moor, the tragic hero of the play, and so, paraphrasing Juliet's famous question to Romeo— "What's in a name?" (*RJ*, 2.2.43)—we can ask what is it about *Othello*, the name, or in it, that makes it what we can call, using a technical term, Shakespearean? Second, if it is right to hear a specific semantic field resonating out of or around the name *Othello*—again, "wish," "want," "will," "desire"; and, however playfully he may have done so, Shakespeare certainly elsewhere liked thus to derive connotation out of designation, or perhaps the other way around: e.g., Bottom is an ass in *A Midsummer Night's Dream*, Perdita is lost in *The Winter's Tale*, to take some obvious examples; or, to take some yet more pertinent examples, the ways in which in several sexy sonnets Shakespeare plays upon his own name, Will—why is this semantic field called up by Shakespeare as something in the past?[8] Why, for Shakespeare, is it O-thello and not *thelō*, i.e., why is it *I wished* or *I desired*, and not *I wish* or *I desire*, that is thus sounded out by the temporally inflecting *O* in this Shakespearean name? Finally, or third, both more generally and more particularly, if, for Shakespeare, *Othello* is at once the personal and personalizing name of desire, why is this generically determined as something

tragic, as, specifically, *The* Tragedy *of Othello*? Why, that is, for Shakespeare, is the story of the man named desire a story that is tragic and not,
for example, something pastoral, or comic, or romantic?

Phrased this way, all these questions address themselves to Shakespeare,
the person, and to his quite literal and personal relation to the name and
naming of desire. Yet the same questions may also be raised, and in straightforwardly thematic ways, in relation to Othello—not himself a person, but
the literary representation thereof—since Othello seems to act out his love
story—a characteristically Shakespearean love story of delusional, paranoid,
and mortifying jealousy—as though it were effectively determined by his
registration of his name. If so, what is the relation between these two distinct relations, that of Shakespeare, the person, and that of the Moor, the
literary figuration of a person, to the same name, *Othello*? To begin an answer to this question, which is a question about the relation of an author to
an authorized persona—the relation, therefore, between a historical subject,
whom we call Shakespeare, and, equally historical, one of Shakespeare's
strongest literary subjectivity effects, whom Shakespeare called Othello—I
want to suggest that the lexical issues I have so far mentioned in connection
with *ethelō* are relevant in more than simply thematic ways to two questions
of motivation regularly raised by or addressed to the play: on the one hand,
why is Othello so gullible; on the other, why does Iago do what he does to
Othello?

Since we know Iago is the motivator of Othello, Othello's first cause, we
know also that an answer to the second of these questions is effectively an
answer to the first. But this is precisely why Iago's motivation—the motive
for his actions which are in turn the motive for all other actions in the play—
has always seemed a central problem, one foregrounded by the play insofar
as all Iago's explanations of the reasons for his actions either seem inade-
quate as motives or, instead, to contradict or undercut each other—e.g.,
Iago's resentful disappointment at Cassio's military promotion over himself, or Iago's expressed suspicions, which he himself suspects, that both
Othello and Cassio have cuckolded him, or Iago's stressedly homosexual
envy of the "daily beauty" (5.1.18) in Cassio's life. This enigma attaching
to the motives of Iago was the cue for Coleridge's famous characterization
of Iago's diverse and conflicting rationalizations as "the motive hunting of
motiveless malignity." The phrasing points to the fact that the question of
Iago's motivation has regularly been posed in moral terms, which is why, as
developed Vice-figure, the particular motive for Iago's particular evil is so
readily assimilated to the general motive of generic evil as such. In either
case, however, particular or general, the question of Iago's motivation presents itself as a familiar question about the motive at the origin of evil, a
question about the origin of the energy for originary sin, and the reason why
this question is familiar is because traditional psychology can only understand
desire, that is, that which motivates an action, as an impulse or a pulsion

toward the good.⁹ Speaking very broadly, we can say that for the tradition of philosophical and faculty psychology that extends from Plato to the Renaissance, it is relatively easy to explain the motive for an action by reference to an ultimately instrumental reason that conduces toward the satisfaction of a rational desire. In this tradition there is, therefore, necessarily, a good reason for doing something good, since Reason is the reason for doing anything whatsoever, and, moreover, Reason is, by definition, something good. For this very Reason, however, there can, in principle, be no good reason, and therefore no reason whatsoever, for doing something bad, which is why, for all intents and purposes, that is, as a matter of intentional or purposeful action, we can say that in this tradition there is no such thing as evil. Hence, for example, the familiar ontological definition of evil as the absence or privation of the good, and the corresponding psychological explanation of an agent's evil motivation in terms of either his mistaken or his thwarted movement toward the good.

If we take this tradition seriously, and if we agree Iago is the motivator of Othello's actions in the play, we can begin to understand how and why Othello acquires both his large and at the same time empty grandeur. At the very beginning of the play, Iago explains himself to Roderigo, and does so in terms of his relation to Othello: "I follow him to serve my turn upon him" (1.1.43), "It is as sure as you are Roderigo,/Where I the Moor, I would not be Iago" (1.1.56-57), and, finally, a pregnant phrase, the opposite of Yahweh's self-denomination, "I am not what I am" (1.1.65). Thus defined, Iago presents himself as a being whose being consists in being that which is not what it is, an entity—here we can think either of Jacques-Alain Miller's discussion of the Lacanian zero in Frege or of Shakespeare's arithmetic of *Will* in sonnet 136: "Among a number one is counted none"—that is nonidentical to itself.¹⁰ And it is this principle—"I am not what I am"—a principle of seeming-being—to be *as* not to be—that, we can say, Iago, as complementary opposite of a less complicated Othello, introduces to or into Othello in the course of the play. Given the tight economy of their stipulated relation—"I follow him to serve my turn upon him," "Were I the Moor, I would not be Iago"—we can think if Iago, precisely because he is the motivator of Othello, as the inside of Othello, as a principle of disjunct being—"I am not what I am"—introduced into the smooth and simple existence of an Othello who, at least at the beginning, is, whatever else he is, surely what he is.

It is in this way, through the idea of a "one" inhabited by "none," that we can understand *The Tragedy of Othello* as, specifically, *The Tragedy of Desire*, and at the same time understand how a specifically Shakespearean conception of tragic motivation conduces towards a specific subjectivity effect. The play unfolds so as to show the passage of Othello from being, as Lodovico describes him, and as we see him at the start, "all in all sufficient" (4.1.265)—"Is this the noble Moor whom our full senate/Call all in all sufficient?" (4.1.264-265)—to being, instead, eventually, the empty shell of a hero self-proclaimed by Othello at the end as "That's he that was Othello, here I am" (5.2.284). This evacuating clarification of Othello, most fully realized at this moment when the hero names his name, is what gives Othello his heroic, tragic stature, at the same time, however, as it specifies the way in which Othello, as a tragic hero, is inflated with his loss of self. This subject who speaks, in the third person and in the past tense, of "he that was Othello," is at the same time present, deictic referent of the *I* who tells us "here I am." And yet this *I* who stands and speaks before us can only speak about himself in terms of how he now survives as retrospective aftermath of what was once the "all in all sufficient," as though the name *Othello* only served to warrant or to measure how Othello, now, as speaking I, is absent to the self that bears his name. Speaking, therefore, of himself as *he*, because his I—what Roman Jakobson would call a shifter, what Bertrand Russell would call an egocentric particular—is thus subjectively discrepant to the "Othello" *I* recalls, Othello thus assumes his name only through his registration of his distance from its designated reference. And if it is Iago's *I* to which the play initially accords the paradoxical condition of an entity unequal to itself—"I am not what I am"—then we can see the way in which it is Iago—whom I will now define as *ego*—who leads Othello thus explicitly to speak about—indeed, to name—his structured difference from his own denomination: "That's he that was Othello, here I am not what I am." The image from *The Voyages and Travels of Sir John Mandeville*, a picture of what Othello describes to Desdemona, when he woos her, as "the Cannibals that each other eat,/The Anthropophagi, and men whose heads/Do grow beneath their shoulders" (1.3.143-144), is an illustration of the way this kind of materialized absence of self to itself might be imagined to inhabit or to inhere in the experience of self, thereby generating the substantialized emptiness that motivates and corroborates precisely that psychologistic interiority for which and by means of which Shakespeare's major characters are often singled out. The picture schematically illustrates an anorectic, homophagic economy of subjectifying self-cannibalization, "feed[ing] thy light's flame with self-substantial fuel,/Making a famine where abundance lies," to use the carefully considered language of Shakespeare's very first sonnet.[11]

I have elsewhere argued that Shakespeare is not only responsible for first introducing this kind of literary subject, compact of its own loss, into literary history, but that the literary features through which this Shakespearean subject is constructed and imagined are, for more or less formal reasons, strictly circumscribed.[12] Summarizing that claim very briefly, I have argued that Shakespeare writes at the end of a tradition that identifies the literary, and therefore literary language, with idealizing, visionary praise, a tradition in which there is, at least figuratively speaking, an ideal Cratylitic correspondence, usually figured through motifs of visual or visionary language, between that which is spoken and that which is spoken about. Registering the conclusion of this tradition of the poetry of praise, a tradition that reaches back to the invention of the "literary" as a coherent theoretical category, Shakespeare, *to be* literary, is obliged to recharacterize language as something duplicitously and equivocally verbal rather than something truthfully and univocally visual, and, as a consequence, Shakespeare is both enabled and constrained to develop novel literary subjects of verbal representation for whom the very speaking of language is what serves to cut them off from their ideal and visionary presence to themselves. More clearly and starkly than any other Shakespearean tragedy, *Othello*, the play, is organized or thought through precisely such a large disrupting and disjunctive thematic opposition between visionary presence and verbal representation, not only when Iago determines, as he puts it, "to abuse Othello's ear" (2.1.385), or to "pour this pestilence into his ear" (2.3.356)—and such poisoning through the ear is of course a Shakespearean commonplace; think of Hamlet's father—but, more generally, in Iago's plot to substitute for the "ocular proof" (3.33.360) Othello demands—"I'll see before I doubt" (3.3.190)—the indicators or the signifiers whose "imputation and strong circumstances . . . lead," Iago falsely says, "directly to the door of truth" (3.3.406-407).[13] Because, as Iago explains to Othello, there are things, especially sexual things, "It is impossible you should see" (3.3.403), Othello will receive instead the signs—like the misplaced, fetishistic handkerchief, ornamented with aphrodisiacal strawberries—which, conceived and conceited as something verbal, "speak against her with the other proofs" (3.3.441). We can say, speaking very abstractly, that this arrival of the specifically and corruptingly linguistic—through the instrument of Iago—is what determines the details of Othello's destiny as well as the two morals of the play, summarized at the end, after Othello's suicide, as, on the one hand, "All that is spoke is marr'd" (5.2.357), and, on the other, "The object poisons sight,/Let it be hid" (5.2.364-365). So too, we can also say, speaking formally, that it is only to the extent the play manages to make its own language perform, as does the Liar's paradox, the truth of its own falseness, that Othello, as the representation of a person, exudes a powerfully psychologistic subjectivity effect.

This performative aspect of the play's language accounts for my concern with the sound of *O* in *Othello*, for I understand the sound of *O* in *Othello* both to occasion and to objectify in language Othello's hollow self. Thus it is that the line I took as one of my epigraphs—Othello's "O, Desdemon dead, Desdemon dead,/O, O!" (5.2.282)—is not only the conclusion of Othello's discovery of Iago's plot, but is also immediate preface to the line in which Othello names his absence to himself "That's he that was Othello, here I am" (5.2.284). In some respects, my insistence on the importance and significance of this sound is not a novel claim. Frank Kermode, for example, in his introduction to the *Riverside* edition of the play, makes something like, or almost like, this point when he says: "*Othello* no less than the other great tragedies invents its own idiom. The voice of the Moor has its own orotundity, verging, as some infer, on hollowness.''[14] Yet if we initially agree that what Kermode calls Othello's "hollowness" is materialized in the sound of *O*, it is important also to realize that this peculiar voicing is sounded out throughout the entirety of the play, that is, that *Othello's O* is by no means restricted to Othello's mouth. We hear it, for example, in almost all the names of the character—Brabanti*o*, Gratian*o*, Lodovic*o*, Othell*o*, Cassi*o*, Iag*o*, Roderig*o*, Montan*o*, Desdem*o*na; again, most of these so-called by Shakespeare—and so, too, is it evoked or invoked as a continual refrain, often metrically stressed, throughout the dialogue, for example, these lines from Act 5, Scene 1:

> *Iago:*   *O* treacherous villains! What are you there? Come in and give some
>   help.
> *Roderigo:*   *O* help me there!
> *Cassio:*   That's one of them.
> *Iago:*   *O* murd'rous slave! *O* villain!
> *Roderigo:*   *O* dam'd Iago! *O* inhuman dog! (5.1.57-63)

or, a few lines later:

> *Bianca:*   What is the matter h*o*? . . .
>   *O* my dear Cassi*o*, my sweet Cassi*o*!
>   *O* Cassi*o*, Cassi*o*, Cassi*o*!
> *Iago:*   *O* notable strumpet! Cassi*o*, May you suspect
>   Who they should be that have thus mangled you?
> *Cassio:*   N*o*.
> *Gratiano:*   I am sorry to find you thus; I have been to seek you.
> *Iago:*   Lend me a garter. S*o*.—*O* for a chair
>   To bear him easily hence!
> *Bianca:*   Alas he faints! *O* Cassi*o*, Cassi*o*, Cassi*o*! (5.1.74-84)

These are representative examples, which could be multiplied, of the way the sound of *O* is sounded out throughout the entirety of the play, and not just by Othello.

Why is it, then, that this sound—these abject *O*s, which I will soon want to associate with Lacan's *objet a*, that is, what for Lacan is the occasion of desire and the mark of the real—is, both for Shakespeare and for Othello, constitutive of Othello's self? This is a more precise way of asking the questions I asked earlier as to why, for either Shakespeare or Othello, Othello's tragic passage into empty, retrospective self occurs at the climactic moment when the hero names his name? In search of an answer, I want now to turn to some of Lacan's remarks concerning proper names, beginning with what is perhaps the most well known of these, the passage in "The Subversion of the Subject and the Dialectic of Desire in the Freudian Unconscious," where Lacan explains the relation of a subject to a signifier:

> My definition of signifier (there is no other) is as follows: a signifier is that which represents the subject for another signifier. This signifier will therefore be the

signifier for which all the other signifiers represent the subject: that is to say, in the absence of this signifier, all the other signifiers represent nothing, since nothing is represented only *for* something else.[15]

Lacan speaks here, more or less straightforwardly, of the way, as he understands it, the speaking subject is constitutively precipitated, as ruptured or as broken subject, as an effect of the language in which he finds himself bespoken—and no more so self-evidently than when this subject speaks explicitly about himself. For Lacan, as he explains in this section of "The Subversion of the Subject," the subject comes to be a subject through his dialectical relation to a generalized Other conceived to contain or to comprise, like a thesaurus or treasury, the entirety of signifiers that for one single and particular signifier represent the subject. This unique and distinct signifier— distinct because within the treasury of signifiers in the locus of the Other, it represents the subject for another signifier, indeed, for *any* and for *every* other signifier—is at once the mark of the totality of language for the speaking subject and of the totality of the subject thus bespoken. In either case, however, speaking either of the subject or of the Other, the entirety thus marked as something total is for that very reason lacking that which marks it as complete. Lacan explains:

> Since the battery of signifiers, as such, is by that very fact complete [what Shakespeare would call "all in all sufficient"], this signifier [i.e., that which represents the subject for another signifier] can only be a line (*trait*) that is drawn from its circle without being able to be counted part of it. It can be symbolized by the inherence of a (—1) in the whole set of signifiers. As such it is inexpressible, but its operation is not inexpressible, for it is that which is produced whenever a proper name (*nom propre*) is spoken (*prononcé*). Its statement (*énoncé*) equals its signification. ("Subversion of the Subject," pp. 316-317)

It may seem odd, a kind of vestigial Cratylism, for Lacan to say of the operation of the proper name that its statement equals its signification, but this is because, for the subject, the paradoxical statement of the proper name, like the Liar's paradox, is that its statement is *not* equal to its signification. We can say that this is the *only* statement language can speak truly to and for a subject. Hence the precision, which is only slightly comic, of Lacan's algebraic formulation of the signification, for the subject, of the signifier that represents him for another signifier:

$$\frac{S \text{ (signifier)}}{s \text{ (signified)}} = s \text{ (the statement), with } S = (-1), \text{ produces } s = \sqrt{-1}$$

where the signifier, understood as minus one, is to be divided by the signified it equals, which is therefore also understood as minus one, yielding as the product of division the imaginary but still useful number we have learned to call the square root of minus one ("Subversion of the Subject," p. 317). Lacan immediately explains what this means for the subject: "This [i.e., the

√—1] is what the subject lacks in order to think himself exhausted by his *cogito*, namely, that which is unthinkable for him" ("Subversion of the Subject," p. 317).

This lack in the subject—on the one hand, unthinkable for the subject; on the other, responsible for His (his/her) constitution *as* subject, specifically, as a desiring subject—is, at least in this formulation, occasioned by the subject's registration of His (his/her) proper name, the *trait unaire*, as Lacan explains in "The Subversion of the Subject," "which, by filling in the invisible mark that the subject derives from the signifier, alienates this subject in the primary identification that forms the ego ideal" (p. 306). This alienation is a function, Lacan says, of "the relation of the subject to the signifier—a relation that is embodied in an enunciation whose being trembles with the vacillation that comes back to it from its own statement" (p. 300); "An enunciation that denounces itself, a statement that renounces itself, ignorance that dissipates itself, an opportunity that loses itself, the trace of what *must* be in order to fall from being?" (p. 300). And this fall therefore determines, Lacan says, the being of the subject, determines it as "Being of non-being, that is how *I* as subject comes on the scene, conjugated with the double aporia of a true survival that is abolished by knowledge of itself, and by a discourse in which it is death that sustains existence" (p. 300). Or, to cite one of Lacan's many glosses of Freud's "*Wo es war, soll Ich werden*," but which might equally well serve to gloss the temporal structuration of "That's he that was Othello, here I am," *not* what *The Standard Edition* translates as "where id was there shall ego be," but, instead, and more Shakespearean, "There where it was just now, there where it was for awhile, between an extinction that is still glowing and a birth that is retarded, 'I' can come into being and disappear from what I say" (p. 300).

Lacan always, by no means only in "The Subversion of the Subject," returns to this necessary lack, gap, absence, disjunction, hole, determined for the subject by the very registration or denomination of the all, the complete, the total, the one, the whole, in which the subject finds himself, and therefore finds himself as lost. Elsewhere, in the *Seminar on Identification* (1961-1962), Lacan develops the same point, again in connection with proper names and the unitary trait, in terms of the paradox of classes with which Russell confounded Frege.[16] Lacan uses the diagram of an inverted figure-eight to

$$\Sigma^B \text{ ensemblesqui se comprennent eux-mêmes}$$

$$\int B \text{ ensemblesqui ne se comprennent pas eux-mêmes}$$

schéma

illustrate the paradox that results when one asks, as inevitably one must, whether the class of classes that do not contain themselves is itself contained in the class of classes that do not contain themselves.[17] If so, then it is contained in the class of classes that do not contain themselves, which is paradoxical, and, if not, then we come upon an analogous impasse. We can note the way Lacan's inverted figure-eight reproduces the structure of subjective inversion imaged by the Mandeville drawing of "the men whose heads do grow beneath their shoulders"—the circle within and without that which it circles—an inversion Lacan explains in terms of a redoubling, or turn, or return, by means of which, in Russell's paradox, the interiority of the inside is rendered homogeneous with the exteriority of the outside in a systematically aporetic way.[18] Between the one and the other, between, that is, an inside and an outside that are both turned inside out, stands the tangential, placeless, auto-differential mark that is neither the one nor the other, but, instead, the lack in both that derives from their disjunctive conjunction, the same lack that is disclosed, Lacan says in the *Seminar on Identification*, by the fact that "a signifier, insofar as it might serve to signify itself, is obliged to pose itself as different from itself."[19]

This determination of the auto-differential mark—which Lacan alternately develops in terms of the post-Cartesian difference between the subject who speaks and the subject who is bespoken, or in terms of the difference between the subject of the signifier and the subject of the signified, or in terms of the desire precipitated by the infinite discrepancy between finite need and infinite demand, or in terms of the fading of the subject in the intersubjective dialectic between the intersaid (*interdit*) and the intra-said (*intradit*), or in terms of the disjunctive intersection of the imaginary and the symbolic (I say in passing that all this can be directly related to the by now familiar quarrel in Anglo-American philosophy between discriptivist and causal-chain theorists of proper names)—is for Lacan the mark of the real: "the cut in discourse, the strongest being that which acts as a bar between the signifier and the signified" ("Subversion of the Subject," p. 299). As Lacan puts it in "The Subversion of the Subject": "This cut in the signifying chain alone verifies the structure of the subject as discontinuity in the real" (p. 299). And it is around this cut, experienced *as* cut, that the subject finds the motivating lack around which his desire circulates in a structurally asymptotic and vain effort to plug up the hole within the w-hole that is its on-going, constituting cause, as does Othello, when, entering the bedroom to strangle Desdemona, he explains: "It is the cause, it is the cause, my soul;/Let me not name it to you, you chaste stars,/It is the cause. Yet I'll not shed her blood,/Nor scar that whiter skin of hers than snow,/And smooth as monumental alabaster" (5.1.1-3). On the one hand, the mark of this cut determines what is erotic in the so-called "erogenous zone": "the result of a cut (*coupure*) expressed in the anatomical mark (*trait*) of a margin or border— lips, 'the enclosure of the teeth,' the rim of the anus, the tip of the penis, the vagina, the slit formed by the eyelids, even the horn-shaped aperture of the ear" ("Subversion of the Subject," pp. 314-315); on the other, "this mark of the cut is present in the object described by analytic theory: the mamilla, faeces, the phallus ([as] imaginary object), the urinary flow." (An unthinkable list, if one adds, as I do, the phoneme, the gaze, the voice, the nothing) ("Subversion of the Subject," p. 315). And so, too, says Lacan, is this the " 'stuff,' or rather the lining . . . of the very subject that one takes to be the subject of consciousness. For this subject, who thinks he can accede to himself by designating himself in the statement, is no more than such an object" ("Subversion of the Subject," p. 315). It is for this reason, also, that I associate the sound of *O* in *Othello*, insofar as this is sounded out as mark of a subjectifying name, with the mark of the real, the *objet a*, that occasions desire in the first place, as well as its subjective temporality as aftermath, also in the first place.

But what kind of desire is this, really? Lacan, though he says it elsewhere, offers an answer in *Television* when he says, stressing the banality of the observation that "there is no sexual relation," that is, that there is no sexual rapport, by which he means, at the very least, that the ideal unity of two is precisely that which forecloses the possibility of union, thereby provoking a desire for precisely that which it prevents.[20] The topos brings us back to Othello, the representation of a person, and through him back to Shakespeare, the person.

It is often remarked that Othello's jealousy is necessarily delusional, for, given the compressed and double time-scheme of the play, there is literally no time for Cassio to have cuckolded Othello. It is not so often noticed, however, that, for the same reason, there is no time in the play for Othello ever to have consummated his marriage to Desdemona.[21] What should have been the lovers' first married night together, in Venice—in Venus—is interrupted by the announcement of the Turkish threat, whereupon Othello and Desdemona both set out for Cyprus in separate ships. In Cyprus, the postponed honeymoon night is once again delayed and interrupted by Cassio's noisy, drunken riot, and the interruption occurs at precisely that moment when Iago says, "the General hath not yet made wanton the night with" Desdemona (2.3.16). Affectively, that is to say, Othello never consummates his marriage until the climactic moment in which he strangles Desdemona, when the marriage bed, in characteristically Shakespearean fashion, becomes the death bed. This consistent instantiation of Othello's *coitus interruptus*, an interruption specifically signaled by noise, is emblematized in a small scene, often cut in production, in which some wind musicians, at Cassio's behest, come on stage to serenade Othello and Desdemona from beneath their bedroom window. No sooner do they start to play, however, than Othello's clown comes out to tell them to be silent: "The General so likes your music, that he desires you for love's sake to make no more noise with it"

(3.1.11-12). Instead, says the Clown, "If you have any music that may not be heard, to't again," but, if not, "Go, vanish into air, away!" (3.1.15-16).[22]

I stress the emblematic significance of this scene because I take its evoked "music without sound" to be a definition, "for love's sake," of the sound of *O* in *Othello*. And the reason why this seems important is that this "music without sound" returns again to the play, and does so in a passage that, for purely vocal reasons, has always seemed, to critics and to audiences, profoundly strange and haunting. I refer to Desdemona's "Willow Song," which she sings just prior to her murder and where even the "wind" of the wind musicians reenters the diegesis of the play, and reenters it again *as* interruption:

> *Desdemona.* "The poor fool sat sighing by a sycamore tree,
> Sing all a green willow;
> Her hand on her bosom, her head on her knee,
> Sing willow, willow, willow.
> The fresh streams ran by her, and murmur'd her moans,
> Sing willow, willow, willow;
> Her salt tears fell from her, and soft'ned the stones,
> Sing willow"—
> Lay by these—
> [Signing.] "—willow, willow"—
> Prithee hie thee; he'll come anon—
> [Singing.]
> "Sing all a green willow must be my garland.
> Let nobody blame him, his scorn I approve"—
> Nay, that's not next. Hark, who is't that knocks?
> *Emilia.* It's the wind.
> *Desdemona.* [Singing]
> "I call'd my love false love; but what said he then?
> Sing willow, willow, willow;
> If I court moe women, you'll couch with moe men."—
> So get thee gone, good night. Mine eyes do itch;
> Doth that bode weeping?
> *Emilia.* 'Tis neither here nore there.
> *Desdemona.* I have heard it said so. (4.3.40-60)

The central, we can say the most Shakespearean, fact about this "Willow song" is that it is *not* by Shakespeare, and would have been recognized as such, i.e., as non-Shakespearean, by the original audience for the play.[23] What is called Desdemona's "Willow Song" is, in fact, a traditional ballad, reproduced in miscellanies, that appears to have captured Shakespeare's aural imagination—inspired him, we can say, thinking of the wind—and which he here introduces into the play as though to sound out something that comes from a literary place outside the literariness of the play. Recognizing this, my claim is a simple one, but one with several consequences: namely, that the "willow" of Desdemona's "Willow Song" amounts to Shakespeare's literal and personal translation of the Greek verb *ethelō*, and that this is a significant translation because Desdemona's "Willow Song," understood in this way, therefore marks the place where Shakespeare's own name, Will, is itself marked off by the invoked, cited sound of the sound of *O* in *Othello*—"Sing will-ow, will-ow, will-ow." If this is the case, then we can say, at least in this case, precisely what there is in a Shakespearean name that makes it Shakespearean. It is specifically the *O*, calling to us from an elsewhere that is other, that determines the Shakespearean subject as the difference between the subject of a name and the subject of full being, or, even more precisely, as the subject who exists as the difference between the *Will* at the beginning of Will-iam and the *I* of Williams's *I am: Will-O-I am.*[24]

In Desdemona's "Willow Song," therefore, we can say the real of the subject of Shakespeare enters the play, informing with the force of its contingency the otherwise merely formal literary exigencies with which and through which the subjectivity effect of the hero is constructed. And this is important because we can thereby account for the powerful investment, specifically at the level of subjectivity, of both author and audience in the character of Othello, for in both cases what is necessarily and structurally at stake in the representation of a persona whose subjective evacuation is substantiated by the sound of *O* in *Othello* is the way in which, in the words of Lacan that I took as epigraph, "The sexual impasse exudes the fictions that rationalize the impossible within which it originates." For both author and audience these fictions—what I will elsewhere call the "alibi" (*alius ibi*, i.e., the elsewhere) of subjectivity—really are "the invitation to the real that underwrites them," but of a specifically Shakespearean real, the willful legacy of which continues to determine, as the example of Lacan makes evident, not only the erotic contents but also the tragic contours of the literature of person. Hence the concluding answer I propose to the question I raised earlier as to whether we should see in Othello and Shakespeare the corroborating proof or evidence of Lacan's theorizations about subjectivity or, instead, whether we should see in Lacan's theorizations an epiphenomenal consequence of the powerful literary subjectivity effect Shakespeare invents toward the end of the English Renaissance: given the historical force of the sound of *O* in *Othello*, I say the latter and call him, Lacan, Shakespearean.

Psychoanalysis and Feminism

4

Why Does Freud Giggle
When the Women
Leave the Room?

Jane Gallop

There is something funny going on in Freud's work, *Jokes and their Relation to the Unconscious (Der Witz)*.[1] This strange business and its relation to women was signaled to me by an article in *New Literary History* (Winter, 1975), in which Jeffrey Mehlman pursues an analogy between Freud's joke theory and sexual theory, by following Freud's mythical genesis of the sexual joke.

Although for Freud and his peers ("The higher social levels," "Society of a more refined education" pp. 99-100) dirty jokes are not told in the presence of women, Freud posits that this exchange between men has its origin in smut uttered by man in order to seduce a woman. If the woman resists seduction, the sexually-exciting speech itself becomes the aim. Freud writes that "the ideal case of a resistance of this kind . . . occurs if another man is present at the same time—a third person." This third person (specified by Freud as another man, not another woman) becomes of "the greatest importance" (p. 99). The joke is addressed to the other man, and can even go on quite well in the woman's absence. This marginally-derived case ("Can go on in the woman's absence") returns us to precisely the context of sexual jokes as Freud knows them. In fact, not only are sexual jokes not told to women at the "higher social levels," but what goes on at lower levels is elsewhere characterised by Freud as smut or jests, and not jokes proper. So the sexual joke which originates in a mythical scene between a man and a woman, never takes place except between two men.[2]

Mehlman's analysis goes on to derive a structural model of this transference from the woman (second person) to another man (third person), comparing it to the Oedipal triangle: the structural Oedipus, the child's loss of

49

the imaginary one-to-one relation to the object (mother) upon the child's insertion into the circuit of exchange, into the symbolic order of the Name-of-the-Father. That intrusive third term is simply the Law: that is, the structural necessity of the irremediable loss of the original, mythic, pre-Oedipal object. So we see that Freud's jokebook contains the very dynamics which French Freudians, specifically Jacques Lacan and Jean Laplanche, have outlined as insistent/persistent in Freud. At the end of the article, there is a fleeting moment of regret for a certain lost object as Mehlman writes: "For it will be seen that the further we pursued our analysis of *Der Witz*, the more did the apparent object of Freud's analysis—jokes—disappear. Like the woman—the second person—in Freud's paradigm of the joke. I confess that this homology between Freud's model and our own undertaking strikes me as sufficient consolation for that loss."

The woman is lost, but the man consoled. Rather than a woman, he has a homology. The second person, the other sex, has been irretrievably lost. But no matter, it was worth it to gain a sameness, to find an identification (with the father, Freud/Lacan/Laplanche). The Oedipus is good: one loses the mother, but gains the Father's Name, entry into the world, into the exchange between men—Lévi Strauss's exchange of women, Freud's exchange of dirty jokes. The Oedipus is good, for the man. He escapes from his difference with the resistant, other sex into the world of homologies; man's economy.[3]

Mehlman is not the only one in pursuit of an analogy. Freud's articulation of the mechanisms of jokes is based on an analogy (*Analogie*) he discovers between joke-work and dream-work. There seems to be some guilty pleasure in this analogical gratification, homological acquisition. For Freud, analogy is dangerously seductive: "Shall we not *yield to the temptation* to construct [the formation of a joke] on the analogy of the formation of a dream?" (p. 195, my emphasis). He repeatedly defends himself against the imagined complaint that "under the influence of the model" he is abusing the material, "looking only for techniques of joking which fitted in with it, while others would have proved that this conformity (*übereinstimmung*) is not invariably present" (p. 167). Freud works to fend off the suspicion that he excludes otherness, difference, in pursuit of an analogy, a conformity.

In speaking of the similarity between the jokework and the dreamwork, he alternates between the two terms *Analogie* and *übereinstimmung*. The latter term reappears in the explanation of how the teller of the joke (the first person) can give pleasure to the hearer (always referred to as the third person, although he corresponds to the grammatical second person, whereas the joke's second person is generally absent). In order for the joke to work there must be psychical accord (*übereinstimmung*) between the first and third person. Rather than tell a joke to a woman, who would resist, not be in agreement (*übereinstimmung*), not be analogous, the man tells it to another man.

Analogy (in this case a translation of *Gleichnis*, from *gleich* meaning same, equal) is the last technique considered in the chapter on the technique of jokes (chapter II). The section on analogies begins with an apology; Freud is not certain that analogies ever are really jokes, rather than merely comic. But he nonetheless pursues this dubious section, citing various uncertain examples of joking analogies. The last one is a lengthy quotation which Freud attributes to Heinrich Heine's *Bäder von Lucca*. (*The Baths of Lucca*). After that analogy, he declares, "In the face of this . . . example, we can no longer dispute the fact that an analogy can in itself possess the characteristic of being a joke." (p. 87) Analogy (elsewhere seductive and guilty, here dubious and equivocal) has been justified, doubt dispelled. However . . . the paragraph Freud quotes is not to be found in the *Bäder von Lucca*.

This doubtful Heine *Gleichnis* ends chapter II, which many, many jokes earlier began with another joke from the *Bader von Lucca* (this one correctly attributed). Hirsch-Hyacinth, a character in the *Bader von Lucca* says: "I sat beside Salomon Rothschild and he treated me quite as his equal, quite famillionairely" (*ganz wie seinesgleichen, ganz familionär*—"equal" here translates the word *gleich*, as in *Gleichnis*).[4] Freud "reduces" this joke to the meaning: "Rothschild treated me quite as an equal, quite familiarly, that is, so far as a millionaire can." This joke about an apparent equality, an apparent analogy between two men with undertones of humiliation for one of them allows Freud to explain the process of condensation in jokes. Because there are similarities between familiar and millionaire, because there is conformity, en entire thought—"that is, so far as a millionaire can"—is reduced to a small change in a word, an addition of one syllable. The joke about a certain humiliation underlying the relation between likes (*gleichen*) reveals itself as a condensation, a technique in which one thought can be subordinated by another (humiliated, so to speak) because of a conformity.

The famillionairely joke is capital in this book. It is the first joke of the book, the only example in the first chapter. Freud makes his first return to this joke in chapter II, where he begins: "Let us follow up a lead presented us by chance" (p. 16)—chance translates the word *Zufall*. There follows the lengthy explanation of the mechanism of this joke, summarized above. Freud returns to the joke again in chapter V: "It is a remarkable coincidence that precisely the example of the joke on which we began our investigations of the technique of jokes also gives us a glimpse into the subjective determinants of jokes" (p. 140). "It is a remarkable coincidence" translates "ganz zufällig trifft es sich"—*zufällig* is the adectival form of *Zufall*, the word for "chance" in chapter II. The emphasis on chance seems to deny any responsibility for the importance of this joke, treating it as if it just kept coming up without being solicited. And so this joke, which is not particularly funny, but is a great example of condensation, becomes more uncanny than it seems to need to be. Was it not logical to consider first and then repeatedly the joke whose mechanisms Freud understood best?

The analogy-joke from the *Bäder von Lucca* is not to be found there. The Rothschild joke is, but is treated as uncanny, as if its repeated appearances were surprising coincidences. A third mention of the *Baths of Lucca* is found in chapter II, in the section on allusion as a joke technique. Freud praises Heine's ingenious use of allusions for polemical purposes. The polemic is against Count Platen, a homosexual poet who wrote a satirical work on the romantic movement. According to Freud, the *Bäder von Lucca* contains frequent remarks alluding to anal and homosexual concerns, providing an insistent subtext until finally those themes are made explicit. Freud and Heine treat anal and homosexual almost interchangeably; the two are interwoven into one theme. Indeed, Freud is right about the pervasiveness of this closet thematic; the Baths of Lucca fairly reek of the anal and the homosexual.

Hirsch-Hyacinth, the hero of the famillionairely anecdote, is the servant of the Marquis Christophoro di Gumpelino, originally the banker Christian Gumpel. In the chapter after the Rothschild joke, Gumpelino gets a letter from his lady-love, a married woman with a watch-dog brother-in-law. The letter says that tonight the brother-in-law will be gone and Gumpelino can finally consummate his love, but in the morning the lady must leave Lucca for good. However, just before the letter arrives, because his master was depressed about the possibilities of satisfaction in his love affair, Hyacinth gave him Glauber salts, a tremendously powerful laxative. So when the letter comes, Gumpelino cannot go, because he "has to go." He cannot satisfy his desire for the lady, and instead must spend the night on the pot. (Were I a simple-minded Freudian I might point out—with an ah ha!—this regressive substitution of anal satisfaction for genital, but I won't yield to the temptation of that analogy.)

In the morning, however, the lover is no longer sad. The lady is gone forever, but Gumpelino has found consolation (Heine's translator uses that word). Mehlman's consolation was a homology, Freud's an analogy. Gumpel's consolation is an anal orgy and a book of Count Platen's homosexual poetry which he read all night on the pot—a book so fine Gumpel tells Heine that, although sorely tempted, he never used a page to wipe his ass. Heine remarks that Gumpel is not the first to be thus tempted.

Freud uses another joke from the *Baths of Lucca* in chapter II, but this time he does not name the work, but merely writes: "Heine said of a satirical comedy: 'This satire would not have been so biting if its author had had more to bite'" (p. 37). The line is from the *Bäder*'s last chapter, and refers to the satire Platen wrote against the romantic poets. Freud makes a small mistake in his quotation, he uses the word *Dichter* for author, whereas Heine had used *Verfasser*. Condensing *Dichter* and *Verfasser*, we reach *Verdichter*, a word itself meaning "condenser." *Verdichtung* is what leads Freud to the seductive, guilty analogy between dreams and jokes.

As I said before, condensation and the famillionairely joke share a structure of humiliation/subordination between similars (*gleichen*), which would be precisely Freud's view of male homosexuality. Two likes, two people in psychical accord, two analogues are debased to the level of the anal—the level of humiliation.

What is the name of this satire, occasion for such a rich network of slips, properly Freudian slips? Platen called his satire of the romantics *King Oedipus*. Oedipus is not mentioned in Freud's jokebook, but Mehlman's reading has shown us its operation here.

Heine suggests that Platen's play might have been better if "instead of Oedipus murdering his father Laius, and marrying his mother Jocasta, on the contrary, Oedipus should murder his mother and marry his father." Thus here, in the *Bader von Lucca*, in the text that manifests itself so uncannily throughout Freud's jokebook, in this Heine text functioning like an unconscious in Freud's book, we can read what Freud would only postulate much later, what Freud would someday call the negative Oedipus. Freud was to find that besides the familiar Oedipus, every child also has the desire to murder his mother and marry his father.

The negative Oedipus never was fully integrated into the Oedipus complex. It merely disturbs the calm homologies of the structural Oedipus. Should we return to the mythic origin of the sexual joke, we might see another sense of Freud's statement that "the ideal case" is when there is another man present, and especially when the woman is absent.

Mehlman's Freud has the myth (that is, the fantasy) of heterosexuality in an economy of homology, analogy. Men exchange women for heterosexual purposes, but the real intercourse is that exchange between men. The heterosexual object is irretrievably lost in the circuits, and the man is consoled by the homology. But the pleasure in the joke, in the homology, the temptation of the analogy points to the homosexual, the anal. Freud's Heine points to Freud's heinie.

5

The Female Subject: (What) Does Woman Want?

Jerry Aline Flieger

Lacan's seminar of the year 1972-73 centered around the question "What does woman want?," a question that he claimed Freud expressly left aside. But in a sense, of course, it is this question—of sexual difference and female subjectivity—which insists throughout Freud's work, even if it remains a stumbling-block. Indeed it is this question which opens the history of psychoanalysis, since Freud's earliest work with female hysterics represents an effort to make the patient a speaking subject, able to recognize and articulate what she really (that is, unconsciously) wants. Significantly, it is this same question—what does woman want?—which is central to feminist theory and practice, underlying the debate on goals and strategy.

Thus psychoanalysis and feminism have a great deal in common, the heart (of darkness?) of each of their endeavors being the exploration of what Freud called "the dark continent" of femininity, female subjectivity, and female sexuality. Perhaps it is this common interest, this "disputed territory," which makes the potential for mutual misunderstanding and mutual hostility so great. For some feminists contend that psychoanalysis seeks only to colonize the dark continent, whereas feminism seeks to liberate it to and for itself. The sources of feminism's distrust of psychoanalysis are well known: the Freudian dogma of female anatomical inferiority and penis-envy, and the attendant privileging of the male model in the Oedipal drama; and, in Lacanian theory, the status of the phallus as privileged signifier as well as the crucial

A first version of this paper was presented at the Convention of the Modern Language Association, December 1985.

importance accorded to the paternal function in the Symbolic register, with an accompanying disparagement of the Imaginary, the preoedipal, and the maternal. Moreover, many feminists express a general distrust of rigid methodology, finding that the will to theory itself is a patriarchal value. Perhaps the most serious feminist objection to psychoanalysis, however, concerns its claim to a non-ideological objectivity, as science exempt from political concerns; thus many feminists have addressed themselves to analyzing the bias of the science of psychoanalysis, and have done so, of course, in the name of their own expressed political orientation, since feminism is by its very nature resolutely political, goal-oriented, and ethical. Some Freudians and Lacanians, on the other hand, have read feminism's political and prescriptive agenda as a "symptom" of repression of the discovery of the Unconscious, a desire to be without desire. (See, for example, Jane Gallop's critique of Juliet Mitchell's "ethical discourse," the subject of the opening chapter of Gallop's book *The Daughter's Seduction: Feminism and Psychoanalysis*.) Thus the question of "what woman wants" is framed by other questions of authority and ideology: who wants to know, and why?

Thus those of us who are feminists dealing with psychoanalytic theory sometimes find ourselves in a precarious position, required to arbitrate between a "phallocratic" theory which, at worst, either disparages woman or effaces her, and a perhaps equally authoritarian feminist doctrine, which, at its worst, threatens to deny the specificity of woman in the name of equality. In other words, as feminists we must demand a certain equality (the demand itself of course being a tricky concept, enmiring us in intersubjective desire), even while as psychoanalytic theorists, we must insist on difference. Both efforts require a questioning of the status of female Subject—not only concerning what she wants, but *if* she wants at all, indeed, in Lacanian theory, if "she" (as "woman") even exists at all.

To further complicate matters, the question of what woman wants signals a deep and sometimes bitter rift among feminists themselves, concerning the nature of power and the feminist way (if any) to play and win the game of power. For feminist demands range from a demand for full equality and enfranchisement to a complete rejection of man's world (summed up by Luce Irigaray's injunction, "Frenchwomen, stop trying," the title of one essay in *Ce sexe qui n'en est pas un*). The politics of power relations often seem to present an untenable choice between silence and cooptation, of how, in Catherine Clément's formulation, "to be a woman and be in the street," without succumbing to phallocratic modes of opposition and oneupmanship. For some feminists, these questions occasion a critique of the women's movement itself and its claim to equality (Julia Kristeva, for one, has called "a certain feminism" a "naive romanticism" and a "vulgar trap" in her 1974 interview published in *Tel Quel*), either on the grounds that the movement is contaminated with phallocratic goals of power, or on the grounds that it is insufficiently theoretical, unconcerned with a higher political mission. (This

the authority of paternal law altogether, by implicitly or explicitly contesting the importance of the paternal function in the Symbolic order. Cutting herself off from psychoanalytic orthodoxy, this paternal orphan often turns to the other parent, in a kind of "affirmative action" which seeks to rehabilitate the preoedipal, the Imaginary, and the maternal (and which, unfortunately, often collapses the three concepts into one). This, then, is the Mother's Daughter, whom in her revolt against paternal law often models herself after Antigone rather than Oedipus (a theme of the work of Irigaray, for example), and whose theory is sometimes separatist or even "terrorist" in tone (the term is K. K. Ruthven's, in *Feminist Literary Studies: An Introduction*). Hélène Cixous, for one, writes (in "The Laugh of the Medusa") "Now, I-woman am going to blow up the Law: an explosion henceforth possible and ineluctable; let it be done, right now, *in* language" (cited from Marks and de Courtivron's *New French Feminisms*, p. 257). The Mother's Daughter will use language itself as weapon against (Lacanian) linguistic Law, and will usher in a new non-ordered order.

Perhaps the best-known proponent of this new order, this "parole de femme" (Annie Leclerc's term), is Luce Irigaray, who claims (in *Speculum of the Other Woman*) that woman has always been effaced by patriarchal culture, and continues to be effaced in Lacanian theory, in order to serve as a blank canvas upon which the image of Man is projected. In *This Sex Which is Not One*, she argues that woman's sexuality has been defined by psychoanalysis as a lack or an atrophy of male sexuality, and that woman herself has been consigned, especially in Lacanian theory, to an underground, spectral existence: "She never has a proper name; she has no right to public existence except in the protective custody of mister X" (*This Sex Which is Not One*, p. 22). Since language itself is male, custodial, Irigaray counsels woman to remain "unnamed, forgotten, without ever having been identified—i—who? will remain uncapitalized. Let's say 'Alice' *underground*" (p. 22).

Irigaray and others propose a new "fluid" language, free from phallic logic, a "m(other) tongue," characterized by openness rather than closure. (The term is borrowed from a recent anthology of essays on psychoanalysis, feminism, and literature, and suggests the maternal aspect of woman's language. Irigaray herself has resisted the equation of "female" with "maternal," but as Jane Gallop has pointed out in a discussion of Irigaray, her writing nonetheless often seems bound up in the relation with her own mother.) From the concept of a woman's language, grounded in female anatomy—Naomi Schor has posited, for instance, the "clitoral" basis of synecdoche as female trope; Irigaray has theorized a kind of "vaginal" language; Annie Leclerc has emphasized fluidity and cyclic rhythms—it is a short step to the elaboration of a female poetics, the equation of a certain writing itself with "the feminine" (or, to use Alice Jardine's term, with *Gynesis*). Irigaray, Kristeva (in her concept of the semiotic), and Cixous all to some extent participate in this vision of a female expression which represents the "other" of phallic or monologic systems. Rather than repressing difference, the "m(other) tongue" is by nature heterogenous, fluid, plural, open.

The value of the approach of the Mother's Daughter lies in her affirmative stance, her elaboration of the "maternal subtext" (Coppélia Kahn) in psychoanalysis, reinterpreting the mother-child relation, and her appreciation of female language and creativity. But such theorizing, at worst, risks a fetishization of the female body, a privileging of maternity at the expense of non-procreative sexuality, or even an *equation* of feminine creativity with maternity (as Kristeva seems to do), coming full circle to the worst of Freud. Indeed, the privileging of the Imaginary may neglect the Symbolic altogether, promoting a new fiction of unified subjectivity, experienced in a golden semiotic age of infant fusion with the mother. Similarly, the mystification of woman's language as a locus of incoherence or antitheoretical immediacy (Chantal Chawaf writes, for instance, that "we must deintellectualize writing," for "theories deprive us of whirlpools sparkling and free which should carry us naturally toward our full blossoming," in "La chair linguistique," [*Nouvelles littéraires*, May 1976]), may ellide the question of woman's responsibility or even complicity in social life, or may abdicate any real entry into history or political debate. Such positions may end up reconsigning women to a role at worst passive or separatist (as when "Psych et Po" rejects the "naïvité" of the notion of equality), at best indirect and manipulative (as when Irigaray suggests "mimicry" of male language as a strategy, a kind of crafty submission without subjugation).

Thus much of feminist psychoanalytic theory seems to propose a choice between Father and Mother, system and silence, rigid structure and anarchy. (As Jane Gallop puts it, in her account of the continuing appeal of patriarchal concepts, including that of the Phallic Mother, "the need for the Phallus is great. No matter how oppressive its reign, it is more comforting than no one in command" [*The Daughter's Seduction*, p. 131].) But are these the only available alternatives—oppressive structure or lack of order; the reign of the Phallic Parent or its flip side, the reign of the fetishized Maternal Body as chora, locus of incoherence? Put in political terms, such a choice would seem to be between totalitarianism and anarchy. Is there no hope of another sexual politics, which may valorize difference without abdication or "terrorist" tactics? Are the only responses to the persistent question of what woman wants to be in parental terms (the solace of a "mystic Mommy" or the authority of a "strong Daddy")?

In all of the feminist writers to whom I have alluded thus far, and in many other feminist psychoanalytic theorists as well, we find signs of a fourth possible position—beyond that of the Father, the dutiful daughter, or the illegitimate "mother's daughter"—to which I will refer as the position of the Prodigal Daughter. She is a daughter still, who acknowledges her heritage: or rather, like the prodigal child of the Biblical account—who is of course a son in the original parable—she goes beyond the fold of restrictive paternal law, only to return. But unlike the prodigal son of legend, who returns repentent, she returns enriched—for she is "prodigal" in the second sense of the term as well: she is lush, exceptional, extravagant, and affirmative. To be prodigal in this sense is to alter the law, to enlarge its parameters and recast its meaning (even in the patriarchal parable, let us recall, the prodigal is forgiven his outlandish behavior, and reassimilated—thus changing forever the limits of what is permissible). Thus the law to which the prodigal daughter accedes—yes, in the name of ethics and responsibility, however phallic some may consider those terms—is an altered ethics; her subjectivity is indeed "hers," rather than a deficient version of his. What, then, does such a woman want? What are the directions in current psychoanalytic and feminist theory which enable *her* to pose the question, from the position of speaking subject?

There are first, for example, the efforts at redefining maternity from the mother's point of view, rather than as object of the child's desire or stage in the child's development (see, for example, the essay of Susan Suleiman, "Writing and Motherhood," in *The (M)Other Tongue*, or Marianne Hirsch's work on the role of Jocasta in the Oedipal scenario). There are also those new feminist efforts at rereading cases of female psychic "illness," and particularly hysteria, not as the "histories" of maladjusted "subjects," but rather as *histoires* of cultural heroines, victims of the patriarchal Symbolic whose very illness is a testimony to the creativity of female desire and female subjectivity, which *will* speak when repressed, even if only in somatic symptom. It is no wonder that for many feminists Dora and Anna O. are prodigal daughters par excellence, who either refuse the patriarchal version of their illness, or actively particpate in the invention of their own treatment, forever transforming the psychoanalytic "law." (See, for example, the collection of essays edited by Charles Bernheimer and Claire Kahane, entitled *In Dora's Case: Freud-Hysteria-Feminism* [Columbia University Press, 1985], or Naomi Schor's essay on "Eugénie Grandet: Mirrors and Melancholia," in *The (M)Other Tongue*, cited above.)

The prodigal daughter of today, I would suggest (and in this regard Juliet Mitchell and Jacqueline Rose are both examples), insists on the cultural nature of Freud's and of Lacan's discoveries, even when the Fathers themselves are blind to it. One of the most promising efforts at this kind of cultural interpretation is to be found in the work of Luce Irigaray, when she analyzes Lévi-Strauss's findings concerning the cultural position of women as objects of exchange and circulation among men ("women on the Market," in *This Sex Which is Not One*). For Irigaray performs her analysis with an eye to securing "a place for women within sexual difference," rather than simply proposing to eschew culture and cultural transaction because of their heretofore sexist character. Such a project implies a willingness to assume the responsibility of speaking subject, as agent of culture (even if, for the moment, women are still "subjects-in-the-making," as Kristeva has suggested). Irigaray emphasizes the positive side of Lévi-Strauss's findings: woman is not only an object of exchange, but a speaking subject as well; she may then make use of her unique position, her double perspective, to critique and reshape the culture which tends to objectify her. It is a question, perhaps, as Madeleine Gagnon has written, of "taking over a language which, although it is mine, is foreign to me" ("Corps I," in *La venue à l'écriture*, translated in *New French Feminisms*, p. 179). It is then a question of owning up to one's identity as speaking subject, rather than rejecting "identity" and "logic" as naïve or phallocentric terms, a question of assuming active responsibility for societal and cultural processes. In other words, even if we are not yet ready to claim, with Cixous and others, that there is no such thing as a female essence (preferring to consider, with Alice Jardine and others, that the question of specificity is of necessity a question of the future), even if we do not on the other hand wish to claim to be the *same* as male subjects, we must nevertheless be willing to lay claim to a "full and equal" subjectivity, without undue squeamishness about the terms, stemming from our habit of defining "full" as exempt from desire and "equal" as phallic.

It is perhaps in this effort of redefinition that Lacanian theory is of most use for feminist theory and practice, and to a recasting of the law by the prodigal daughters of psychoanalysis. For Lacanian theory, phallocentric as it is (even if, for Lacan, the phallus is merely a Symbol of its own inaccessibility to all Subjects), allows feminists to affirm the bisexuality of all speaking subjects (as Kristeva and Cixous, for example, repeatedly do), or to deconstruct the notions of male and female altogether (as Sarah Kofman's work, *The Enigma of Woman*, does), thanks to the Lacanian emphasis on the instability of gender identification and the fluidity of sexual aim and object. Indeed, for many Lacanians, this fluidity of gender is the principal lesson of Dora's case—in which Freud both identifies with and desires his patient—and it is an important aspect of Lacan's celebrated reading of Poe's "The Purloined Letter" as well. (I think this is one implication of Barbara Johnson's essay on Derrida on Lacan on Poe, appropriately titled "The Frame of Reference"; and it is the explicit position of my own essay "The Purloined Punchline: Joke as Textual Paradigm," in *Lacan and Narration*, Robert Con Davis, ed.). Significantly, even when a writer like Hélène Cixous mordantly criticizes Lacan and Lacanians as "cops of the Signifier" (in "The Laugh of the Medusa"), her call for a new "bisexuality" of open exchange and shared vulnerability between sexes is in fact *enabled* by the Lacanian challenge to fixed unitary sexuality. For this "bisexuality" is a celebration of difference, both intersubjective and intrasubjective.

Thus it need not be a question for feminist psychoanalytic theory of accepting or apologizing for the "phallic disproportion" (Gallop) in Freud and in Lacan, as daughterly duty might seem to require, but rather of showing how that which is most radical in psychoanalytic thought renders such "phallicism" and "disproportion" obsolete, by proposing a new sexual relation, too frightening for the Fathers themselves fully to recognize. As Madelon Sprengnether writes ("Enforcing Oedipus: Freud and Dora," in *In Dora's Case*, Bernheimer and Kahane, eds., p. 271): "If the indeterminacy of sex roles, like the indeterminacy of narrative form, represents the state of not being in control, then it is no surprise that Freud is unable to imagine love as something not taken but given." For this indeterminacy, so frightening to the Fathers, means a sharing of control, or an alternating vulnerability, since sexual relations may always be an affair of a certain "power." But the reading of the prodigal daughter alters this power, expands the Psychoanalytic Law, and opens the closed familial circuit, even while showing the exchangeability and fluidity of its roles.

This is, for example, what Irigaray does when she "inverts" the Oedipus complex by exposing the incestuous desire of the Father, cloaked in Law, or when she calls for a restaging of the analytic act itself, exposing *both* transferences and thus upsetting the illusion of neutral authority of one party. It is what Jacqueline Rose does when she asserts, after Lacan, that the Father is a function rather than a gender, and thus concludes that the phallus is the privileged signifier only because the culture itself is androcentric (Introduction to *Feminine Sexuality: Jacques Lacan and the école freudienne*. And this observation raises another possibility: the questioning of the association between the Mother and the Imaginary register—why must the nurturing parental function be maternal/female, and the disciplinary function of Law (the Symbolic) be paternal?) It is also what Jane Gallop does when, in her reading of Dora, she expands the family circuit to include the fourth term, the governess, and thus opens the case to political, economic, and class questions (*The Daughter's Seduction*, Chapter 9).

Such prodigal uses of psychoanalysis—for which "mother" and "father" no longer mean "female" and "male," "passive" and "active"—no longer necessarily point to a tragedy of sexual difference (reflected in Lacan's famous dictum, "there is no sexual relation"), but open to a comic celebration of difference. In my own work, for instance, I have discussed the comic nature of Lacan's concept of locus, in which the masculine place in the joke-transaction, the position of joker or agent, is given over in turn to all players, and in which all players share in the role of object, the "dispossessed" butt of the action. Freudian joke theory, then, when read through Lacan, can help rid us of the notion that the position of object is insolubly feminine or castrated, opening the drama of subjectivity to female players, and reexamining the question of "dispossession" as a political (rather than strictly biological or even psychic) act.

What all of these examples suggest, is that even if Law is indeed the psychological and cultural base of human interaction, such law is not necessarily patriarchal. For Lacan's lesson, and Freud's, is perhaps finally that the Unconscious is a function or process rather than a content; and it is thus not a denial of the Unconscious, as some have argued, to insist on the culturally determined nature of this content or its interpretation by patriarchal society. So perhaps, as Juliet Mitchell suggests (in *Psychoanalysis and Feminism*), we may indeed alter the content of the Unconscious scenario, creating a new unconscious with other "privileged" signifiers. But for the moment, we need to reassert our right to the old one; that is, our right to *have*, rather than to *be*, the Unconscious (to respond to Irigaray's query to Lacan concerning woman's relation to the Unconscious). Above all, we need to realize that the prodigal daughter need not decline subjectivity in the name of difference, since she may interpret subjectivity as a working of difference. That is, she may read Lacanian subjectivity as an irrecuperable schism, a *Spaltung*, but she need not accept the terms of that division as "male" and "female," or consider gender itself as a fixed boundary, a wall. She need not shun feminist ethics as an authoritarian discourse, an attempt to be the absolute authority, exempt from desire; she may rather "own up" to her own status as desiring subject, including her desire to see some political goals actually accomplished, without confusing that claim with a claim that human *desire* itself will ever be finally sated, or sutured.

What, then, does such a woman want? From psychoanalysis, she seeks a theoretical base for that reciprocal sexual relation which she has already begun to live. For "full" subjectivity is not freedom from desire, but a freedom to desire: the agency to want, as well as to be wanted, is the act of human signification itself. What "we" want is to say "we," as subjects, and to envision the day what that pronoun may include those on the other side of the wall of gender.

Psychoanalysis and Lacanian Theory

6

Lacan's Seminars on James Joyce: Writing as Symptom and "Singular Solution"

Ellie Ragland-Sullivan

My purpose is to try and convey in some detail the fruit of Jacques Lacan's seminars given on James Joyce, principally in 1975 and 1976, but also as early as 1971. When Lacan first spoke at Yale University in 1975 he began: "Ce n'est pas facile" ("It is not easy for me") ("Kanzer Seminar"). Indeed Lacan's words on Joyce depict a Joyce that will be perfectly strange for many, including Joyce scholars. You will hear ideas such as these. There are real knots in Joyce's prose that are not metaphorical, but have to do with metonymical signifying chains surrounding the Name of the Father. These knots denote the "thing" (*das Ding* or *point de capiton*) stuck at a point of impasse or encounter. But what is a knot? For Lacan the knot has the structure of a symptom, defined in at least three ways. But for the moment we will describe it as that in a person's life history which conscious knowledge does not account for, but which leaves its imprint anyway. That is, the symptomatic knot is Real, extrinsic in the first place to the cord it ties. It has to be put in. As such it is a Real referent. Thus one can say that psychoanalytic resistance has the shape of a knot, the structure of a symptom, the structure of something that is an obstacle or blockage in various aspects of a person's life.

This lecture was first published in *Joyce & Paris: Actes Cinquième Symposium International James Joyce*, Paris, June 16-20, 1975, eds. J. Aubert and Maria Jolas (Paris: C.N.R.S., 1979). It is referred to in my essay from the most recent collection of some of Lacan's seminars given on James Joyce which have been edited by Jacques Aubert in *Joyce avec Lacan*. In Aubert's collection it is referred to as "Joyce le symptôme I." The article called "Joyce le symptôme II" in Aubert's collection was previously published in *L'Âne: Le Magazine Freudien* 6 (1982): 3-5. Many other selections on Joyce from Lacan's year-long seminar on *Le Sinthome* have been published in *Scilicet* and *Ornicar?*.

In 1987 Jacques-Alain Miller described the symptom in *Joyce avec Lacan* as an enigma written in secret characters which in and of themselves say nothing to anyone ("Préface," 11). Secondly, the symptom is also the pure *jouissance*—which Freud discovered as the limit of the power of interpretation—of an *écriture* that Lacan called the Real ("La psychanalyse," 445). Among other things, Lacan says fantasy is separable from *écriture* and gives rise to desire [($ \diamond$ *a*)]. Miller adds later that both interfere in language ("Préface," 11). In Joyce's case, the effects are knots that denote an unconscious memory bank of signifying associations derived from the unsymbolized Real particular to James Joyce alone. These *objet a* are actively suspended within his prose, but resist revealing themselves as transparent "knowledge." Jacques Aubert has suggested that Joyce, like Lacan, developed an "art of suspension" ("Galeries," 83). In such a context "truth" is the *savoir* of a particular subject's unconscious and serves a paradoxical function: to provide a knowledge base and to stop up a hole in the Other from which a subject's *jouissance* arises, not as a signifier, but as an effect of the Real. The unconscious signifying chains or *savoir* contain some elements that make sense and others that are nonsensical, the nonsensical significations producing a *jouissance* effect rather than a clear grammatical or informational communication.

I shall speak of Joyce's prose, then, as arising from the discourse that constituted the author in the first place as a subject poised between oblivion and the signifier. Jacques-Alain Miller once called "discourse" a process of language that truth constrains ("Avertissement," 5). In his 1975 Kanzer lecture at Yale, Lacan spoke of the truth in Joyce's discourse by referring to an article that had just appeared in a French literary journal whose thesis was that the English language did not exist any longer after Joyce's prose. Lacan's opinion was that, on the contrary, up until *Finnegans Wake*, Joyce had respected what Noam Chomsky has called grammatical structure ("Kanzer Seminar"). *His* interest in Joyce was not in the linguistic intricacies of his prose, Lacan said, but rather in the connection of the "truth" that is Joyce's unconscious *savoir* to Joyce's language. One of Lacan's many characterizations of truth is of some *thing* that affects the place from which we are speaking ("The Freudian Thing," 121). Freud understood that the unconscious produces symptoms, but did not grasp that those same symptoms cannot be easily revealed as meaningful truths because they do not arise from anticipated models or meanings such as the various ones he proposed in trying to relate mind to body and truth to an unconscious.

Freud's assumptions of what constituted identity and mentality were typical of the positivistic thinking of his day, assumptions that led him to overlook the meaning (*jouis-sens*) in nonsense that he had cast aside as irrelevant by 1923. He chose instead an id-ego-superego model to replace his earlier search for the cause of symptoms in dreams, jokes, wordplay, slips of tongue and pen (*The Psychopathology of Everyday Life*), in myth (*Totem and Taboo*), or even in the "pathological" sublimation of art. While Freud saw the artist as necessarily neurotic, Lacan meant something quite different from Freud when he attributed symptoms to artists. While Freud elevated the artist to a sacrificial position, one whose repressed neurosis provides others with cathartic release, Lacan argued the opposite. The purpose of art is not to permit repression, but to pose a question that the artist him or herself has not answered or resolved. Artistic productions are not then in and of themselves pathological or neurotic.

Lacan taught that symptoms return retroactively as the *objet a* in a person's life, an effect of the Real as distinct from ego fictions. But what are the *objet 'a*, first derived from Imaginary identificatory material and Symbolic order language and codes? They are the Ur-objects of desire and "drive": the breast, the feces, the urinary flow, the (imaginary) phallus, the voice, the phoneme, the gaze, and the void ("Subversion of the subject," 315). By object Lacan never meant the phenomenologically totalizable object, but something to do with desire and *jouissance* as they inhabit language and the body, joining them. The *objet a* dwell in *jouissance* at the limit of the powers of conscious interpretation. As a surplus or *jouissance*, the *objet a* link the Real to the Symbolic and Imaginary by the Symptom, a fourth order that permits the unknotting of the material that holds symptoms together in the first place. Slavoj Zizek has defined the symptom as a particular element which gives the lie to the Universal of which it is a part ("The Marxist Symptom," ms 12). Some such particulars show up as fictions, desires, or prohibitions whose final referent is the signifer of the Father's Name, the first countable signifier as a referent for identity. Yet these "fillers" make it seem there is no lack in the universe of self, image, language, or consciousness. The human tendency is to try to explain what *is* by things from the outside or by impersonal innate tendencies, rather than by deficiencies and dissymmetries in being and knowing.

Unlike many critics who comment on Joyce, Lacan was not interested in the images in Joyce's work. He argued in his Kanzer Seminar that like any other *apparent* unity, images always block truth. In Lacan's teaching, grammatical language and images merely produce the illusion of a consistent universe. But the unconscious disrupts these illusions, by dissociating meaning that only seems full from our pretenses that it functions smoothly. The unconscious produces, instead, a glimpse of the void underlying our sense productions. On the other hand, truth does show up in spoken language, just as in dream or literary language, when it is linked to the *objet a* as they lean against chains of signifiers. Lacan taught that signifiers lean against the primordial objects of desire or *objet a* and enable us to think against a backdrop of desire. If language is, indeed, infiltrated by *objet a* as Real punctuation points around which articulable matrices of desire cluster, it becomes clearer what Lacan meant when he described truth as that which makes knowledge stumble. Fiction may have the structure of truth, but it is not truth in a theological or essentialist sense.

In 1975 Lacan gave a seminar titled "Joyce le symptôme" at the Fifth International James Joyce Symposium.[1] In this lecture Lacan considered the difficulty of *Finnegans Wake* through describing a split in Joyce himself, but not the famous split of the subject divided between conscious and unconscious awareness. Rather, Lacan pointed to a split between a Real *jouissance* with which one is familiar, and truth which is repressed as an unconscious *savoir* ("The agency of the letter," 169). Moreover, the Real is stronger than the true ("Kanzer Seminar," *Scilicet* 617, 42). Joyce, he suggested, was more attached to the Real suffering caused by the *jouissance* that lies beyond repression than to any wish to ascertain the true reasons for his own psychic pain. It will perhaps be helpful to recall a definition of *jouissance* given by Jacques-Alain Miller: "Truth resisting knowledge of *jouissance*" ("A and a," 25).

In his 1987 introduction to the screening of Lacan's *Television*, Jacques-Alain Miller points out that *jouissance* is not Other-related, but is egotistical ("Introduction to *Television*," 14). Joyce's deteriorating eye condition (glaucoma), his daughter's psychosis, and his increasingly arcane prose were all symptoms of a man whose desire was encumbered by an excessive oppression of *jouissance*. And *jouissance* always concerns the relation of desire to the position of the Father's Name (or the phallus). The issue of fathers was paramount in Joyce's life and work. His own father had been an alcoholic, indebted, and an embezzler. Catholic Church fathers were also constantly disappointing Joyce. In Lacanian terms, his masculine identity was continually beseiged by questions regarding the worthiness of his (father's) name, the worthiness of his national identity, and so on. Disappointed by Imaginary order models and by the Symbolic order itself, Joyce sought to make a *name* for himself chiefly as an artist, thereby depending on his own creativity rather than what others had created for him. Lacan argued that the character Stephen Dedalus was Joyce's Imaginary alter ego through whom he fictively and unconsciously sought to decipher his own life enigmas. This argument is developed at length by Hugo Rotmistrovsky in "Joyce, el nombre." When an enunciation contains the enigma of the *énoncé* (or unconscious knowledge), Lacan denoted this phenomenon in his mathemes as E^e. A particular enunciation is not just talk or information, but itself announces that an unconscious enigma is in play. Rotmistrovsky refers to one such enunciation from *Portrait of the Artist as a Young Man*. "The cock crew, the sky was blue, the bells in heaven, were striking eleven. It's time for this poor soul, to go to heaven?" (35).

By the time he wrote *Finnegans Wake*, shattering his ego into dispersed voices, Joyce had dispensed with Imaginary and Symbolic fathers. Leaving sense behind, the Lacanian Real father (otherwise thought of as the dead

Father or *jouissance*) takes over Joyce's language. Lacan described *jouissances* as unassimilated pieces of knowledge that act as symptoms and cause people to invent myths concerning their origins, bodies, desires, being, and so on. The Real symptom or *objet a* is a universal "negative" positivized as *das Ding* that is terrifying in its full presence—a lack of lack—and thus obscured by the *savoir* that generally masks it for the purpose of protecting a subject from knowing what constitutes his being and desire in reference to a cause. The symptom is the more-than-us in us which destroys us. But we cling to our symptoms because they are familiar and give us a sense of being unified and consistent. In the case of Joyce, Lacan described one of his symptoms as his doubt. He was a Saint Thomas who progressively demonstrated what Lacan taught: that our sins, like our uncertainties, place all of us on the same side as analyst and analysand. We all live behind the wall of language, inhabited by a fault or flaw or lack, or in the language of the Church, a sin. Every subject is an effect caused by this wall of language (Lacan's structure of alienation) behind which he or she lives more or less confidently, not knowing that they retrieve the words by which they live at the expense of a lack in being that constitutes them as speaking beings. Lacan gave Joyce a new name: "Joyce the symptom." By rewriting the spelling of symptom (a late-learned Greek borrowing) with the letters of its archaic Old French spelling—*sinthome*—Lacan said he was giving Joyce a new (old) name. The *sinthome* is that which is singular in each person, as ordered by every subject's experiences of taking on a gender identity.

As early as 1953 in his *Discourse of Rome* Lacan described a symptom thus:

> The symptom is here the signifier of a signified repressed from the consciousness of the subject. A symbol written in the sand of the flesh and on the veil of Maia, it participates in language by the semantic ambiguity that I have already emphasized in its constitution. But it is speech functioning to the full, for it includes the discourse of the Other in the secret of its cipher. It was by deciphering this speech that Freud rediscovered the primary language of symbols, still living on in the suffering of civilized man (*Das Unbehagen in der Kultur*). ("The function and field of speech," 69)

By the 1970s Lacan spoke of the symptom as a happening of the body where language joins symbol in such a way that the Imaginary and Real bodies combine appearance and enigma. It is important to note, however, that he does not make a simple symbol of the symptom. The symbol gives rise to the symptom, and the symptom refers to the symbol that gave rise to it. These are pulled along by the Real with which the Imaginary combines by passing above the symbol (representation of the sun, an elephant, etc.), and below the symptom (the fantasy that interprets the symbol). The link between an unsymbolized Real and a representational Imaginary is thus expressed by an opposition: *they must be taken together.*

In Lacan's redefinition of terms symbol does not mean a second sense or a hidden meaning, but as I have put it elsewhere: "a discrete unit, both autonomous and irreducible, which speech sounds endow with meaning in reference to other units" (*Jacques Lacan*, 170). Lacan has rejected neopositivistic symbologies and redefined symbol as the lowest common multiple of meaning that imposes itself through projection/introjection in the building up of unconscious networks of signifying ensembles. In Lacanian terms, when one encounters an enigmatic use of language such as Joyce's *Finnegans Wake*, the author's language speaks an opaque symptomatology: a *jouissance* of the Real where language conceals (and reveals) the presence of a blockage within itself.

Joyce has called such a phenomenon "consubstantiality," referring to the theological theory that the three persons in the Trinity or Godhead—Father, Son, and Holy Ghost—are of the same substance. Their Flesh made word is celebrated in communion (*Ulysses*, 32). Lacan frequently spoke of the word made Flesh. Yet one cannot read the unconscious of a text, but rather the symptom which has the structure of metaphor. As in metaphor one thing substitutes for another. In Lacan's view, Joyce substitutes the materiality—that which gives weight, density, and motion—of the voice for a cohesion between language and a lacking identificatory signifier for a worthy Father's Name. One can read this through the materiality of the voice as *objet a*, linked to the signifier for the Father's Name. Put another way, the unconscious bites into language. Lacan named this stylistic phenomenon common to Rabelais, Joyce, and himself an *écrit*: a place between speaking and writing where the timbre and resonance of the voice as a libidinal organ resides. As symptoms wax and wane they are linked to the voice. As *objet a* the voice is a cause of desire that refracts the tension between desire and *jouissance*. It produces an echo in the body of the fact that something resonates in language, demonstrating that the word has impact both as cause and effect. *Finnegans Wake* is, for Lacan, a dream, an enigma of signifiers and the silence of a *jouissance* bequeathed us by Joyce. This monumental work is not an awakening, but a dream full of sorrow and death: a wake. After Joyce's other works his *Bildung* or substitute ego (that Lacan designated as Dedalus) was finally ready to collapse in the sense that Joyce's own ego was fading, unraveling, abandoning Joyce to the unconscious signifying networks that spoke him as if from afar.

Lacan loved Joyce for his attempts to shred academic myths and conventions, to make litter of the letter, to retrieve bits of verbal garbage to add to the garbage can of *poubellication* (publication). But he loved him most for his ability to live his symptoms through a sheer will of words. Joyce's discourse was one of contingency, said Lacan, going so far as to suggest that Joyce published *Finnegans Wake* in order to become Joyce the *sinthome*: that is, Joyce the *enigma*. In this effort Joyce gained a mastery over the signifying deficiency that brought him close to lack and loss, that Lacan attributed to a foreclosure òf the signifier for the Father's Name. Joyce's art became a supplement that would give birth to Modernism as that which provokes, but does not answer, and thus pushes "supposed" masters to interpret, according to Slavoj Zizek ("Limits," 38).

The inert energetics of a *jouissance*, both unsymbolized and empty yet totally dense and full, that Lacan attributes to the Real, constitutes the painful, silent symptom behind Joyce's language. Lacan sees this symptom as the flip side of the signifier, one side giving life, the other showing death or an "extimacy" that he described as an intimate alienation emanating from within us (Miller, "A and a," 25). The life-giving side of a word suggests that infinite meanings are possible. Yet when a word ceases to mean, we confront the side of a text or an author that is not open to all meanings. On the contrary, one finds here the point at which all meanings can be abolished. The limits of a language are the limits of the subject. For Lacan this means that the signifier can occasionally, as in dreams or psychotic discourse, take over and begin to function either agrammatically or without reference to a listener, as if functioning on automatic pilot. In these contexts the signifier speaks the subject in such a way as to reveal the Other speaking, as if for no one.

In Joyce's texts that Lacan read and reread over a period of decades, he found both sides of what Jacques-Alain Miller has clarified as the Lacanian symptom. On one side, the symptom is a mark or tic that replaces or substitutes for a trauma (a knotting in the Real). The symptom may be a word, sound, event, detail, or image that acts in a way peculiar to a given subject's history. It will always involve some part of the body, if only as an *objet a*. On this slope, the enigmatic symptom belongs to the sign or the unconscious signifying chain of language because it is susceptible of being deciphered or decoded. But on the other slope, the symptom becomes more problematic because it concerns a *jouissance—hors-sens* or beyond language—that is both extra-utilitarian and inaccessible and does not wish the "good" of the subject it inhabits. Insofar as James Joyce was concerned, Lacan ventured the theory that his first symptoms concerned an unconscious position taken toward the signifier for the Father's Name which he could still enunciate in *Portrait of the Artist as a Young Man* and *Ulysses*. Stylistically speaking, characters served Joyce in these two novels as metaphors—or the double structures that constitute ego or meaning—by negotiating the author's unconscious desire and taking up varying positions regarding his *jouissance*. But in *Finnegans Wake* Joyce had cancelled his subscription to the Other. His recognizable ego—with its substitutive or metaphorical structure—disappears.

In *Ulysses* Joyce's father figures still ground him in a representational lineage, thereby giving him a way to subsist in language as a coherent (that is, desiring) subject. Up until *Finnegans Wake* the Father's Name signifier was represented by a country, a race, a religion, and a name for Joyce himself: *the Artist*. On the first side of the symptom—the side signified by a signifier—Joyce's search for an identity adequate to his desire is only too visible in his texts. On the other side of the symptom *jouis-sens* comes into play as an excess left behind in the wake of the constitution of an ego, pointing here to the referent of the Father. Although Lacan finds this key referent foreclosed, one could not determine that this was the "psychic" structure at issue before *Finnegans Wake*. Moreover, Lacan argues that Joyce is a curiosity like no other. Even the foreclosure of this central signifier is not necessarily sufficient to give rise to a psychotic rupture (Ragland-Sullivan, "La forclusion lacanienne," 199-227). Joyce's great desire to be *the Artist* makes a supplement (a kind of *objet a*) of the *sinthome*. In *Portrait* and *Ulysses* an Imaginary denigration of Joyce's own father becomes a Symbolic order deficiency which the son will try, albeit unconsciously, to rectify by creating Stephen Dedalus. Taken as a cipher for Joyce's unconscious quest "to know," Stephen's ventures lead him along the path of trying to find out how to act, how to be "as a man." It is crucial to Lacan's importance for literary studies that one note his rethinking of creativity (sublimation). Unlike Freud, he did not view invention as neurotic displacement for Oedipal lack. Rather, a creation can function as a supplement or a bridge built between the "partial drives," the *objet a*, desire, and language. Art is a way to *dwell in* language as a subject of unconscious desire, as well as a way to adorn the void. Unlike psychosis or neurosis, art does not equate artist to symptom. Art offers an edifice built over suffering, a something extra that has a life of its own. Lacan theorized that the mental representations—the *Vorstellungsrepräsentanz* or *savoir* (S$_2$)—which ground or frame every subject's identity question, his or her "who am I?," show up ultimately as a gender problematic that can be deciphered by a scanning of how language uses that subject.

It seems fantastic to suggest that the syntactical discontinuities in *Finnegans Wake* come from disturbances in Joyce's body and being, and that these are traceable to insufficient representational grounding for a masculine identity. Lacan's idea that the *objet a* are woven into language, indeed, materialize language, from infancy on—language which structures being by the signifier in the first place—seems outrageous. Yet, Lacan argued from clinical data, from philosophical treatises, from literary texts, from artistic artifacts of all sorts, from theology, and from everything else, that unquantifiable effects and enigmas—*not substantive essences*—create human *being* as an alienated set of fictions and myths that only seem essentialized because our language and bodies are connected by the *objet a*. We are structured as the creatures of an Other desire. This desire is itself lacking as a fullness of knowledge. Moreover, it is perforated by the hole of loss itself from which the *objet a* fall. In *Joyce avec Lacan* Lacan reminds us of this when he speaks of the "drive" as an echo in the body to the fact that there is a *dire* which resonates through the agencies we call being or meaning ("Le Sinthome, Séminaire du 18 novembre," 42). Lacan said the same thing in other words in "Joyce le symptôme I.": "Subjects are spoken in a way that creates their destiny, surely not by chance" (23; my translation). A subject is predetermined—not entirely, of course—by the discourse of his origins.

But does this not return us to a retrograde version of Freud's Oedipus complex? No, we have, instead, encountered Lacan's rewriting of the Oedipal symptom as the paternal metaphor or the fourth term that links networks of associative and combinatory meanings, tying Imaginary identifications to Symbolic language. These are pulled along by the Real of symbol and symptom which Lacan defined as a universal lack or negative kernel at the heart of all being, meaning, language, and desire. The appearance of a symptom points to an imbalance in the interrelatedness of R.S.I. (Real.Symbolic. Imaginary) and denotes what Lacan termed the particular negative. One sees that a Lacanian reading of texts will pay heed not only to jokes, puns, slips of the tongue, and so on, but also to the appearance of the gaze, the voice, the void, or to any equivocation which points to the issue of identifying signifiers. It is in this sense that Lacan proposed in his 1975-76 seminar *Le Sinthome* that the increasing difficulties of Joyce's prose represent the degree to which Joyce becomes progressively detached from the Symbolic or grammatical order ("Kanzer Seminar"). Yet, as Danielle Bergeron points out, Joyce's production of a work of art, viewed as an object presented to the gaze of the Other, served the author as an effort to inscribe himself in the Symbolic order ("Jouer sa vie sur," 172).

An *écrit* as defined by Lacan is something which gives language weight and the semblance of autonomy. Such language is to be located somewhere between speech and writing. For Joyce an *écrit* might be said to reside between language and the voice. We know that he even called his wife "Nor Voice" (O'Brien, 33). If we look at Joyce's difficult prose within a Lacanian context, rather than from the recently familiar deconstructive one, we will end up with a different view of it. Whereas poststructuralist theories have privileged metonomy within language itself, often describing language as the search for metaphor, Lacan placed substitutive desire on the side of metaphor and recast metonymy as a fading into enigma. Language does not so much slip, according to Lacan, as it swims in the water of desire that functions like Freudian condensation, according to the primary law of metaphor. Metaphor spawns metonymies which do not simply open up to yet another signifier on to infinity. Rather, metonymies dwell on the side of the Real and the *objet a*, some of which can be pinned down. While desire is on the side of the unconscious, the Real is on the side of the ego. That is, its effects are palpably strong, albeit mysterious, such as in anxiety. Not only is the Other misrecognized as the unconscious subject of desire, but it is not realized that the Real causes of desire are themselves effects or products of loss marked in the Other as a hole. Lacan spoke of *Finnegans Wake* as language rushing in to fill up a hole in Joyce's being, a hole that revealed a void behind the appearance of unities.

Paradoxically the underweave of discourse in *Finnegans Wake* gave birth to an artist like no other. Here Joyce is *WRITING*. The metaphorical and metonymic slopes of language fade rapidly in and out of each other like kaleidoscopic plays of being and nothingness. Joyce is dispersed into bits and pieces of the *objet a* as phoneme, voice, gaze, and (imaginary) phallus. "The point of unintelligibility there is, however, the ladder by which one shows oneself as master," Lacan said in "Joyce le symptôme II," continuing,

> I am enough of a master of the roots of language [lalangue], the one called French, to have myself arrived at what is fascinating in bearing witness to the *jouissance* particular to the symptom. Opaque *jouissance* of excluding meaning [*sens*]. One suspected it all for a long time. To be a post-Joycian, is to know it. There is no wakening except through this particular *jouissance*. . . . The extraordinary thing is that Joyce arrived there, not without Freud (although it would not suffice that he had read him), but without recourse to the experience of analysis (which would have trapped him into some flat ending). (36)

The two faces of the symptom as designated by Lacan appear clearly in *Finnegans Wake*. On the communicative side, one finds the radical *non-sens* of Other signifying chains. On the *jouis-sens* side, the Name of the Father shows up as destructive of law ("Joyce le symptôme I," 27). The Real, in other words, is an obstacle that fragments and shatters appearances of unity into chaotic bits, its final term being that of the contradiction of the signifier for authority, "Father." When annulled, this signifier shows its structural underpinnings. "Father" signifies desire only in reference to prohibition. Such is Lacan's interpretation of Freud's myth in *Totem and Taboo* in which the primal hoard wishes to destroy the Father, yet feels guilty for this desire. This myth, like many others, served Lacan as a setting out of the conditions of meaning and being, seen as things that will not run smoothly. In this purview, every person's unconscious reserve is ordered by experiences that make of them a symptom, insofar as the symptom is a fourth order or final term by which a subject exists with any sense of being subject to or of some limit. In "Joyce le symptôme I" Lacan says, "All psychic reality, that is to say the symptom, depends on the last term, of a structure where the Name of the Father is an unconditioned element" (27).

Art is an artifice, Lacan suggested, that serves artists in singular ways. In *Portrait* Joyce used Stephen to ask his public for love for himself as author, to hollow out a position for himself in the social sphere. But in *Finnegans Wake* language has itself become a kind of ego. Joyce's unconscious is no longer structured like a language that doubles as a "self" fiction. Rather, language contiguities link pieces of voice to letter and phonation, enabling Joyce to become master of the debris coughed up into his discourse from the Real. In his seminar *Le Sinthome* Lacan wrote: "One thinks against a signifier. This is the meaning I have given the word *appensé*. One leans against a signifier to think" (*Ornicar?* 11,9). So while Joyce's art may be the quintessence of Modernism for literary critics, for Lacan his art elaborated an ego already positioned at the breaking point, but an elaboration that enabled him to live with some Imaginary identificatory consistency in the world of others. Joyce's art did not cure his symptoms nor stop his suffering. For his readers Joyce's language is, however, an interpretative delirium that stretches to infinity, in the words of Slavoj Zizek, "from the time when each stable moment reveals itself to be only an effect of the congealing of a plural signifying process" ("Limits," 38-39).

Zizek has called Joyce the writer of the fantasy in Lacan's sense, where "fantasy" closes off the space of a painful inert presence he called "non-dialectisable *jouissance.*" The prose of *Finnegans Wake* becomes the fantasy of language knotting together images, words, and traumas to (re)constitute knots into which signifying associative chains from the Real, Symbolic, and Imaginary can hook themselves. In this context Lacan described *Finnegans Wake* as a book about the "polyphony of the *parole*" that manifested Joyce's *sinthome* in all its pristine purity. *Finnegans Wake* is anything but a book about play and humor, as some Joyce critics have argued. It is a book about the *sinthome,* itself a kind of writing that is irreducible. Symptom and symbol coalesce in the Real at a place where a signifier's meaning is not intended to be communicated to another as interpretable ("Le Sinthome, Séminaire du 18 novembre," 47).

Lacan's innovative conception of the *sinthome* refers to a kind of writing that is completely empty of meaning, noninterpretable, but still does not lose its aptitude for correlating the subject with something of the unconscious: the sexual nonrelation (Lajonquière, 23). Another innovation in Lacan's reading of Joyce's prose is the idea that *Finnegans Wake* is not intended to mystify readers, but is Joyce's desperate effort to try to keep a link to the Symbolic order intact. This writing on the slope of metonymy gave its author a way to live without falling into the abyss of psychotic *jouissance.* As long as he could chain letters together and substitute sounds for images and voices in prose that resembled metaphorical language (just as one can forestall psychosis in the transferential or Imaginary realm by imitating Imaginary order models), Joyce could reconstitute himself as a double structure for others, even if those others could not grasp what he meant. The polyphony of voices in *Finnegans Wake* creates a kind of border or limit, a simulated superego, whose continuing murmurings allow Joyce to make a pact between the *objet a* as cause of desire and the foreclosure of the Father's Name in the Real (there where no clear limits are set).

In *Portrait* Lacan saw Joyce as still engaged in substituting others in sexual relations for the underlying nonrelation of every subject to the Other. Dedalus represented Joyce's effort to face the gaze of Woman who evoked in him the horror of the Other's desire. Although certain women—particularly those whose standing in the Church was worthy—portrayed the "essence of truth" for Joyce, sexual women threatened him with the "gates of hell." In this sense, Woman was for him, as for other men, a symptom of masculine fantasy relations to the *objet a* Lacan called the void. In a complicated set of arguments Lacan has argued that there is no the in the Woman for she reaches into the ineffable realm of the Real and is, in consequence, villified, deified, or in other ways symptomatic for men (see Lacan, *Encore*; André Aubert, "Avent Propos," 18). In a Lacanian interpretation of literary texts, one can never dismiss figurations of women. It is not that Woman (or women as figures) is synonymous with "truth" or is essentialized in any other way. But she is close to the realm of a "truth" that lives us mysteriously, as an inwardness we recognize but whose source or meaning we cannot quite grasp. In *Portrait* Joyce uses Stephen's voice to block out the female gaze with all its intimations of seduction and judgment. Yet not only do the names of Molly and Nora open onto feminine sexuality, Joyce goes beyond names or characters in his grasp of the feminine when he confronts the Woman in his epiphanies. Catherine Millot has called the epiphanies "trivial vulgar moments" when they concern masculine desire or Woman and sexuality. They indicate Joyce's use of *jouissance* to show the emptiness of phallic meaning in a return that marks the place of *das Ding* as invisible space (Millot, 94). By the time he writes *Finnegans Wake*, Woman is no longer Joyce's major threat. The Real or the hole in the Other is. Instead of making Woman the solution and battleground for his life epic, Joyce took the turn toward the Father, the turn that required him to try to contain the overspill of the unbarred gaze of the Real.

In 1976 Lacan's clinical and theoretical orientation toward the Real does not bear any longer on the Name of the Father, but on the foreclosure of meaning in relation to his axiom that there is no sexual relation at the heart of sexual relating. Rather there are "partial drives" that appeal to others, after having gone through the circuit of the Other. These drives constitute the unconscious desire that conditions each subject (Lajonquière, 22-24). Joyce himself names the foreclosure of the signifier for a Father's Name "the legal fiction of paternity." Not only external invaders—the British Empire, the Church, and so on—but also Joyce's own deteriorating eyesight and his daughter Lucia's psychosis, give a certain meaning to his prose. To read Lacan with an artist is to read art with life. To read *Finnegans Wake* with Lacan's theory of the symptom is to rethink the question of identity in relation to the concept of a signifier for law or limits.

Although Lacan first theorized the potential infinitization of the signifier in 1953, his interest in Joyce in the 1970s bears on the death drive rather than on the play of the signifier. What Freud called the "silence of the drives" in *Beyond the Pleasure Principle*, Lacan named the Real points of an irreducible movement in a subject's primary symbolizations, concerning the residue surrounding the signifier of the Father's Name. A Real knot blocks Symbolic differentials and Imaginary collusions. But Lacan knew that neither analyst nor literary critic—nor author for that matter—can get to the Real (which never ceases writing itself) by simply deconstructing texts or merely by decoding enigma or making innumerable puns. Put another way, language produces a Real which does not have any *corresponding* reality. Thus, it is difficult even to know when one is in the presence of the Real. Yet, paradoxically, even though the Real is the expulsion of, even the aversion to, meaning, Millot points out that the only way it can be treated is by being symbolized (91). In this context perhaps one can better understand that Lacan would take Freud's allegory in *Totem and Taboo* of a mythic father to be a Real father who signifies the paradoxical circumscription of law by desire (Aubert, "Le sinthome, Séminaire du 20 janvier," 66).

One enters the Symbolic order in the first place at the price of submission to an Imaginary father whose superego images are initially (for any child) incomprehensible, if not ferocious and obscene. No child is born understanding that someone must "lay down the law." Although one of the Names of the Father is "mother," Lacan's larger point is that Father signifies law because he is the diacritical opposite of mother, making male/female seem a natural opposition or at least a differential. But the effects of this seemingly equal opposition are structured asymmetrically in terms of gender identity, not as a clear equality. Because law actually dwells in some third position apart from mother and father alike, never equal to itself, yet seemingly attached first to a family structure and then to a social one, the signifier for law always appears to be attached to familial requisites. Freud called it the internalized superego and saw it as necessary to social functioning. Lacan emphasized that without an internalized representation of a border or an identity limit, a subject is open to the chaos of the Real which wreaks havoc on subjects who have little or no sense of a self that has a name and some characteristic properties. Without our "legal fictions," Lacan argued, psychosis waits in the wings, attesting to the human incapacity to think oneself human unless one already has a firm conceptualization of a position in a given Symbolic order. When psychosis appears the individual and particular character of the Real destroys Symbolic systems and Imaginary pacts that seemed adequate to subject functioning when no severe challenge to identity—who are you and what are you worth?—occurred.

The Symbolic Father is a pure signifier, for Lacan, to which there is no correlative representation. Insofar as the mother is a natural signifier, the father is the first signifier for culture, a human interpretation imposed on nature to structure and shape it. This signifier, sometimes called the phallic signifier, denotes its own lack, as well as the possibility of its denotation. "In this respect the Name of the Father is one of the minimal elements of any signifying network whatsoever. Lacan, like Freud, situates the Name of the Father in 'prehistory,' though he instead calls it 'transcendent,' a term that needs to be treated with caution. In calling this signifier transcendent he is claiming that while it has no correlate in any representation it is nevertheless a condition for the possibility of any representation" (Grigg, 120).

In many of his own *Ecrits*, Lacan, like Joyce, pushed at normative linguistic borders where conventions and grammar rules point to some authoritative referent. By pushing style to its limit, both men created a language where the mark of a lack in the Other can evade the Imaginary and attach itself to the Symbolic by the Real. In turn, language can be used to hook into the Real in an effort to avoid and evacuate Imaginary relations. Such writing dwells outside the "human," as if suspended from nowhere. It reveals that language can play around the void of lost objects that return as *objet a*. *Finnegans Wake* dramatizes a "beyond" Joyce's aesthetic, into Lacan's Real. Joyce's efforts to construct an aesthetic remain mimetic and imitative—Imaginary images and Symbolic codes—while the Lacanian Real is a savoir faire linked to the practice of the signifier joined to the *objet a*: "An action planned by man which places him in the situation of treating the Real by the Symbolic" (D. Miller, 34).

Insofar as an aesthetic implies distance and perspective, Lacan's theory that metaphor and the subject of desire function by the same substitutive movement or law confronts us with a "materialization of language" where the word becomes the flesh of being, precisely because meaning must take up the burden of supporting *jouissance* as well as the unconscious signifying chains that speak us. When a signifier refers to the Father's Name, the Real suddenly becomes stronger than ordinarily so. The *objet a* shows its face as a *point de capiton* (anchoring button), making of the subject the same object that causes his desire. But since desire and *jouissance* are at odds, human subjects are asymmetrical (that is, dialectical or contradictory) within their very being. This is because subjects are the causes of Real effects that inhabit them intimately, but as if from afar. If a subject is his own *sinthome*, one can see that actions—including artistic acts—that one performs without necessarily understanding why, may have a *cause* in an Elsewhere with its own meaning and logic. It becomes possible to imagine that James Joyce could have written *Finnegans Wake* to resist the void at the center of his being, as a survival action. In this act his tools or weapons would be words and sounds. In Lacanian terms, the return of the Real always perforates the Symbolic and Imaginary as nonlinear interferences. But for those who are potentially psychotic, the *objet a* can have the paradoxical function of replacing a hole in representation and being, possibly forestalling a psychotic episode or suicide. But would a "supposed" use of the Real in language not merely be a stylistic trick played by Joyce? Worse yet, one which might make of him a neoplatonist trying to unify his being and thinking by seeking an aesthetic in essences thought to dwell in language, or in the Irish people, or in some ideal Form? Lacan's answer would be no. Joyce's goal is not to totalize, nor idealize, but simply to escape the rawness of anxiety produced by the effects of the Real that live him.

Lacan saw language as creative of being in the first place, leaving certain minimal structures in its wake. When language, identifications, and experience are not sufficiently tied together, the Real (or *objet a*), which is usually obscured by apparent unities and by being tied to the other orders, becomes visible. It returns as a gaze or voice or act. Thus, even psychotic language is full of meaning, although its meaning might seem chaotic or peculiar. Yet, the Real as we ordinarily experience it in anxiety, dreams, *jouissance*, and so on, has no explicable meaning at all. In this context, Lacan read Joyce as exemplary of his theory that the Oedipal complex is a symptom that subsists only in relation to language: only because the Name of the Father is the father of the name, and "at least one" element by which we knot together a fiction of being. Through his art Joyce gave life to the archaic fathers in his memory network. Dead persons and failed beliefs are joined to the vitality of the voice, making a signifying knot for the Father's Name foreclosed in Joyce's unconscious. Lacan argued in his seminar on *Le Sinthome* that Joyce's writing actually established a secondary knot between the Imaginary, Symbolic, and Real that tied lack to voice, being, and letter. One might call this a prosthetic knot.

Although Lacan discounts most of Joyce's explanations of how he established his aesthetic, one aspect of his aesthetic did help him to turn *jouissance* or suffering into art: his creation of the epiphany. These joyful moments of mastery become less joyful in *Finnegans Wake* where puns are not so imitative of speech as they are exemplary of linguistic "free association" taken to its breaking point. Lacan's interpretation of Joyce's epiphanies looks at the flip side of what Millot termed trivial vulgarities. When brilliant irradiance is attached to these textual moments they unveil a manic joy of elation and liberation. Lacan called this, quoting Thomas Aquinas, *claritas.* Such "clarity" is a return of the Real, said Lacan, that shows the Wizard-of-Oz shibboleth of phallic law. As such the epiphanies are a "singular" writing, an *écriture* placed at the limits of the Real that touch on the mystical. In Millot's view, Joyce's epiphanies are like "holophrases," which Lacan redefined as the summing up of everything in a few words that seek to grasp an absolute: God, Woman, the All (Aubert, "Avant Propos," 15). Aubert writes that Joyce's epiphanies try to organize what Joyce does not consciously understand, although he seeks to construct what he cannot see or say by trying to control what actually controls him ("Galeries," 83).

Lacan says Joyce in *Finnegans Wake* gave up his belief in a substitute or pseudofather and took the third-person position of one listening to onself write, rather than the usual second-person position of writer to text. The voice becomes palpable, if not visible, as a libidinal object that carries signifiers along. Indeed, for Lacan, Joyce identified with the underwoven vocal tones in his own discourse and in this way escaped the actual death of his ego. Moreover, his writing enabled him to maintain and reconstitute a seemingly unified Imaginary body. In Lacan's thought, the body is an Imaginary signifier that demarcates one kind of limit to thought and desire. By linking language, unconscious signifiers, and body, Joyce created a world where a relationship between ear and eye could exist, even though he had difficulties in seeing. He invented a prose reduced to the torsion of the voice joined to phonation. Sayings such as "you are—very—baa-aa-dd" open up a split between words used for meaning and the voice as a desiring part of the body. In this final text Joyce fully assumes Lacan's name for him: Joyce the *sinthome*.

By viewing Joyce as one who poses his identity question in art, Jacques-Alain Miller sees him as one who succeeded in passing from contingency to a kind of consistency ($ \mathcal{S} \longrightarrow $ (a)]. But the consistency at issue is not perverse or hypocritical because it entails building a language on the side of the *écrit*: something not written to be read in an ordinary way. As Zizek puts it, such language has the status of the *objet a* or cause of desire out of which signifying textures arise in the first place ("Why Lacan is Not a 'Post-Structuralist'," 31-39). One cannot, however, comfortably describe such language as a Lacanian signifier—that which represents a subject for another signifer—because it does not represent a subject coherently. More apt for Lacan is Philippe Sollers's description of *Finnegans Wake* as an exploding and regrouping of language. The art object is no longer as aesthetic artifact, but an *objet a*, itself made of separable parts: voice, name, symptom, palpable *jouissance*. That Joyce could come so close to writing down the unwritable becomes an unwitting revelation of the *équivoque* that ordinarily characterizes language. That is, language can lie, pun, overdetermine meanings, make homophones, turn the phoneme into an empty letter. Seen this way, the letter no longer resides on the side of *l'être* (being), but on the side of trash or litter (Schreiber, 10). This Real of the letter can be taken as an evisceration of meaning, a model of Joyce's epiphanies taken to their extreme point.

One might argue that when Joyce's unconscious desire and his *jouissance* come together in his writing he cannot offer a unified theory of aesthetics for the simple reason that he cannot close the space between the word and the "letter," insofar as the *lettre* is that of the *objet petit a* that goes beyond transparent meaning. When Lacan spoke at a colloquium on Joyce in France in 1975 he spoke of Joyce's symptom as a dream-wish to mark an end or final term with *Finnegans Wake*, linking the Symbolic, Imaginary, and Real by the Symptom in the form of a knot. One can speak of a knot, Lacan said, because it too has a limit ("Joyce le symptôme I," 29). Insofar as he accomplished the goal of showing himself to be a *Master of the English language*, one might ask what interpretation psychoanalysis might give such an achievement? If Lacan is correct in his theory that language is received by humans as an alienating wall from which they, nonetheless, take the meanings they live by, but can only ever speak as half-truths or as truths half hidden, James Joyce's art revealed that writers create or invent in order to live, not the reverse. Such an understanding of Joyce's art adds something to our comprehension of what the literary is or what the aesthetic might be. Moreover,

Joyce reveals that *writing* at its own limits meets—and reveals—the *objet a*. His daughter Lucia's name stands for an *objet a*: the gaze. Lucia means the goddess of seeing or light. The choice of her name, as well as the fact of her psychosis, are evidence for Lacan that she herself is a clue to the enigma that is her father (Kuberski, 49-66).

Lacan was also interested in Joyce's insistence that his daughter was not psychotic, but was telepathic. While Joyce meant that Lucia was endowed with superior intelligence, that she could inform him miraculously of future events through secrets only she knew, Lacan understood something different by "telepathic." Although Lacan found no magic in the idea of telepathy, he did not dismiss the phenomenon, and suggested in his 1953 "Discourse of Rome":

> That the unconscious of the subject is the discourse of the Other appears even more clearly than anywhere else in the studies that Freud devoted to what he called telepathy as manifested in the context of an analytic experience. This is the coincidence of the subject's remarks with facts about which he cannot have information, but which are still at work in the connexions of another experience in which the same psychoanalyst is the interlocutor—a coincidence moreover constituted most often by an entirely verbal, even homonymic, convergence, or which, if it involves an act, is concerned with an "acting out" by one of the analyst's other patients or by a child of the person being analyzed who is also in analysis. It is a case of resonance in the communicating networks of discourse, an exhaustive study of which would throw light on similar facts presented by everyday life. ("Function and field," 55-56)

In Lacan's estimation, Joyce unconsciously looked to his child, even as he chose her name, for help with what he could not see/understand. As his ego gradually unraveled, dissolving borders between whether or not he was controlling language or being controlled by it, it must have seemed to Joyce that he received words in a somewhat hallucinatory—if not telephatic— manner. Moreover, his glaucoma ebbed and flowed, depending on whether or not he was writing, giving it a strangely psychosomatic aspect (Guir, 17). Insofar as *jouissance* is unpleasure, yet the secret satisfaction at the heart of a symptom that attaches a subject to his pain, even serving as the pivot around which he turns, in Joyce's case, not seeing would equal not wanting to know what was written indelibly in his unconscious. Dominique Miller has written that "it is in the measure that the symptom makes an enigma for the subject that a knowledge, in the name of the unconscious, is suspended" (34).

Lacan speculated that Lucia's psychosis was an extension of Joyce's own forestalled psychosis. She lived the suffering he was able to keep at bay by his art. Of course many questions remain unanswered in such speculations. Is Lucia schizophrenic as diagnosed, or severely hysterical? Lacanian analysts find many women hospitalized in the Anglophone world and misdiagnosed as psychotic or borderline patients because the diagnostic category of hysteria is not used clinically or theoretically by the analysts in question. Moreover, in a Lacanian purview, a psychosis is passed on to a child through the mother's desire to close out the father, not directly from the father's inadequacies. The recent book by Brenda Maddox on Joyce's wife Nora, *The Real Life of Molly Bloom,* suggests that the mother may well have been a cause of Lucia's psychosis, although Maddox's viewpoint is that given the difficulties of living with James Joyce, Nora is not to be blamed for any problems she may have caused her daughter (O'Brien, 33). In any event, Lucia's letters to her father reveal an extreme care to avoid a kind of "psychic incest," a care that perhaps cost her a normal life. If Lucia's very life was constituted so as to protect her father's fragile ego, she dwells on the same side as the fictional character Stephen Dedalus. Both would bear witness to Joyce's final failure to project enough Imaginary material onto others in order to survive in any mimesis of normalcy. Yet, by double, I do not refer to the split in the subject where conscious and unconscious *savoir* fades in and out.

In *James Joyce and the Revolution of the Word* Colin MacCabe has written: "To speak is to have accepted a symbolic castration; to have accepted difference and absence. To enter into language is thus to have denied to the father his self-sufficiency and it is this denial which constitutes the guilt associated with language" (145). Lacan teaches the opposite of what MacCabe has written. To speak or write with coherency or consistency demonstrates adequate confidence in an unconscious paternal representation to be able to ignore its effects on language. Lacan saw the relationship between symptoms and language as a kind of half-speaking between primordially repressed representations and a master discourse which is normative and based on further repression of the paternal signifier for any lack or division at all.

In his third theory of the symptom, Lacan thought there was more to *jouissance* than he had previously suggested. Even in analysis, he said, excess *jouissance* remains excessive. It resists cure. Unlike unconscious *savoir*, it is another kind of truth that wants no knowledge of itself. No one, himself included, wants to be cured of their symptoms because the death drive—which Lacan translates as *jouissance*—lies beyond the pleasure principle and beyond the principle of repetition. Freud called this phenomenon negative transference or unconscious masochism. Lacan called it the Real, or the existence of displeasure, discontent, enjoyment in the breach of the pleasure principle that places a stubborn obstacle in every life and a discontent or malaise in civilization. Lacan called the satisfaction of this death drive, as distinct from instinct, *jouissance* (Miller, "A and a," 23). While unconscious desire is connected to speech, *jouissance* dwells on the side of the silence of the drives. Indeed, *jouissance* is the very principle of symptom formation that appears as the "drive not to know."

In Lacan's many lectures on Joyce, he mentions the extraordinary accomplishment of devising a magisterial *dire* that enabled him to avoid his own imminent dissolution. In thinking of this picture of Joyce, I envision a man carrying on his back a mountain of monumental proportions, actually carrying his own mountain with him, rather than merely rolling some mythic stone up and down a mountain like Sisyphus. Lacan has said that sometimes the only adequate way to speak about the adequacy of language to itself is to speak about the manner of its movement. In this concept, language is an affected action, a trajectory, a path-forger, a constituting and reconstituting medium. At first glance a Lacanian might take the movement of Joyce's language to resemble that of an obsessional discourse, a usually masculine structure where the feminine seems all-consuming and is to be avoided at any cost, even though obsessional men are paradoxically overly dependent on the women they hold at arm's length. The obsessional's goal is to use language as a weapon to close out desire. Information systems, encyclopedic knowledge, ritualization of words and things, the use of sex to avoid speaking of love, are all welcome in this use of language that tries to exclude the unbearable threat of desire. Language itself becomes a fortress with potentially double-barred doors from which the all-too-present Other discourse is denied entrance.

On the other hand, one might view Joyce's language movement as typically hysterical, although hysteria is generally the feminine version of obsession (although they act differently). While masculine normativity is based on an accepted identification between father and sons, where desire and law are united in an ego ideal, in hysteria the Imaginary father engenders frustration at the level of ideals and leaves usually the female hysteric with a ferocious superego. Her duty is nothing less than to unconsciously support the desire of a denigrated father who gains his power of death over her life by his very shame which she takes on as her special burden to bear. In the end result, as Jacques-Alain Miller has put it, hysteria is itself dissatisfaction with knowledge as it stands ("A and a," 20).

Although there may be hysterial and obsessional traits in some of Joyce's texts, in the overall movement of his language something else occurs. A kind of tape-recorded double of sounds and voices appears behind and within regular language. The shadow language points to a prepsychotic structure where language is broken down into pieces in order to serve grammar as a missing superego or border that will prop up the ego, lest it collapse into the sterility of psychotic speech where there is no distance from the Other, no metaphorical law of the double. In the 1970s Lacan argued that foreclosure of the signifier for the Father's Name was not enough to cause a psychotic breakdown. Although the Real returns in the symptom to satisfy the superego which demands the right to *jouir* in the field of the Symbolic, and the *objet* returns in the Real by way of the Imaginary in fantasy, in psychosis the Real becomes detached from the Imaginary and Symbolic. Thus when there is a failure of—in Joyce's case masculine—identity, when any semblance of phallic authority disappears, it is still possible for a person to identify with the symptom as the terminal point of a failure of their desire (Aramburu, 171-73). This theory led Lacan to rewrite his formula regarding the sexual unrelation, to say that there is no sexual relation which is not supported by the *sinthome* that supports the Other sex of a particular subject. That is, because every subject is the subject of a symptom, thanks to the particularity of a *sinthome*, he or she can have a relation to the Other, from which an identity is forthcoming. The *sinthome* can stand in for the "number" of the Father which Lacan called the fourth term (Grisolia, 31). Only in the outbreak of a psychotic episode does the symptom become synonymous with itself because a relation to the Other disappears. When the ego breaks down and psychosis ensues, the psychotic person becomes the Other. Joyce died at age 58 and never had a psychotic break. In the broadest conception of the symptom that one can find in Lacan's teaching, the *sinthome* played the displacement role for Joyce of building simulated relations to others, as in ordinary (sexual) relations, thus maintaining some distance from the Other. There may have been foreclosure of the signifier for the Father's Name in James Joyce's unconscious, but Joyce never became psychotic as did Judge Daniel Schreber, for example, because Joyce's *sinthome* is itself the knot that ties together the Borromean topology (R.S.I.) requisite to subject functioning, creating the illusion of a relation to the Other.

We are no longer speaking of Oedipus, but of the difference between a *sinthomal* and a *nonsinthomal* structure where the foreclosure of the paternal reference is compensated for by art ("Lajonquière," 23-24). Perhaps we are speaking of the case of "one," if not the only one, at least one of few writers who have shown that literary art is not the unconscious, but can respond to unconscious drives (the *objet a*) to create against the odds. As such, artistic creation shows itself to be the greatest achievement of mankind. In speaking of James Joyce in Lacanian terms, we speak of the *sinthome* of invention, then, not the symptom of pathology. In this sense, James Joyce becomes a *saint homme*.

Psychoanalysis and Semiotics

7
The Limits of the Semiotic Approach to Psychoanalysis
Slavoj Zizek

Le point de capiton

Lacan's best-known proposition is surely the famous "unconscious structured like a language," which is usually understood as pointing towards a semiotic reinterpretation of psychoanalytical theory and practice. The aim of the present paper is to demonstrate that, contrary to this widely assumed proposition, Lacan's theory, at least in its last period, is far from endorsing any kind of language reductionism: his central effort is precisely to articulate the different modes of the real kernel (*das Ding, objet petit a*) which presents an irreducible obstacle to the movement of symbolization. We will try to exemplify this deadlock of symbolization by some ideological and artistic phenomena.

Let's begin on the opposite end: with the elementary *semiotic* operation as it is articulated by Lacan—the operation of *point de capiton*. Lacan introduces this concept in chapter XXI of his seminar on the *Psychoses*, with regard to the first act of *Athalia* by Racine: to the lamentations of Abner about the sad fate which awaits the partisans of God under the reign of Athalia, Joad replies with these famous lines:

> The one who puts a stop to the fury of the waves
> Knows also of the evil men how to stop the plots.
> Subservient with respect to his holy will,
> I fear God, dear Abner, and have no other fear.

Translated by Sylvie Newman. Edited by Ellie Ragland-Sullivan.

which bring about a true conversion of Abner: from an impatient zealot (*zélé*) and precisely for that reason uncertain, they create a calm believer (*fidéle*) assured of himself and of a great divine power. How does this evocation of the "fear of God" succeed in effecting the miraculous conversion? Before this conversion, Abner sees in the earthly world only a multitude of dangers which fill him with fears, and he waits for them to lend them their help and allow him to conquer the many difficulties of this world from the opposite pole, that of God and his representatives. Faced with this opposition between the earthly realm of dangers, uncertainty, fears, etc., and the divine realm of peace, love, and assurance, Joad does not simply try to convince Abner that divine forces are, despite everything, powerful enough to have the upper hand over earthly disarray; he appeases his fears in a quite different way: by presenting him with their very opposite—God—as a more frightening thing than all earthly fears. And—that is, the "miracle" of the *point de capiton*—this supplemental fear, fear of God, retroactively changes the character of all other fears, it

> accomplishes the magical trick of transforming, from one minute to another, all fears into a perfect courage. All fears—*I have no other fear*—are exchanged against what is called the fear of God.[1]

The common marxist formula—religious consolation as compensation or, more precisely "imaginary supplement" to earthly misery—would be taken literally. In this case we are dealing with a dual imaginary relation between the earthly below and the celestial beyond, without the intervention of the moment of symbolic "mediation." The religious operation would consist, according to this conception, in compensating us for earthly horrors and uncertainties by the beatitude which awaits us in the other world—all the famous formulas of Feuerbach on the divine beyond as a specular image, reversed, of earthly misery. For this operation to work, a third moment must intervene which somehow "mediates" between the two opposite poles. Behind the multitude of earthly horrors the infinitely more frightening horror of God's anger must show through, so that earthly horrors take on a new dimension and become so many manifestations of divine anger. One has the same operation, for example in fascism: what does Hitler do in *Mein Kampf* to explain to the Germans the misfortune of this epoch, the economic crisis, the moral "decadence," etc.? Behind the multitudes of these miseries he constructs a new terrifying subject, a unique cause of evil: the Jew. The "Jewish plot" "explains everything" so that all earthly miseries, from the economic crisis to the family crisis, become manifestations of the "Jewish plot": The Jew is Hitler's *point de capiton*.

The "Dreyfus Affair" unfolds this effect of the "miraculous curve" of the discursive field, produced by the intervention of the *point de capiton* in a paradigmatic fashion. Its role in French and European political history already resembles that of a *point de capiton* for it will restructure that entire field and release, directly or indirectly, a whole series of displacements which still even today determine the political scene. Some displacements which ensued are the final separation of Church and State in bourgeois democracies, the socialist collaboration in bourgeois government, and the split of social democracy into socialists and communists. One can also point to the birth of Zionism, the elevation of antisemitism to the key-moment of "right wing populism."

But here one will only try to indicate the decisive turn in its development: the intervention which made a judiciary quarrel bearing on the equity and legality of a verdict the stake of a political battle which shook national life in its entirety. This turning point is not to be sought, as one usually believes, in the famous *J'accuse* that appeared in the *Aurore*, January 13, 1898, where Zola took up once again all the arguments for Dreyfus's defense and denounced the corruption of the official circles. Zola's intervention remained in the cadre of bourgeois liberalism, that of the defense of liberties and rights of the citizen, etc. The real upset took place in the second half of the year, 1898. On August 30th, Lieutenant Colonel Henry, new Chief of the Second Bureau, was arrested. He was suspected of having forged one of the secret documents on the basis of which Dreyfus had been condemned for high treason. The next day, Henry committed suicide with a razor in his cell.

This news provoked a shock in public opinion. If Henry confessed his guilt thus—and what other meaning could one give to his suicide?—the act of accusation against Dreyfus must, in its entirety, lack solidity. Everyone expected a retrial and the acquittal of Dreyfus. For the moment, let us repeat the poetic description of Ernest Nolte:

> Then in the midst of the confusion and consternation, a newspaper article appeared which altered the situation. Its author was Maurras, a thirty-year-old writer hitherto known only in limited circles. The article was entitled "The first blood". It looked at things in a way which no one had thought or dared to look.[2]

What did Maurras do? He did not present any supplementary evidence, he did not refute any fact. He simply made a global reinterpretation by means of which the whole "affair" appeared in a different light. He made a heroic victim of Lieutenant Colonel Henry, who had preferred patriotic duty to abstract "justice." That is to say, Lt. Col. Henry after having seen how the Jewish "Syndicate of Treason" exploited a little judiciary error in order to denigrate and undermine the foundation of French life, for the purpose of breaking the force of the Army, did not hesitate to commit a small patriotic falsity in order to stop this race towards the precipice. The true stake in the "affair" is no longer the fairness of a sentence but the shock, the degeneration of the vital French force from the Jewish financiers who hide behind corrupt liberalism, freedom of the press, autonomy of justice, etc. As a result, its true victim is not Dreyfus but Henry himself, the solitary patriot who risked everything for the salvation of France and on whom his superiors, at the decisive moment, turned their backs: the "first blood" spilled by the Jewish plot.

That intervention changed, the right wing united its forces, and "patriotic" unity rapidly took the upper hand over the disarray. Maurras provoked this upset by creating the triumph, the myth of the "first victim," from the very elements which, before his intervention, roused disorientation and amazement (the falsification of documents, the inequity of the sentence, etc.), and which he was far from contesting. It is not surprising that up until his death he considered this article as the best work of his life.

The elementary operation of the *point de capiton* should be sought in this "miraculous" turn, in this quid pro quo by means of which what was just prior the very source of the disarray, becomes the proof and the testimony of a triumph—as in the first act of *Athalia* where the intervention of the "supplementary fear," that of God, suddenly changes all the other fears into their opposites. Here one is dealing with the act of "creation" in its strictest sense: the act which turns a chaos into a "new harmony" and suddenly makes "comprehensible" what was up to then only a senseless and even terrifying disturbance. It is impossible not to recall Christianity—less the act of God which made an ordered world out of chaos—than this decisive turning from which the definitive form of Christian religion, the form which showed its worth in the tradition which is ours resulted. This is, of course, the Paulinian cut. Saint Paul centered the whole Christian edifice precisely on the point which up to now appeared, to the disciples of Christ like a horrifying trauma, "impossible," non-symbolizable, non-integrable in their field of signification: his shameful death on the cross between two bandits. Saint Paul made of this final defeat of his earthly mission which annihilated the hope of deliverance (of Jews from the Roman domination) the very act of salvation. By his death Christ has redeemed, saved humankind.

Tautology and its forbidden

One can bring light to the logic of this operation by a small detour through the detective story. What is the principal charm of the detective story concerning the relationship between law and its transgression, the criminal adventure? We have on one side the reign of law, tranquillity, certainty, but also the triteness, the boredom of everyday life, and on the other side crime as—Brecht was already saying it—the only possible adventure in the bourgeois world. Detective stories, however, operate at this time a terrific trick, already uncovered by Gilbert Keith Chesterton:

> To the old Adam, who whispers continuously in front of a phenomenon as universal and as automatic as civilization, and always advocates escape or revolt, they teach that civilization is the most moving escape and the most romanesque of revolts . . . By showing us the policeman alone and without fear in a den of bandits, surrounded by knives and tight fists, they remind us that this agent of

social justice is an original and poetic figure, while the thieves and the pieds-feutrés (quiet feet) are only the cold conservators of the avatism of apes and wolves. Thus, the novel of the police is a novel of man. It rests on this declaration that morality is the darkest and the most audacious of conspirations.[3]

The fundamental operation of the detective story then consists in presenting the detective himself—the one who works for the defense of the law, in the name of the law, in order to restore the reign of the law—as the greatest adventurer, as a person in comparison to which it is the criminals themselves who appear like indolent petit-bourgeois, careful conservators. . . . It is a true miraculous magic trick: there are, of course, a great number of transgressions of the law, crimes, adventures which break the monotony of everyday loyal and tranquil life, but, the only true transgression, the only true adventure, the one which changes all the other adventures into a careful petit-bourgeoise, is the adventure of civilization, of the defense of the law itself.

And it is about the same with Lacan. For him also, the greatest transgression, the most traumatic, the most senseless thing, is law itself: the mad, superegotistical law which inflicts, which commands enjoyment. One does not have on one side a plurality of transgressions, perversions, aggressivities, etc., and on the other side a universal law which regulates, normalizes the cul-de-sac of transgressions and makes possible the pacific co-existence of subjects. The maddest thing is the other side of the appeasing Law itself, the law as a misunderstood, dumb injunction to enjoyment. One can say that Law divides itself necessarily into an appeasing law and a mad law. The opposition between the Law and its transgressions repeats itself inside the Law itself. Thus one has here the same operation as the one in *Athalia*. In Chesterton, law appears, in the face of ordinary criminal transgressions, as the only true transgression. In *Athalia*, God appears, in face of earthly fears, as the only thing which is really to be feared. God thus divides himself into an appeasing God, a God of love, tranquillity and grace, and into a fierce, enraged God, the one who provokes in man the most terrible fear.

This turn, this point of reversal where the law itself appears as the only true transgression, corresponds exactly to what one calls, in Hegelian terminology, the "negation of the negation." We have the simple opposition between the position and its negation, first in our case, between the positive, appeasing Law, and the multitude of its particular transgressions, crimes. The "negation of the negation" is the moment when one notices that the only true transgression, the only true negativity, is that of the Law itself which changes all of the ordinary, criminal transgressions, into an indolent positivity. That is why Lacanian theory is irreducible to any variant of transgressism, of anti-oedipism, etc. The only true anti-oedipism is the Oedipe himself, his superegotistical reverse. . . . One can follow this "Hegelian" economy up to Lacan's organizing decisions. The dissolution of the *Ecole freudienne de Paris* and the constitution of the *Cause freudienne* could have given the impression of a liberating act—an end to bureaucratization and regimentation of the school. Now, one would only worry about the Cause itself, liberated from all the earthly hindrances. . . . Indeed, very quickly, one noticed that this act enhanced the restoration of an *Ecole de la Cause elle-même*, much more severe than all the other schools, just as the surpassing of earthly fears by divine love implicates the fear of God, more terrible than all earthly fears.

The most appropriate form to indicate in ordinary language this curve of the *point de capiton*, of the "negation of the negation," is, paradoxically, that of the tautology—"law is law," "God is God." Here the tautology functions precisely in the Hegelian sense, as one's identity which reveals the supreme contradiction. In the tautology "God is God," the first God is the one of tranquillity, grace, and love, while the second God is the one of an unsustainable rage and fierceness. Likewise, the tautology "law is law" shows the illegal and illegitimate character of the establishment of the reign of the Law. Blaise Pascal probably was the first to detect this subversive content of the tautology "the law is the law":

> Custom completely makes equity, for this sole reason that it is received; it is the mystical foundation of its authority. Whoever brings it back to its principal, annihilates it. Nothing is so wrong than those laws which rectify faults; whoever obeys them because they are just, obeys the justice they imagine, but not to the essence of law: it is completely gathered in itself; it is law, and nothing more . . . That is why the wisest of legislators used to say that, for the good of men, one must often snare them; and another, good politician: "Since he ignores the truth which frees, it is good that he is fooled." He must not feel the truth of the usurpation; it had formerly been introduced without reason, it has become reasonable; one must look at it as authentic, eternal, and hide its beginning if one does not want it to soon be at an end.[4]

It is useless to underline the scandalous character of these propositions: they subvert the foundations of power, of its authority, at the very moment when they give the impression of supporting them. The illegitimate violence by which law sustains itself must be dissembled at any price, because this dissemblance is the positive condition of the functioning of the law. The law functions insofar as its subjects are fooled, insofar as they feel the authority of the law as "authentic, eternal" and do not feel "the truth of the usurpation." That is why Kant is forced in his *Metaphysique des moeurs* to forbid, each question concerning the origins of legal power. Through precisely such questioning the stain of this illegitimate violence would appear which always soils, like original sin, the purity of the reign of the law. It is not surprising, then, that this prohibition receives in Kant the paradoxical form, well known in psychoanalysis. It forbids (*interdit*) something which is at the same time given as *impossible*:

The origin of supreme power is for the people, who are submitted to it, unfathomable (*insondable*) practically speaking, in other words the subject must not discuss (*ne doit pas discuter*) actively this origin. . . . It is for the people, already submitted to civil law, ratiocinations totally empty and yet dangerous for the state. . . .

It is in *vain* to seek the historical origins (*origines historiques*) of this mechanism, in other words one cannot go back to the very beginning of civil society. . . . But it is a thing that deserves to be punished to undertake this research.[5]

Well, one cannot (ne *peut* pas) go back to the origin of law because one must (*doit*) not do it. One knows the Kantian formula of duty: "You can because you must" ("Du kannst, denn du sollst"). The so-called prohibition is an exact inversion of this famous formula: "You cannot because you must not." The elementary model of such a prohibition is, of course, that of incest. Furthermore, it is, nevertheless, not foreign to philosophical discourse. A whole series of examples shows that, up to the famous proposition which ends the *Tractatus* by Wittgenstein: "Whereof one cannot speak, thereof must be silent." One must ask a totally naive question here. If one declares that one cannot, at any rate, say anything about the ineffable, why add again the totally redundant statement that one must not say anything about it, that one must be quiet? Where does such a fear of not saying too much about the inexpressible come from? The paradox of this "nothing," of this pure semblance, is, of course, the very paradox of the object: cause of desire in the Lacanian sense of the *objet petit a*.

Kant with Sade

"At the beginning" of the law, there is a certain outlaw, a certain reality of violence which coincides with the act itself of the establishment of the law. All of politico-philosophical classical thought rests on the denial of the reverse of the law. That is why one must read "Kant with Sade." If Kant did not manage to articulate the lack in the Other, the big A crossed out, he has however—taking J.-A. Miller's formulation—articulated the big B crossed out under the form of inaccessibility, of absolute transcendance of the supreme Good, the only object and legitimate, non-pathological motor, of our moral activity. Every given, determined, represented object which functions as a motor of our will, is already pathological in the Kantian sense: an empirical object, related to the conditions of our finished experience and not having an a priori necessity. That is why the only legitimate motor of our will remains the very form of the law, the universal form of the moral maxim. The fundamental thesis of Lacan is that this impossible object is nevertheless given to us in a specific experience, that of the *objet petit a*, object-cause of desire which is not "pathological," which does not reduce itself to an object of need or demand. And that is why Sade is to be taken as the truth of

Kant. This object whose experience is eluded by Kant appears precisely in Sade's work, under the appearance of the hangman, the executioner, the agent who practices his sadistic activity on the victim.

The Sadean executioner has nothing to do with pleasure. His activity is in the strictest sense ethical. Beyond each "pathological" motor, he only fulfills his duty. The lack of wit in Sade's work really shows this. The executioner always works for the enjoyment of the Other and not for his own. He becomes a sole instrument of the Will of the Other. In the sadistic scene, near the executioner and his victim, there is always a third, the Other for which the sadist practices his activity, the Other whose pure form is that of the voice of a law which addresses itself to the subject in the second person, with the imperative "Fulfill your duty!"

The greatness of the Kantian ethic is to have formulated for the first time the "beyond of the principal of pleasure." The categorical imperative of Kant is a superegotistical law which goes against the subject's well being. More precisely it is totally indifferent to his well being, which, from the viewpoint of the "principal of pleasure" as it prolongs the "principal of reality," is totally non-economical and non-economizable, senseless. Moral Law is a fierce order which does not admit excuses—"you can because you must"— and which in this way receives an air of mischievous neutrality, of mean indifference.

According to Lacan, Kant avoids the other side of this neutrality of moral law, its meanness and its obscenity, its mischievousness which goes back to the enjoyment behind the law's command; Lacan ties this dissimulation to the fact that Kant avoids the split of the subject (subject of speech/subject of grammar) implicated in moral law. That is the meaning of Lacan's criticism of the Kantian example of the deposit (*dépot*) and of the trustee (*dépositaire*). There the subject of speech is reduced to the subject of grammar, the trustee reduced to his function of trustee: Kant presupposes that we are dealing with a trustee "doing his duty," with a subject who lets himself be taken without remaining in the abstract determination of being the trustee.[6] In the second seminar, Lacan tells a small joke which goes in the same direction: "My fiancée never misses the rendezvous, because as soon as she misses it, she would no longer be my fiancée." Here also, the fiancée is reduced to her function of fiancée. Hegel had already detected the terrorist potential of this reduction of the subject to an abstract determination.

The presupposition of revolutionary terror is indeed that the subject lets himself be reduced to his determination as Citizen who is "doing his duty," which brings about the liquidation of subjects who are not doing this duty. Therefore, Jacobean terror is really the consequence of the Kantian ethic. It is the same with the command word of real socialism: "All the people support the Party." Such a proposition is not an empirical declaration and as such is refutable. It functions, on the contrary, performatively, as the definition of true People, of People "up to their duty." The true People are those who support the Party. The logic is thus exactly the same as that of the joke about the fiancée. "All the people support the Party because the elements of the People who agitate against the Party have in that way excluded themselves from the community of the People." One is dealing after all with what Lacan, in his first seminars, called the founding word (*la parole fondatrice*), the symbolic mandate, etc. (the "you are my fiancée, my trustee, the citizen . . ."). This should be read again from the perspective of the ulterior conceptualization of the S_1, of the master-signifier. The stake of Lacanian criticism is that there is in the subject who takes on himself the symbolic mandate, who accepts to incarnate an S_1, always an excess, a side which does not let itself be taken into the S_1, in the mandate. This excess is precisely the side of the *objet*. As long as he escapes being caught in the signifier, the mandate which is conferred on him by the socio-symbolic tie, the subject of speech functions as an object.

That, then, is the split between the subject of grammar and the subject of speech of law. Behind the S_1, the law in its neutral, pacifying, solemn, and sublime side, there is always a side of the object which announces mischievousness, meanness, and obscenity. Another well-known short story illustrates perfectly this split of the subject of the law. In response to the question of explorers researching cannibalism, the native answers: "No, there aren't any more cannibals in our region. Yesterday, we ate the last one." At the level of the subject of grammar, there are no more cannibals, and the subject of speech is precisely· this "we" who have eaten the last cannibal. That then is the intrusion of the "subject of speech" of the law, elided by Kant: this obscene agent who eats the last cannibal in order to ensure the order of the law. Now we can specify the status of paradoxical prohibition which concerns the question of the origin of law, of legal power. It aims at the object of the law in the sense of its "subject of speech," of the subject who becomes the obscene and fierce agent-instrument of the law.

Kant with McCullough

That is precisely what Kant misses, this philosopher of unconditional Duty, the greatest obsession of the history of philosophy. But what Kant did not know, the vulgar sentimental literature, the *kitsch*, of today knows well. This is not surprising, here, if one realizes that it is precisely in the universe of such a literature that the tradition of "amour courtois" has survived whose fundamental trait consists in considering the love of the Dame as a supreme Duty. Let us take an exemplary case of this genre, *An Indecent Obsession* by Colleen McCullough (a novel completely unreadable and for that reason, published in France in the collection *J'ai lu*), the story of a nurse in charge of psychiatric patients in a small hospital of the Pacific around the end of the Second World War, divided between her professional duty and her love for one of her patients. At the end of the book she figures out things concerning her desire, gives up love and goes back to her duty. At first glance, then, the most insipid moralism: the victory of duty over passionate love, the renunciation of "pathological" love in the name of duty. The presentation of the motives for this renunciation is nevertheless a little more delicate. Here are the last sentences of the novel:

> She had a duty here. . . . This wasn't just a job—her heart was in it, fathoms deep in it! This was what she truly wanted. . . . Nurse Langtry began to walk again, briskly and without any fear, understanding herself at last. And understanding that duty, the most indecent of all obsessions, was only another name for love.

One is dealing then with a true dialectical Hegelian trick: the opposition of love and duty is surpassed when one feels duty itself to be the "other name for love." By means of this reversal—the "negation of the negation"—duty, at first the negation of love, coincides with supreme love which abolishes all other "pathological" loves, or, in order to express oneself in Lacanian terms, it functions as the *point de capiton* in relation to all other "ordinary" loves. The tension between duty and love, between the purity of duty and indecency, the pathological obscenity of love passion, is resolved at the moment when one has experienced the radically obscene character of duty itself.

The essential part rests in this change of place of the "indecent obsession" in relation to the opposition between duty and love. At the beginning it is duty which appears as pure, universal, contrary to the pathological, particular, indecent, love passion. It is duty itself then which is revealed as being *"the most indecent of all obsessions"*. That is the Hegelian logic of "reconciliation" between the Universal and the Particular. The most radical, absolute Particularity is indeed that of the Universal itself as far as it has a negative rapport of exclusion towards the Particular: in other words, in as much as it opposes itself to the Particular and excludes the wealth of its concrete content. And that is how one should also take the Lacanian thesis according to which Good is only the mask of radical, absolute Evil, the mask of "indecent obsession" by *das Ding*, the atrocious-obscene thing. Behind Good, there is radical Evil, Supreme Good is the other name for an Evil which does not have a particular, "pathological" status. As far as it obsesses us in an indecent, obscene way, *das Ding* makes it possible for us to untie ourselves, to free ourselves from our "pathological" attachment to particular, earthly objects. The "Good" is only one way to keep the distance towards this evil Thing, the distance which makes it bearable.

That is what Kant does not know, unlike the *kitsch* literature of our century. The other side, the obscene side, of Duty itself. And that is why it was only possible for him to evoke the concept of *das Ding* in its negative form, as an absurd (im)possibility—in his treatise on negative grandiosities, for example, concerning the difference between logical contradiction and real opposition. Contradiction is a logical relationship which does not have a real existence while, in the real opposition, the two poles are equally positive. In other words their relationship is not that of something in its lack but indeed that of the two positive givens which constitute the opposition. For example, the example which is not accidental at all, insofar as it shows directly the level at which we are, namely that of pleasure, the principal of pleasure—pleasure and pain.

"Pleasure and pain are not compared to each other like gain and absence of gain (+ and −). In other words they are not opposed simply like contradictory (*contradictoire s. logice oppositum*), but also as contraries (*contrarie s. realiter oppositum*)."[7] Pleasure and pain are then like poles of a real opposition, in themselves positive facts. One is negative only in relation to the other, while Good and Evil are contradictory, their rapport being that of + and 0. That is why Evil is not a positive entity. It is only the lack, the absence of Good. It would be an absurdity to want to take the negative pole of a contradiction as something positive, thus, "to think of a particular sort of object and to call them negative things." Furthermore, *das Ding* is, in its Lacanian conceptualization, precisely such a "negative thing, a paradoxical Thing which is only the positivitation of a lack, of a hole in the symbolic Other. *Das Ding* as an "incarnated Evil" is indeed an irreducible object at the level of the principal of pleasure, of the opposition between pleasure and pain. In other words, it is a "non-pathological" object in the strict sense, also the unthinkable paradox of the "critical" step for Kant, for which reason he is to be thought along "with Sade."

The "totalitarian object"

Now, here is our fundamental thesis: the advent of contemporary "totalitarism" introduces a decisive cut in this conjuncture—let's say—classical, a cut which corresponds precisely to the passage from Kant to Sade. In "totalitarism," this illegal agent-instrument of the law, the Sadean executioner, is no longer hidden. He *appears as such* for example in the shape of the Party, agent-instrument of historical will. The Stalinist Party is really and literally an executor of great creations: executor of the creation of communism, the greatest of all creations. That is the meaning of Stalin's famous proposition: "We are, us, communists, people of a different sort. We are carved out of a different material." This "different material" (*the right stuff*, one could say), is precisely the incarnation, the apparition of the object (*objet*). Here, one should go back to the Lacanian determination of the structure of perversion as

> an inverted effect of fantasm. It is the subject who determines himself as object, in his encounter with subjectivity.[8]

The formula for fantasy is written as $\$ \lozenge a$. In other words the crossed-out subject is divided in its encounter with the object—cause of his desire. The sadist inverts this structure, which gives $a \Diamond \$$. In a way he avoids his division to occupy the place of the object himself, of the agent-executor in front of his victim, of the subject divided-hysterized: for example the stalinist in front of the "traitor," the hysterical petit-bourgeois who did not want to completely give up his subjectivity, who continues to "desire in vain" (Lacan). In the same passage Lacan goes back to his *Kant with Sade* in order to recall that the sadist occupies the place of the object "for the benefit of another, for the enjoyment from which he practices his act of a sadistic pervert."[9]

The Other of "totalitarism," for example the "inevitable necessity of laws of historical development" to which the sadean figure of the great Other refers itself, for which the Stalinist executor practices his act, would then be conceived as a new version of the "supreme Being of Evilness" (Lacan). It is this radical objectivization-instrumentization of his own subjective position which confers to the stalinist, beyond the deceptive appearance of a cynical detachment, his unshakable conviction of only being the instrument of the production of historical necessity. The Stalinist Party, this "historical subject," is thus the exact contrary of a subject. The distinctive trait of the "totalitarian subject" is to be sought precisely in this radical refusal of subjectivity in the sense of $\$$, the hysterical-bourgeois subject, in the radical instrumentalization of the subject in relation to the Other. By making himself the transparent instrument of the Will of the Other, the subject tries to avoid his constitutive division, for which he pays through the total alienation of his enjoyment. If the advent of the bourgeois subject is defined by his right to free enjoyment, the "totalitarian" subject shows this liberty to be that of the Other, "supreme Being of Evilness."

One could then conceptualize the difference between the classical, preliberal Master, and the totalitarian leader as that between S_1 and object. The authority of the classical Master is that of a certain S_1, signifier-without-signified, autoreferential signifier which incarnates the performative function of the word (*parole*). The "liberalism" of Enlightenment wants to do without this instance of "irrational" authority. Its project is that of an authority founded entirely in the effective "savoir-(-faire)." In this frame, the Master reappears as the totalitarian Leader. Excluded like S_1, he takes the shape of the object-incarnation of an S_2 (for example the "objective knowledge of the laws of history"), instrument of the superegotistical Will which takes on itself the "responsibility" of producing the historical necessity in its cannibalistic cruelty. The formula, the matheme of the "totalitarian subject," would thus be

$$\frac{S_2}{a}$$

the semblance of a neutral "objective" knowledge, under which the obscene object-agent of a superegotistical Will hides.

The king and his bureaucracy

Hegel was probably the last classical thinker to have developed in his *Philosophie de droit* the necessary function of a purely formal symbolic point, of an unfounded, "irrational" authority. Constitutional monarchy is a rational Whole at whose head there is a strictly "irrational" moment: the person of the monarch. The essential thing, here is the irreducible abyss between the organically articulated rational Whole of the constitution of the State, and the "irrationality" of the person who incarnates supreme Power, by which the Power receives the form of subjectivity. To the reproach that the destiny of the State is abandoned here to the eventuality of the psychic disposition of the monarch (to his wisdom, honesty, courage, etc.), Hegel replies:

> it is indeed the presupposition that one is dealing with the particularity of the character, which does not count here. One is only dealing with, in a completed organization, the peak of the case of the formal decision, and for the monarch, one only needs a man who says "yes" and who says clearly what he wants; because the peak must be such that the particularity of character is not important . . . In a well organized monarchy, the objective side belongs only to the law to which the monarch only has to add the subjective "I want."[10]

The nature of the monarch's act is thus completely formal. The frame of his decisions is determined by the constitution. The concrete content of his decisions is proposed to him by his expert-advisers so that often he has nothing to do but to sign his name. But it this name (*nom*) which is important: "It is the peak that one cannot pass."[11]

Really, everything is already said. The monarch is the "pure" signifier, the master-signifier "without signified." All his "reality" (and authority) rests on the name (*nom*), and that is why his "effectiveness in reality" is arbitrary. It can be abandoned to the biological contingency of heredity. The monarch is the One who—as the exception, "irrational" summit—from the amorphous mass ("not-all") of the people makes the totality of customs concrete. With his ex-sistence of "pure" signifier, he constitutes the Whole in its "organic articulation" (*organische Gliederung*). He is the "irrational" supplement as the condition of the rational Totality, the "pure"-signifier without signified as condition of the organic Whole of the signifier-signified:

> The (*le*) people, considered without (*sans*) their monarch and without the articulation of the Whole which is necessarily and immediately linked here, is an amorphous mass which is no longer a State and to which belong *none* of the determinations present only in a Whole formed in itself (*Formé en soi/in sich geformte Ganze*).[12]

Here, the Hegelian stake is much more ambiguous, even cynical, than we think. His conclusion is almost the following: If the Master is indispensable in politics, one must not condescend to the reasoning of good sense which tells us "that he may at least be the most capable, wise, courageous." One must, on the contrary, save as much as possible of the distance between the symbolic legitimations and the "real" skills, localize the function of the Master in a point rejected from the Whole where it really does not matter if he is dumb. In other words, Hegel says the same thing here as Lacan in his Seminar on *L'Envers de la psychanalyse.* The gap between State bureaucracy and the monarch corresponds to that between the battery of "knowledge" (S_2, the bureaucratic "savoir-faire") and the *point de capiton* (S_1, the "unary" master-signifier) who "upholsters" (*capitonne*) his discourse, who "totalizes" it from outside, who takes on himself the moment of "decision" and confers to this discourse the "performative" dimension. Our only chance is thus to isolate as much as possible S_1, to make of it the empty point of formal "decision" without any concrete weight, in other words to keep a maximal distance between S_1 and the register of "skill qualifications" which is that of the bureaucratic "savoir-(-faire)." If this point of exception fails, bureaucratic knowledge "becomes mad." The "neutrality" proper to the knowledge, in the absence of the *capitonnage*, appears to be "evil." Its very "indifference" provokes in the subject the effect of a superegotistical imperative. In other words, we come to the reign of "totalitarian" bureaucracy.

The decisive thing is thus not to confuse the "irrational" authority of pre-liberal monarchy with that of the post-liberal "totalitarian" regime. The first one is based on the gap of S_1 in relation to S_2, while "totalitarism" comes precisely from the *non-capitonné* bureaucratic discourse of S_2 without S_1. This difference comes out better when one considers the justification of obedience. The "totalitarian" leader demands submission in the name of his supposed "effective" capacities, his wisdom, his courage, his adherence to the Cause, etc. While, if one says "I obey the king because he is wise and just," it is already a crime of lése majesté. The only appropriate justification for this is the tautology: "I obey the king because he is king." Kierkegaard has developed it in a magnificent passage which extends, in an extended arc, from divine authority, through the highest secular authority (the king), up to school and family authority (the father):

> To ask if Christ is profound is a blasphemy and an attempt to destroy him with ruse (either with conscience or without conscience) since the question contains doubt concerning his authority . . . To ask if a King is a genius—for him to be submitted to the case of a positive answer—is actually a lése majesté since the question contains the doubt in the sense of submission to his authority. To submit oneself to school on the condition that this place knows how to be inventive, really means that one doesn't care about school. To venerate one's father because he is a big chief is impiety.[13]

Horkheimer, who cites these lines in *Authorité et famille*, sees in them an indication of the passage of the liberal-bourgeois principal of "rational authority" in the post-liberal "totalitarian" principal of "irrational" and unconditional authority. Against such a reading, one must insist on the gap between symbolic authority and "effective" capacities which alone hold open the non-"totalitarian" space. In other words, Kierkegaard moves here on the terrain of pre-liberal Hegelian argumentation, while post-liberal "totalitarism" is to be taken as an effect of the interior reversal of "liberalism" itself. Namely: When and in what conditions does State bureaucracy become "totalitarian"? Not there where S_1, the point of "irrational" authority, would exert a pressure "too strong," excessive, on the bureaucratic savoir(-faire), but on the contrary where this "unary" point which *"capitonne"* and "totalizes" from outside the field of S_2 fails (*fait défaut*). The bureaucratic "knowledge" "becomes mad." It works "by itself," without reference to a decentered point which would confer to it the "performative" dimension. In a word, it starts to function as a superego.

The "mischievous neutrality" of bureaucracy

When knowledge itself takes on itself the moment of "authority," summons, command, imperative, a short circuit between the "neutral" field of knowledge and the "performative" dimension is produced. Far from limiting itself to a kind of "neutral" declaration of the given objectivity, the discourse "becomes mad" and starts to behave itself in a "performative" way towards the given of the facts themselves. More precisely, it masks its own "performative force" under the shape of "objective knowledge," of the neutral "declaration" of the "facts." The example which comes to mind immediately is the Stalinist bureaucratic discourse, the supposed "knowledge of objective laws" as the ulterior legitimation of its decisions: a true "uncontrolled knowledge" capable of "founding" any decision after the fact. And it is, of course, the subject who pays for this "short circuit" between S_1 and S_2. In a "pure" case the accused with great political trials finds himself confronted by an impossible choice. The confession demanded from him is obviously in conflict with the "reality" of the facts since the Party asks him to declare himself guilty of "false accusations." Furthermore, this demand of the Party functions as a superegotistical imperative which means that it constitutes the symbolic "reality" of the subjects. Lacan insists many times on this link between the superego and the supposed "sentiment of reality." "When the sentiment of strangeness bears on something, it is never on the side of the superego. It is always the ego that gets lost."[14] Does he not indicate by this an answer to the question: where does the confession come from in the Stalinist trials? Since there was not any "reality" outside of the superego of the Party for the accused, outside its obscene and mean imperative, the only alternative to this superegotistical imperative being the emptiness of an abominable reality, the confession demanded by the Party was indeed the only way for the accused to avoid the "loss of reality." Stalinist "confessions" are to be conceived as an extreme consequence which ensues from the "totalitarian" short circuit between S_1 and S_2. In other words, in the way that S himself takes the "performative" dimension on itself, one is dealing with a "mad" variant of the discourse's own "performativity." The signifying work can indeed "change reality," namely, the symbolic reality, by transforming retroactively the signifying network which determines the symbolic significance of the "facts." But here, signifying work "falls into the real," as if language could change the facts outside-language in their "massivity," itself very real.

The fundamental fact of the advent of "totalitarism" would consist then of social Law beginning to function as a superego. Here it is no longer the one which "forbids" and, on the basis of this prohibition, opens, supports, and guarantees the field of coexistence of "free" bouregois subjects, the field of their diverse pleasures. By becoming "mad," it begins to directly command enjoyment: the turning point where freedom-to-enjoy permitted is reversed into an obligatory enjoyment which is, one must add, the most effective way to block the access of the subject to enjoyment. One finds in Kafka's work a perfect staging of bureaucracy under the aspect of an obscene, fierce, "mad" law, a law which immediately inflicts enjoyment: in short, of the superego.

> Thus I belong to justice, says the priest. Since then, what could I want from you? Justice does not want anything from you. It takes you when you come and leaves you when you leave.

How can one not recognize, in these lines with which the interview between Josef K. and the priest ends in Chapter IX of *Trial*, the "mischievous neutrality" of the superego? Already the starting point of his two great novels, *The Trial* and *The Castle*, the call of a superior instance (the Law, the Castle) to the subject—aren't we dealing with a law which "would command: Enjoy, to which the subject could only reply by an: I hear (*J'ouis*), where the enjoyment would be nothing more than an innuendo"?[15] The "misunderstanding," the "confusion" of the subject confronting this instance, isn't it precisely due to the fact that he misunderstands the imperative of enjoyment which resounds here and which perspires through all the pores of its "neutral" surface? When Josef K., in the empty audience room, glances at the judges' books, he already finds "an indecent picture" in the first book. A naked man and woman were sitting down on a sofa. The intention of the artist was obviously obscene" (*The Trial*, chapter III). That is the superego: a solemn "indifference" impregnated in parts by indecencies.

That is why, for Kafka, bureaucracy is "closer to original human nature than any other social institution" (letter to Oscar Baum, June 1922): what is this "original human nature" if not the fact that man is from the start a *"parlêtre"*? And what is the superego—the functioning mode of bureaucratic knowledge—if not, according to Jacques-Alain Miller, what "presentifies" under the pure form of the signifier as the cause of the division of the subject, in other words, the intervention of the signifier command under its chaotic, senseless aspect.

Postmodernism I: Antonioni versus Hitchcock

This reference to Kafka is by no means accidental. Kafka was in a way the first post-modernist. It is precisely post-modernism which, in the field of art, embodies the limits of the semiotic, "textual" approach characteristic of modernism.

"Post-modernism" is a theme of theoretical discussions from Germany to the United States, with the quite surprising effect that it evokes a totally incompatible problematic in the different countries. In Germany, by "post-modernism" one understands the devalorization of universal Reason, of the "modern" tradition of Enlightenment, in the current which starts with Nietzsche and whose last offspring would be the French "post-structuralism" of Foucault, Deleuze, etc. (cf. the many texts by Habermas). In the United States it designates particularly the art stage which follows the expiration of the modernist avant-garde: in other words the different forms of "metro" movements. In all of this diversity, there is, however, the same matrix. One conceives of "post-modernism" as a reaction to modernist "intellectualism," as a return of the metonymy of the interpretive movement to the fullness of the Thing itself, to the instillment in vital experience, to the baroque wealth of the *Erlebnis* before the supposed "prisonhouse of language."

Now, here is our thesis. It is only the Lacanian passage from the signifier to the object, "from the symptom to the fantasy" (J.-A. Miller), which makes it possible to take the advent of post-modernism outside the field of an ideology of authenticity, instillment, etc. Post-modernism marks the rising in the middle of the modernist space of language and its interpretative auto-movement to the infinite, of a "hard" nucleus, of the inertia of a non-symbolizable real. Lacan enables us to see this place outside the symbolic as an emptiness opened by the hole in the symbolic Other. The inert object is always the presentification, the filling of the hole around which the symbolic command articulates itself, of the hole retroactively constituted by this command itself and in no way a "pre-language" fact.

Let's start with *Blow-Up* (1966) by Antonioni, perhaps the last great modernist film. When the hero (the photographer) develops the photographs of a park in the laboratory, his attention is attracted to the stain in the bushes on the side of a photograph. He enlarges the detail, and one discovers the contours of a body there. Immediately, in the middle of the night, he goes back to the park and indeed finds the body. But the next day, when he goes back to see the site of the crime again, the body has disappeared without leaving a trace. It is useless to stress the fact that the body is, according to the detective novel's code, the object of desire *par excellence*, the cause which starts the interpretive desire. The key to the film is given to us however by the final scene. The hero, resigned because of the cul-de-sac where his investigation has ended, takes a walk near a tennis court where a group of hippies pretend to play tennis (without a ball, they simulate the hits, run and jump, etc.). In the frame of this supposed game, the imagined ball jumps through the court's fence and stops near the hero. He hesitates a moment and then accepts the game. He bends over, makes the gesture of picking up the ball, and throwing it back to the court. . . . This scene has, of course, a metaphorical function in relation to the totality of the film. It makes the hero sensitive to consenting to the fact that "the game works without an object." The hippies do not need a ball for their game, just as in his own adventure everything works without a body.

The "post-modernist" way is the exact reverse of this process. It consists, not in showing the game which also works without an object and which is put into movement by a central emptiness, but directly in showing the object, making visible on the object itself its indifferent and arbitrary character. The same object can function successively as a disgusting reject and as a sublime, charismatic apparition. The difference is strictly structural. It is not tied to the "effective proprieties" of the object, but only to its place, to its tie to a symbolic trait (I). One can grasp this difference between modernism and post-modernism with regard to the fright, the horror in Hitchcock's films. At first, it seems that Hitchcock simply respects the classical rule (already known by Aeschylus in the Oresteia) according to which one must place the terrifying event outside of the scene and only show its reflections and its effects on the stage. If one does not see it directly, terror rising as the emptiness of its absence is filled by fantasmatic projections ("one sees it as more horrible than it actually is . . ."). The most simple process in order to evoke horror would be, then to limit oneself to the reflections of the terrifying object on its witnesses or victims. For example, one only hears it (*l'entend*) when one sees (*voit*) the frightened faces of the victims on the screen.

Furthermore, Hitchcock, when he is "doing his duty," reverses (*renverse*) this traditional process. Let's take a small detail of his *Lifeboat* (1944), the scene where the group of allied castaways welcome on their boat the German sailor of the destroyed submarine, their surprise when they find out that the saved person is an enemy. The traditional way of making this scene would be to let us hear the screams for help, to show the hands of an unknown person who grips the side of the boat, and then not show the German sailor, but move the camera to the shipwrecked survivors. It is the perplexed expression on their faces which must show us that they have pulled something unexpected out of the water. What? At that time, when one has already created the suspense, the camera can finally show us the German sailor. But Hitchcock does the exact contrary of this traditional process. Precisely what he does not show is the shipwrecked survivors. He shows the German sailor climbing on board and saying, with a friendly smile, "Danke schön!" Then he *does not* show the surprised faces of the survivors. The camera remains on the German. If his apparition provoked a terrifying effect, one can only detect it by his reaction to the survivors' reaction. His smile dies out, his look becomes perplexed.

That is Hitchcock's Proustian side uncovered by Pascal Bonitzer, because this Hitchcockian procedure corresponds perfectly to that of Proust in *Un amour de Swann* when Odette confesses to Swann her lesbian adventures. Proust only describes Odette. If her story has a terrifying effect on Swann, Proust only shows it with the changed tone of this story when she notices its disastrous effect. One shows an object or an activity which is presented as an everyday, even common thing, but suddenly, through the reactions of the milieu of this object reflecting itself on this object itself (*se reflétant sur cet objet lui-même*), one realizes that one is confronting a terrifying object, the source of an inexplicable terror. The horror is intensified by the fact that this object is according to its appearance, completely ordinary. What one took only a moment ago for a totally common thing, is revealed as Evil incarnated.

Post-modernism II: Joyce versus Kafka

Such a post-modernist procedure seems to us much more subversive than the usual modernist procedure, because the latter, by not showing the Thing, leaves open the possibility of grasping the central emptiness under the perspective of the "absent God." If the lesson of modernism were that the structure, the intersubjective machine, worked as well if the Thing lacked, if the machine turned around the emptiness, then the post-modernist reversal shows the Thing itself as the incarnated, positivized emptiness. It does it by showing the terrifying object directly and then by denouncing its frightening effect as a simple effect of its place in the structure. The terrifying object is an everyday object which started to function, by chance, as a filler of the hole in the Other. The prototype of modernist work would be *Waiting For Godot*. The whole futile and senseless action happens during the wait for Godot's arrival when, finally, "something might happen." But one knows very well that "Godot" can never arrive. What would the "post-modernist" way of rewriting the same story be? On the contrary, one would have to directly show Godot himself: a dumb guy who makes fun of us, who is, to say, exactly like us, who lives a futile life full of boredom and foolish pleasures—with the only difference that, by chance, not knowing it himself, he found himself at the place of the Thing. He started to incarnate the Thing whose arrival one is awaiting.

It is a less known film by Fritz Lang, *Secret Beyond the Door* (1947), which stages in the pure form (one is almost tempted to say distilled) this logic of any everyday object which is found in the place of *das Ding*. Celia Barrett, a young business woman, travels to Mexico after her older brother's death. She meets Mark Lamphere there. She marries him and moves in with him, at

Lavender Falls. A little later, the couple receives his intimate friends and Mark shows them his gallery of historical rooms, reconstituted in his own house. But he forbids anyone access to room number 7 which is locked up. Fascinated by his reservation vis-à-vis this room, Celia gets a key made and enters it. It is the exact replica of her room. The most familiar things receive a dimension of disquieting strangeness from the fact that one finds oneself in a place out of place, a place which "is not right." And the thrill effect results exactly from the familiar, domestic character of what one finds in this Thing's forbidden place. That is the perfect illustration of the fundamental ambiguity of the Freudian notion of *Unheimliche*.

From this problematic, one can also come to the chief motif of the "hard-boiled" detective novel: that the *femme fatale* is "a bad object" par excellence, the object which eats men, which leaves many broken lives as a trace of its presence. In the best novels of this genre, a certain reversal happens when the *femme fatale* as "a bad object" is subjectivized. First she is presented as a terrifying, devouring, exploitative object. But when, suddenly, one is placed in the perspective which is hers, one finds out that she is only a sickly, broken being, one who is not in control of her effects on the milieu (masculine), who, especially when she thinks she "masters the game" is no less victim than her own victims. What gives her power of fascination to the *femme fatale* is exclusively her place in masculine fantasy. She is only "mastering the game" as an object of masculine fantasy. The theoretical lesson that one should get from this is that subjectivization coincides with the experience of one's own powerlessness, of one's own position as that of a victim of destiny. It is the moment detected by Adorno in his superb text on *Carmen* (in *Quasi una fantasia*), concerning the melody on the "unmerciful card" of the third act, the nodal point of the whole opera, where Carmen, this bad-fatal object, is subjectivized, is felt as a victim of her own game.

That is how the beautiful Adornian sentence on the "original passivity of the subject" should be grasped. It is to be taken literally. In other words one is not dealing with the fact that the subject, this center and origin of activity, of the remaking and appropriation of the world, should in some way recognize his limit, his subordination to the objective world. One must, on the contrary, affirm a certain passivity as an original dimension of subjectivity itself. The structure of this passivity is given to us by the Lacanian formula of fantasy ($\$ \lozenge a$). The fascination of the subject in front of *das Ding*, in front of the "bad Thing" which fills the whole of the Other, and the exceptional character of the subjectivization of the *femme fatale*, comes from the fact that she is indeed herself this object in relation to which she feels her original passivity.

However, one must suspend this series of variations in order to notice the socio-political correlation of this passage from modernism to post-modernism: the advent of what we call post-industrial society where all the coordinates of art change, including the status of art itself. The *modernist* work of art loses its "will have" (*aura*) (Benjamin). It functions as a reject without charisma insofar as the "everyday" world of merchandise becomes itself "will-have-like" (*auratique*) (publicity, etc.). The *post-modernist* work regains the "will have." Furthermore, it does it with the cost of a radical renunciation, counter to the modernist utopia ("fusion of art and life") detectable even in its most "elitist" projects. Post-modernism reaffirms art as a social *institution*, the irreducible distance between art and "everyday" life. One is tempted to conceive post-modernism as one of the phenomena of global ideological change which includes the end of the great eschatological projects. As such it is at the same time post-marxist.

This opposition of modernism and post-modernism is, however, far from being reduced to a simple diachronic. One finds it already articulated at the beginning of the century in the opposition between Joyce and Kafka. If Joyce is the modernist par excellence, the writer of the symptom (Lacan), of interpretive delirium taken to the infinite, of the time (to interpret) when each stable moment is revealed to be only a freezing effect of a plural signifying process, Kafka is in a certain way already post-modernist, the antipode of Joyce, the writer of fantasy, of the *space* of a painful, inert presence. If Joyce's text provokes (*provoque*) interpretation, Kafka's blocks (*bloque*) it.

It is precisely this dimension of a non-dialectizable, inert presence, which is misrecognized by a modernist reading of Kafka, with its accent put on the inaccessible, absent, transcendent instance (the Castle, the Court Room), holding the place of the lack, of the absence as such. From this perspective, the secret of Kafka would be that in the heart of the bureaucratic machinery, there is only an emptiness, the Nothing. Bureaucracy would be a mad machine which "works by itself," as the game in *Blow-Up* which can function without a body-object. One can read this conjuncture in two different ways which share a same theoretical frame: theological and immanentist. Either one can take the inaccessible, transcendent character of the Center (of the Castle, of the Court Room) as a mark of an "absent God"—the universe of Kafka as an anguished universe, abandoned by God—or one takes the emptiness of this transcendence as an "illusion of perspective," as a form of a reversed apparition of the immanence of desire. The inaccessible transcendence, its emptiness, its lack, is only the negative of the supplement (*surplus*) of the productive movement of desire on its object (Deleuze-Guattari). The two readings, although opposed, miss the same point: the way that this absence, this empty place, is found always, already filled by an inert, obscene, dirty, revolting *presence*. The Court Room in *The Trial* is not only absent, it is indeed present under the figures of the obscene judges who, during the night trials, glance through pornographic books. The Castle is indeed present under the figure of subservient, lascivious, and corrupted civil servants. Here, the formula of the "absent God" in Kafka does not work at all: on the contrary Kafka's problem is that in his universe God is too present, under a shape, of course, which is not at all comforting, under the shape of obscene, disgusting phenomena. Kafka's universe is a world where God—who up to now has held himself at an assured distance—got too close to us. One must read the thesis of the exegetes according to whom Kafka's would be a universe of anxiety, based on the Lacanian definition of anxiety. We are too close to *das Ding*. That is the theological lesson of post-modernism. The mad, obscene God, the supreme-Being-of-evilness, is exactly the same as the God taken as the Supreme Good. The difference lies only in the fact that we got too close to Him.

Psychoanalysis and Marxism

8

The Politics of Impossibility
Andrew Ross

In recent years, the eye of the critical-theoretical storm has increasingly moved away from the heady anti-positivism of poststructuralism into the relatively more temperate regions of a criticism that is socially, politically, and historically minded. We cannot, however, afford to forget what was learned about the interplay between subject and structure. What ought to be salvaged from these hard-won lessons? And what, in particular, can be reconstructed, for the new cultural politics, from marxism and freudianism, after two generations of readers influenced by poststructuralism have raised themselves on the rereading, translating, libidinalizing, and seducing of these two great parent traditions?

Universal Abandon

While the conjugation of these two traditions remains fraught, as ever, by problems both theoretical and practical, both marxism and psychoanalysis have come to share a similar fate: each has been stripped, finally, of their pseudo-scientific status as discourses of *universality*. At the core of this critique lies the more general challenge of postmodernism to the absolutist or universalist status of the foundational narratives in the West, especially those upon which the Enlightenment, with its boundless faith in rationality, based its social project for global, human emancipation. The result of this faith in rationality had been the reign of positivism in each of the spheres of life in

---

This paper was originally written for, and presented at, a conference on *The Transference: Lacan's Legacy* in June 1985 at the University of Massachusetts, Amherst.

which the progress of this rational transformation of society could be judged: morality, law, aesthetics, economics, etc. While both Marx and Freud discovered logics of determination which threatened to overturn, in every way, the liberal idealism of Enlightenment rationality, their work, and the intellectual and political traditions they endowed, were nonetheless suffused with the spirit of positivism. In either case, this positivism assumed different forms and, of course, offered different solutions. But from generation to generation, and from culture to culture, the "solutions" have produced far from universal effects. In fact, the intellectual renewal of both traditions has been achieved largely through challenges to marxist and freudian positivism, and these challenges have produced a series of crises at the institutional heart of both orthodoxies.

In the case of marxism, which I shall consider first, the most cogent criticism came from those who questioned the dominance of the Hegelian emphasis on totality within marxist thought. The origin of this critique can be traced to the Frankfurt School response to fascism and "totalitarianism" in the thirties and forties. The ensuing debate, especially in French marxist circles, was not without its sensationalist side, best summed up by what came to be known as "the Gulag question"—which proposed that the discourse of totality, dominant within classical marxist theory, is, and always has been, coextensive with the potential practice of totalitarianism, and that the passage from Hegel to the Gulag is a necessary one. In posing such a question, the complex, century-old debate about theory and practice within marxism was reduced to a short fuse: Is marxism the home of totalitarianism or only of theories of totality? If the answer was the former, then a nostrum for emancipation had come to be seen as an apology for the institutionalizing of unfreedom.

For those who have outrightly resisted the question, their response has often been no more helpful. Perry Anderson, for example, acerbically notes that "today, Lévi-Strauss speaks of Marxism as a totalitarian threat even to the animal kingdom."[1] Others have been more rigorous and less defensive. Martin Jay calls for a "truly defensible" and "liberating totalization that will not turn into its opposite," and this at the end, ironically enough, of his panoramic survey of the massive anti-Hegelian impulse within the history of Western marxist thought.[2] And Fredric Jameson responds in kind to the recognition of ideology's role in legitimizing the idea of one "universal culture": "all literature must be read as a symbolic meditation on the destiny of community"—a response which succinctly demonstrates how marxism can still be used to invoke a discourse of the universal that may be just as imaginary as the one it seeks to supplant.[3] For those, on the other hand, who have followed out all the consequences of the various critiques of classical marxism, the bewilderingly diverse, new field of post-marxist thought has, at times, taken on the less strenuous feel of a new liberal pluralism just as the revolutionary horizon of the Western marxist vision has receded.

While the dimensions of this most recent "crisis of marxism" have been precipitated by the political strategies advanced by the new social movements of women, people of color, sexual minorities, ecologists, and peace activists, the term "crisis of marxism" is an old one, first used by Thomas Masaryk in 1898 in response to the early claims of Lassallean social democracy. It points to a debate that is internal to the history and theory of marxism itself, and one that challenges the orthodox claims to universality intrinsic to what, today, is seen as the increasingly contested doctrine of historical materialism: the universal claim of Reason to emerge victorious over the realm of Nature, thereby putting an end to Necessity and proclaiming the rule of Freedom; the slow but inexorable "cunning" of History's rationality; the Jacobin imaginary of revolutionary emancipation in which the proletariat acts as a privileged historical meta-subject; and the universal criteria claimed by scientific socialism for its laws of value. At the historical onset of the orthodox marxist theater of conflict, this discourse of universality was posited against an equally seemless logic of necessity implied in the marxian thesis that the domination of capital was *all*-pervasive. Thus, if the rule of exchange-value was all-powerful, then *all* power could only be seized by an equally totalizing version of political strategy. The consequence was what has come to be known as orthodox marxism, fully institutionalized under the Second International. In effect, one universal narrative engendered and was engendered by its antagonistic mirror image. If this mirror image proved, in true Lacanian fashion, to be historically premature, then it was because the marxist code of historical necessity (describing the inevitabilist triumph of rational emancipation) was to be called into question and, some have argued, ultimately discredited within decades, if not years of its conception in the work of Marx and Engels. By contrast, the discursive terms used ever since to describe the universality of capital's ruling logic have become progressively monolithic in their projection of total domination.

As the credibility of an emancipatory discourse of totality faded, the rhetoric of domination went from strength to strength. From the scepticism of Weber's "iron cage" of rationalization to the nihilism of Baudrillard's image of society as a smooth, reflective surface; from Simmel's "tragedy of culture" to Horkheimer's "instrumental reason"; Adorno's "technological veil"; Lefebvre's "everyday life"; Marcuse's "one-dimensional society"; the fully administered society; the fully disciplined society; and the various post-industrial visions of consumer domination (granted their orthodox marxist form by Ernest Mandel in his version of the grand narrative of "late capitalism," wherein capital logic colonizes the very last corners of our lives and minds through its annexation of *all* social and cultural relations). On the side of emancipation, Habermas remains one of the few major Western marxist thinkers willing to embrace the Enlightenment idea of rationality, and hence it is no surprise that the universal ethics of speech which he upholds should draw upon a neo-freudian adaptation model of discourse—the mythical promise of communicative rationality, or a "full speech." Habermas's positivism presents another mirror image of the discourse of universal domination, and thus further contributes to the history of imaginary vicissitudes associated with a traditional marxist critique that issues from a transcendent or Archimedean point of view.

The problems that arise from such theories of universal domination (or emancipation) are complex but unavoidable. Clearly the paranoic impulse to construct such a monolithic vision leaves little or no room to theoretically develop any kind of oppositional stance; we are left with a poverty of political strategy. Theories about the pervasive rule of commodity logic, for example, often fail to account for the ways in which that logic is obliged to successfully intersect with popular needs and desires, or for the ways in which that logic must absorb, incorporate, or respond to counter-logics in order to renew its power. Such theories tend to see audiences and populations as passive dupes, or as perfectly interpellated, Pavlovian subjects.

Just as important, however, at least for theorists, is the question asked by, and of, epistemology. What is the epistemological value of a statement which proposes that all of our social existence, now, is subject to *one* universal law of regulation—the law of the commodity form? Even the most committed realist would probably conclude that such a statement was empirically unverifiable. But is the truth of this statement, on the other hand, to be reduced to a mere "truth-effect," as discourse analysis would have it? This question is far from abstract, and any response summons up a whole history of marxist thinking about epistemology. The weak argument for a marxism faithful to a materialist epistemology is that there is always a nonidentical relation or gap between concept and object; there is no unmediated access, for example, to objective knowledge of *real* contradictions. To extend this position to its limits is to understand how marxism, in its post-Althusserian flight from empiricism, enabled theory to achieve a conceptual or discursive authority of its own. Even for Adorno, a discursive totality was never coincident with an objective *real* totality. Even in his bleakest descriptions of totalitarian domination there was always an epistemological escape clause which guaranteed that such a description was never "realized." Moreover, if the present totality were "false" in this discursive sense, then it could be further challenged by Adorno's practice of discursive inconsistency: the fragment, the aphorism, and the anti-essentialism of a negative dialectic. A more attenuated form of this epistemology survives in Althusser's reworking of his notion of a "science" which develops according to its own conceptual logic, outside of any empirical guarantees, and in which realm of conceptual objects theory must be seen as its own autonomous productive practice. Similarly, the strength and appeal of the various poststructuralist critiques of universalism can be attributed, on the one hand, to their resolute anti-empiricism, and, on the other, to their maverick attitude towards discursive autonomy: Derrida's ludic counter-logic of semantic instability, Deleuze and Guattari's schizo-cultural decoding of the classic channels of universal exchange, Baudrillard's parodic critique of the simulacrum, the non-essentialist feminist analysis of discursive categories of femininity, Foucault's nominalist descriptions of the discourses of power and their various "truth-effects."

One common criticism, increasinly voiced, of all of these positions, is that of political quietism. The marxist for whom the primacy of the political demands immediate accountability will say—"Perhaps there is indeed a non-identity between theory and practice (or between discursive strategy and the 'real' political struggle), but surely this does not mean that Gulags and Utopias alike are nothing other than effects of discourse? They can and do exist, and something should be done about them!" To properly take up the challenge posed by this kind of question, it would be necessary for the epistemologically minded post-marxist to reject its resurrected demand for an account of objective knowledge; it would be necessary to ignore the call for some empirical recognition of political agency; it would be necessary to show how this critic's question presupposes the form of its answer.

Post-Marxism

To properly address the question of new relations between theory and practice, one would have to provide an account of society as an intelligible structure which could do justice to the need for political agency but which would not appeal to any *a prioristic* assumptions about causal determination, structural totality, or unitary essentialism; which would not appeal, in short, to the logic of necessity that has traditionally been the bedrock of historical materialism. Post-Althusserian theorists like Barry Hindess and Paul Hirst went well beyond the marxist fetish of essentialism in arguing for society as a set of discrete and autonomous practices which lacks any necessary structure, and which rests merely upon the claims of its atomistic (Leibnizian) substantiality. The most significant recent contribution to this tendency has come from the work of Ernesto Laclau and Chantal Mouffe which has attempted to make sense of what they call "a politico-discursive universe that has witnessed a withdrawal of the category of necessity."[4] Laclau and Mouffe proceed from the recognition that society—perceived as a structure that would be intelligible from a single, or sutured, point of view in the classic rationalist sense—is *impossible*. In the absence of any appeal to necessity, a new social logic can only be a logic of contingency which recognizes that it is impossible to fix the meaning of any event beforehand and independently of its articulation in relation to other events. The social is therefore composed of non-necessary or non-essential elements linked by non-necessary relations. Identity is composed of multiple subject-positions, articulated differently from moment to moment: a worker, for example, is not only a worker or proletarian, but also a citizen, a consumer, and tenant of a host of institutional positions defined by his or her various insertions into other social discourses. In theorizing the political nature of this non-positivistic model of society, Laclau and Mouffe make new uses of Gramsci's notion of a "war of position" in which social elements, perceived as elements of discourses, are constantly entering into new arrangements of conflict, and in which everyday inequalities are constantly becoming upgraded into the form of political antagonisms. The struggle for hegemony is thus the struggle to appropriate the meanings of any such discourse that is not fixed in advance and is thus available to groups along the full range of the political spectrum. Society is open, incomplete, and politically unstable, crisscrossed by a plurality of different social logics. In proposing such a model, Laclau and Mouffe have offered a productive, political description of the social that is *based upon a discourse of impossibility*—a project unthinkable on the left heretofore because of its committment to positivist models of thought and action.

Like marxism, the tradition of freudian thought has often been criticized for its "false" universalism, especially where freudians have drawn upon the assumption that certain psychic structures, whether traditionally perceived as "Oedipal" or from the more linguistically oriented Lacanian perspective, can be read off as universal, causal determinants of particular social structures or effects. In order to uphold such a reading, one has to assume that both psychic and social logics are "possible," or complete, and thus structurally compatible in some way. Such a claim, of course, runs counter to the spirit of Freud's discovery that the unconscious is predicated upon the shifting articulation of incomplete psychic processes. In effect, new ways of reading psychic and social effects together must be more attuned to the absence of final, determining relations. Their point of departure will lie in the recognition that the psychic and the social share a logic that denies the positivity of a constitutive identity or rationalist foundation.

Lacan's Politics

In this respect, it would be difficult to ignore the "logic of impossibility" that lies at the heart of Lacan's later work, from the time of the publication of the *Ecrits* until his death, and within which I shall single out the elements of at least three political discourses; sexual politics, an anti-rationalist politics of science, and the politics of the institution.

1) In the realm of sexual politics, Lacan engaged in a relentless critique of the universalism espoused by neo-essentialist theories of femininity in their positing of a common, neo-biologist identity for "all women." It should be noted that this critique was mounted as much in response to the challenges of his women disciples and antagonists, both inside and outside the Ecole Freudienne, as it was articulated in response to any "natural" development of his own psychoanalytic thought. The fundamental challenge of Lacanian

theory rests upon the assumption that the infinite, or the un-finished, is the working limit of all psychic operations inasmuch as these operations either derive from incomplete processes or else produce incomplete formations. Two examples of these respective failures of unicity are suggested by Lacan's translation of *das Unbewusste* (the unconscious) as *l'une-bévue* (mistaken-for-one, or one-at-odds), and his emphasis on the "not'all" (*pas-toute*) of Woman as a universal sexual category.[5] Both these examples can be read as highly qualified critiques of the ways in which concepts like "the unconscious" and "Woman" have been essentialized as fixed and easily available terms of reference for political thinkers and activists alike. The concept of *l'une-bévue* challenges the Reichian, Marcusian, Deleuzian, and other libertarian-freudian attempts to speak about the unconscious as a "collective" or *universal* substratum of vital energy, to be merged with or plugged into, but it equally critiques the practice of referring to an "individual's unconscious" as if it were a *particular* possession. Similarly, the force of *pas-toute* is not only to militate against the idea that all women, by virtue of a common biology, can be represented by one common term, but also to suggest that references to particular or personal experience cannot be presented as if they were natural and unproblematic reflections of a universal, sexual essence. Both these critiques, of course, have complex social consequences which cannot be easily subsumed into unified social consequences or agendas; they do not lend themselves to traditional ideas of solidarity around issues pertaining to sexual politics. In fact, Lacan's insistence on the unfinished at all psychic levels is often seen as a thorn in the side of the political possibilities for feminism.[6] Reinterpreting psychoanalysis on behalf of feminism (a tradition initiated by Juliet Mitchell) has had the effect of problematizing the relation between theory, on the one hand, and practices waged around a politics of identity on the other. One of the consequences has been to see the discourses of essentialism and non-essentialism as not necessarily mutually exclusive, and to use them strategically from context to context.

2) Lacan's second political critique takes its place within and against the long history of psychoanalysis's relation to science, with its origin in Freud's inveterate desire for psychoanalysis to be seen as "serious scientific work carried on at a high level."[7] Because of the need to court respectability for his discoveries, Freud was quick to pose psychoanalysis as a triumph of Enlightenment. As a result, his ubiquitous positivism has stood in the way of an honest assessment of psychoanalysis's relation to rationalist categories, while, in one of the great ironies of intellectual history, it involuntarily anticipated the sway of medicalism over what Freud called "the obvious American tendency to turn psychoanalysis into a housemaid of psychiatry."[8]

As is now well known, Lacan's return to Freud claimed to bypass the "science" of the ego laid out in the later metapsychological systems of the freudian corpus, dating, let us say, from the first emphasis on the subjective structure of narcissism in 1914. Before the post-1914 tendency to codify and systematize set in, it was the unconscious and its formulations which held sway over Freud's interests, particularly in the work on dreams, jokes, and slips of the tongue. Commentators have suggested, however, that it is not only the latter half but the whole of Freud's work which should be read in the light of his epistemophilic will to master and organize a body of knowledge about the real within the limits of a speculative system, and to present this feat as a triumph of scientific resolve.[9] Analysis, by extension, would then be little more than an experimental method, or a "laboratory" technique, designed to substantiate a pre-existing theory, or to provide evidence for any further modifications of that theory. François Roustang, for one, has gone further in arguing that the "science" of psychoanalysis is a *myth* from its very inception, and one which is employed at every turn in order to play down the less reputable aspects of certain psychoanalytic practices, those which have their murky genesis in hypnosis and suggestion, and which bedeviled Freud in his dealings with thought-transference, telepathy, and the like. In soliciting this myth, Roustang argues, a myth that "domesticates what cannot be integrated into a scientific, technological, rational world," psychoanalysis simply extends the limits of science to cover the irrational, a domain from which science had hitherto been excluded. In renouncing this myth, analysis falls back into "occultism and magic. . . . into the unsayable and the ineffable," foredoomed never to rise about the "level of faith-healing and witchcraft."[10] Roustang's point of view is extreme, if cogently argued on the polemical terms it establishes—psychoanalysis is compelled to masquerade in the "emperor's new clothes" of science. But these are terms which appeal to a theory of origin that assumes a totalizing destiny written into psychoanalysis from its onset in a nineteenth-century episteme in which the stifling medicalization of sexual pathology is precariously balanced against the "success" of clinically reprobate practices such as Charcot's hypnosis techniques. Is this origin to be held up to haunt every new interpretive advance in the field of psychoanalysis, or is it, as much a myth as any old family curse, to be historically assumed, worked through, and finally shrugged off?[11] This question is paramount for any "politics of the institution" which psychoanalysis might now mount.

As the most resolute critic of Freud's neo-positivist claims for the scienticity of psychoanalysis, Lacan's position on this question was unequivocal. In fact, he claimed that the practice which Freud conceived as analysis turned out to be the "last flowering of medicine,"[12] at the same time as it was the first recognition of a new epistemological practice, or discourse about knowledge. For Lacan, psychoanalysis could never be a science in the rationalist sense because it is irrefutable, or rather because it is not subject to refutation, and is thus a practice more like an art, the speech-art of "gossiping."[13] The last ten years of his teaching, however, were given over to what he called, with some irony, "the science of the real." These years saw his complex and often inscrutable attempts to demonstrate the *limits* of rationalist possibility within psychoanalytical discourse in the form of a critique undertaken not by reason itself, in the Kantian sense, but through the heady intercurrence of a rather exotic set of discourses—number theory, topology, classical logic, homespun symbolic logic, quantum physics, literary adventurism, etc. Armed with these two critiques—the anti-rationalist "gossiping" of the talking cure, and the "mathematizable minimum" of the later "science of the real"— Lacanian theory set out to put to the sword any distinctions between the scientific and non-scientific; distinctions which can themselves be seen to draw upon the rationalist categories of truth and error and are thus part and parcel of the ideology of science itself.

   3) Lastly, at the level of psycho-social theory, we are obliged to examine Lacan's long and fractious involvement with the institutional discourses of the psychoanalytical establishment, and his subsequent effort to demonstrate the *impossibility* of artificial groups, like the Ecole Freudienne, massively unified by the discursive effects generated by the bonds of transference. On the face of it, his involvement with the institution seems willfully compelled to repeat the earlier patterns of Freudian discord, almost as if to superimpose its new fractures upon the old faultlines. Expelled from the Paris Psychoanalytical Society in 1953, he helped to form the French Psychoanalytical Society from which, in turn, he was excluded in 1964 as the price to pay for its recognition by the IPA. His own school, the Ecole Freudienne, founded in the same year, flourished until internal dissension caused him to dissolve it in 1980, after which the new Cause Freudienne led a much more tenuous existence, caught in the crossfire between loyal and dissident students.

   In dissolving his school in 1980, an event that gave rise to a bout of mass hysteria in Parisian psychoanalytical circles, Lacan hoped to demonstrate two points: first, the dangers involved in the politically necessary act of periodically breaking up a group bound together by the "imaginary servitude" of transference, and, second, the lessons to be learned from psychoanalysis itself about the constitution of such groups.[14] In his *Letter of Dissolution*, Lacan alluded quite specifically to the "horde" effect that Freud noted in his discussion of the psychoanalytical Church, while recognizing his own position as the severed link in the Borromean knot—once cut, the one that frees all the others and puts an end to the "dire mastery" of his disciples' transference.[15] So too, the communiqué issued by his students after his death suggests that his interest in the group was not in how it worked, but rather in its failure and in how "the psychoanalytical formation is put to work" within that failure.[16] The purpose of the dissolution, then, was to allow that formation and its impossibility to "ek-sist," or stand out like a symptom for all to see. In taking the Master's position to its very limits, Lacan had sought to expose the full repertoire of privileges, fears, excesses, and scandals that lay behind it.

Freudo-Marxism

Towards the end of this paper I shall discuss this third critique—Lacan's "demonstrations" of institutional love and/or discord—as a political proposition in its own right. As a prelude, however, it would be useful to recapitulate, with a view to resisting it, the harmonizing impulse that has informed the long history of abortive freudo-marxisms. My point in doing so will be to stress the need to recognize the pluralistic autonomy of different (social) logics of which the psychic is only one, as opposed to assuming that these often contradictory logics can be commonly harnessed either to some neopositivistic law of evolutionary necessity, or alternately to a hermeneutic understanding of repression that could describe and account for the universality of ideological servitude.

Any study of the history of social involvement on the part of psychoanalysis should demonstrate at least one thing—that the meaning of the discourse of psychoanalysis is not fixed in advance, and that it has indeed proved available to right and left alike. Ironically, if not symptomatically, it was the socialist element in Freud's Inner Circle, and Adler in particular, which was to recant the most radical of Freud's advances and fashion instead a somewhat reactionary theory of *personality*. Linked to the concept of social conditioning, this theory, of course, fed into the institutionalized codes of ideological grooming, existential goal-attainment, and the pursuit of a happy, pragmatic, everyday self-wisdom that have become so endemic to American psychoanalysis.

For Freud to characterize Adler's thought as "reactionary and retrograde" is one thing, but how do we reconcile this with his often cited opinion that the unconscious was profoundly conservative? Do either of these opinions have any significance for the subsequent tradition of libertarian psychoanalysis that runs from Reich through Marcuse to Deleuze and Guattari? Or is it enough to conclude that the unconscious doesn't give two hoots for democracy in any of its forms, and even that it is fundamentally asocial? Alternatively, might it not be best to follow the "path not taken" in psychoanalytic history—that of Otto Fenichel—which insists that psychoanalysis is an indispensable tool for understanding how ideological processes in general are lived out by human subjects?

These are only some of the questions that have served to define the historical parameters of psychoanalysis alternately, and often simultaneously, as a discourse of political possibility and impossibility. Take for example the first appearance of psychoanalysis on the stage of Western marxism, where it is invoked by Max Horkheimer to help explain the failure of the European proletarian revolutions, and thus to provide a non-economistic understanding of worker passivism. Psychoanalysis is therefore invoked, on the one hand, because of its privileged knowledge of the experience of failure, and on the other, because it can help to chasten, if not reverse, the failure of the classical positivism of marxism itself. It will provide a discourse of the particular—the freudian theory of subjectivity and psychosexuality—to match, supplement, and shore up a discourse of the universal—the marxist theory of collective consciousness and action. In effect, the freudo-marxist myth of the concrete universal is born and a logic of necessity reaffirmed. Psychic particularity is presented as the new site within which it will be possible to rediscover the universality of the social code.

In the subsequent work of the Frankfurt School, for example, opposition to the mechanistic logic of historical materialism is celebrated through the irreducibility of the individual to the collectivity.[17] A newly strengthened subjectivity could then act as a bulwark against the growing totalitarianism of collective authority. The antidotal strength of this individualism was a redemptive lesson learned from the Frankfurt study of Fascism. In Fascist mass culture the Frankfurt critics saw what Leo Lowenthal called "psychoanalysis in reverse"—the propensity to spawn authoritarian personalities rather than to cure them—and hence a seemingly irrationalist politics in which mass populations willfully surrendered rather than competed, as liberal capitalism would surely teach them to do.

Adorno's response, however—to reclaim the voluntarist autonomy and the practical agency of individualism—might seem retrogressive and naive to us now, recoiling from the "feelgood" excesses promoted in the name of autonomy by the social engineering of ego psychology. In the current political and ideological climate it is a program that would be hard put to contest the strident claims about individualism propagated as articles of American faith by neo-conservatism. Nonetheless, the Frankfurt analysis of "psychoanalysis in reverse" should strike a responsive chord with those familiar with the debate, most recently activated by the work of Roustang, about the "dire mastery" or "fatal destiny" of psychoanalytical groups to generate interpersonal relations of utter discipledom, akin in many ways, as he sees it, to totalitarian social structures.[18]

Roustang's argument rests upon the proposition that the bonds established by transference are never dissolved, only strengthened, and that the psychoanalytic group institutionalizes and lives this proposition up to its psychotic hilt, at which point no one speaks in his or her name, but merely reproduces the discourse of an other—the Master. Not only does this transference preclude the possibility of free speech, but it also induces a psychosis in the analyst-disciple whereby he or she is deliriously bound to the thought and discourse of an Other. In the case of Roustang's example, that discourse is Lacanian theory, which, far from being experimental, then becomes no more than "a symptom or system of defense" against the furthering of true analytic work. He describes the "sterility" of Lacan's followers, reduced to "intransigence, pretension, crass ignorance and fanaticism" before the gaze of their "master-hysteric-educator-analyst." This description evokes a familiar freudian scene, described at least once before by Alfred Hoche—"a fanatical sect blindly submissive to their leader"—a description Freud took pleasure in quoting in his history of the psychoanalytic movement.[19] Roustang's impatience with this alarming model of servitude is designed to appeal directly to our emancipatory instincts. Whether or not one accepts his analogy—analyst/analysand = State/citizen—the structure of that analogy is already assumed to some extent in Roustang's argument. More importantly, this analogy is derived from the utopian promise of a state of analytic investigation that would provide a truly representative knowledge of the facts, as opposed to what Lacanianism generates—a distorted or "repressive ideology" of false theoretical speculation. No matter how effective his appeal to freedom, it is clear, then, that Roustang's argument rests, ultimately, upon the very same categories of truth and error which Lacanian theory, in its style and purpose, sought to challenge and discredit. If the act of challenging these categories is like a "science," then perhaps it would be more useful to think of Althusser's notion of science as a theoretical practice which *breaks up*, rather than confirms, a set of natural or imaginary ties to a given reality. Althusser employs this notion of science in his own critique of a rationalist construction—the correspondence theory of economic determinism. In the case of psychoanalysis, "science" would then be a theoretical point of view which attacks the seemingly "natural" relation between metapsychological theory and the given "reality" of the facts as they appear.[20]

Love Letters

Roustang's conclusion, however, is a worthy one—a psychoanalytic society is impossible, at least if the possible (conceived as the best of political worlds) has anything at all to do with egalitarianism. But how can we interpret his thesis about the impossibility of a small artificial group in the context of a similar but larger proposition that society itself is *impossible*, if, again, by the possible we mean the emancipated, egalitarian imaginary of a universal free speech? If, as Roustang and others have insisted, the transference relation is conceptually unthinkable without a power inequality, and if that relation is resident in every social bond, as Freud argued in "Group Psychology and the Analysis of the Ego" and elsewhere, then it would indeed be impossible to think of society as anything other than a perpetual structure of domination and servitude. To accept this conclusion would mean the unwanted return of the universal picture of domination which I sketched out earlier. However, we do not want to discard the valuable insight into power relations offered by the study of transference, especially if it bears upon contemporary discussions of citizenship. How, then, to avoid the universalist conclusion?

It would be a fundamental mistake, for example, to assume that the "artificial" structure of an artificial group like the psychoanalytical community is too much the product of particular or local conditions to be of any general social significance. So too, it would be wrong to conclude that these "artificial" relations, even if they proved to be socially universal, were "merely" artificial, and thus, as in the orthodox marxist critique of the so-called "false consciousness" of all ideological relations, would be swept away by the coming of an "organic" social totality. On the contrary, the solution I want to offer here stems from the proposition that *a psychoanalyst is never only a psychoanalyst.* He or she occupies many other subject-positions in a number of other social discourses of which the discourse of psychoanalysis and the transferences peculiar to it are only one. At any moment, the transferences specific to other discourses—the discourse of love, teaching, citizenship, consumerism, the Internal Revenue Service, etc.—will vie for dominance, often in direct conflict with each other. Social transference, then, far from being seen as a relatively fixed and universal network of psycho-social relations, overwritten by a master-code of necessary domination, could instead be viewed according to a logic of contingency whereby different subject-positions are articulated from moment to moment, depending on the changing and, I suppose we could say, hegemonic configuration of transferences that are operative at any one time.

The theoretical advantage of such a thesis is that it retains the concept of "dire mastery" peculiar to the transferential network of a *particular* discourse, in this case, that of the analytic institution, while refusing to acknowledge the same fatal destiny for society as a whole. To conclude with an appropriate example with which to demonstrate this critical pluralism, one need look no further than the bizarre and hybrid formation of Lacan's Cause Freudienne, set up after the dissolution of the Ecole Freudienne in order to break up the authoritarian "group effect" of the latter. Under the newly instituted code of "love," Lacan asked all of his students to write him a letter of allegiance. Far from resolving anything, this new "letter-box effect" actually provided an exemplary model of the very discursive relations that generated the group effect in the first place. What is important about this, however, is *not* that (most of) his students *did* send their letters to Lacan. What is more important is that they did not send *all* their letters to Lacan; they sent their income tax returns, their parking fines, and their other love letters elsewhere.

Psychoanalysis and Deconstruction

9

Psychoanalysis
Modern and Post-Modern
Henry Sussman

In the inevitable comparisons between philosophy and literature, the latter often ends up in the secondary and subordinate position: as the field where philosophical concepts are "illustrated," as the diluted and popularized handmaiden of "pure reason." Freud, among others, understood, however, that literature also serves the preemptive function of a divining-rod for the issues and processes that will find what Hegel termed a *"stilles Abbild,"* a quiescent image in philosophical conceptualization. In its at times disorderly intuitions, literature may usurp the seminal and anticipatory role in the chicken-and-egg dialogue between the two discourses.

Studying the development of psychoanalytical theory in the twentieth century may well furnish us with a case in point, illustrating both the vertiginous battle of two types of books, and literature's uncanny ability to predicate order where it seems to nurture whimsy. I have elsewhere suggested that psychoanalysis, while linked inextricably to the person and personality of Freud, may be regarded partly as an extension of modern philosophy and partly as a hybrid fusion between esthetic intuitions and clinical practice. As an outgrowth of philosophical operations, psychoanalysis may be philosophically analyzed and placed in context, as in very different ways, Lacan and Ricoeur have done. I would nonetheless argue that the history of literature in the twentieth century may more vibrantly and in the end more analytically illuminate the transition between certain stages of psychoanalysis than the overtly conceptual explorations into the psychoanalytical subject, its experiences, and into the objects to which it binds.

The literary history that I would apply to certain developments within the psychoanalytic field is not sequential or biographical. It proceeds by the rarely orderly interchange between two models achieving particular prominence during our century, the modern and the post-modern. While modernity, as Paul de Man eloquently establishes,[1] is not bound to any age or century but is, rather, a moment of textual configuration (or disfiguration), the twentieth century is nevertheless noteworthy for the intensity and experimentation of its attempts to violate the limits of the modern. The writings of, among others, Kafka, Joyce, Proust, Musil, and well as Beckett, Artaud, Bataille, and Borges abound both with awareness and instances of what may be termed the modernist project and with attempts to delimit it—and break its momentum.

I have elsewhere described the twentieth century as beginning—and now ending—with a firm sense, as firm as possible, of the linguistic constitution of reality and the conceptual systems erected to qualify, modify, and contain it.[2] There is an uncanny affinity, a grandparental closeness, between, say, the fragmentary Kafkaesque experiments made into the nature of fictive language at the outset of the century and Jacques Derrida's sweeping yet unsystematic philosophical survey of the positions and roles of language during the epoch of Western thought. Paradoxically, it is in the "core" of the century where the intuitions regarding the constitutive role of language are subjected to their most rigorous testing. Between the linguistic intuitions with which twentieth-century literature and theory begin and end occurs a structuralist moment, when the actual translation of the qualities and processes of language into the discourses of criticism and the human and natural sciences takes place. This structuralist moment is exemplified by the impasses that Lévi-Strauss and Foucault reach as their frameworks for reading, respectively, "primitive" cultures and intellectual history "buckle," or "bubble" under the strain of the language whose play their analyses accommodate. A series of literary productions, by writers as diverse as Albert Camus and Jorge Luis Borges, also marks the fundamental structuralist transition, in which a primary concern with systems passes to the language in which they are articulated.[3]

The discourse of psychoanalysis, replete with its conflicting prognoses and sectarian battles, rarely has a rhetorical access to the "modern," "structuralist," and "post-modern" stages in which the literary history of the century unfolds. Like a well-wrought administrative intervention, however, these models may clarify a situation while circumventing affect, specifically the investments and stakes held by various clinical and theoretical schools. What would it mean to say that psychoanalytic theory initially arises as a modernist construction with moments of structuralist intuition? What would it mean to assert that certain post-Freudian revisions of psychoanalytic theory are tantamount to its post-modern updating? It is to these and similar questions that we turn as we test the competence of literary discourse to illuminate the stages of philosophical conceptualization.

As the century terminates (this is, after all, a psychoanalytical publication), it appears that no apter insignia was conjured for it than the "Angelus Novus" that Walter Benjamin culled from the late images of Paul Klee. Childlike in its simplicity, this angel is propelled on the winds of futurism, but with its face straining toward the past.[4] Force, in its physical and conceptual dimensions, is the form of the future at the outset of the century, the style with which it emerges. The twentieth century is born in an act of arbitrariness, almost violation. The figure of a backward-looking angel whose own wings compel it toward an unbounded future captures the ambivalence with which a hypothetical historical collectivity gazes ahead in time.

The century begins, then, in a form of separation *Angst*, one of whose compelling instances is triggered by an absent kiss, the one that the narrator of Proust's epic *Recherche* doesn't get when, as a child, his nightly rituals are interrupted by Swann's invasion of his household. Beneath the bourgeois facet that he presents to Marcel's family, Swann is an Ali Baba presiding over a treasure-trove of artifacts and artistic knowledge. The traumatic separation episode of the narrator's childhood consists of the deprivation of his mother's physical presence and love through the intrusion of a far more indirect and undependable medium. The foreign element is language, whose involution is figured in the herbal tea-leaves that will, at a later moment in the narrator's life, reactivate, as if by magic, certain lost memories. The critical literature has long recognized that Swann is, by virtue of his name, a fictional advocate for the sign. (The French word for swan is *cygne*, which is homonymically related to the sign or *signe*.) Ironically, the narrator, tormented as a child by the disarray and absence that language introduces into his life, chooses this medium as his adult vocation. A good deal of the novel is devoted to the erudition that he attains in above all esthetic (Vinteuil's music, Elstir's canvases, Bergotte's writing, la Berma's theater) but also socio-political sign-systems.[5]

However the seminal works of modernism may shatter the formal specifications they inherited, they are also pervaded by a yearning for the security and reassurance of presence that a strategic kiss would provide. Proust shatters the formal constraints of the novel and the French sentence; Kafka, on the other hand, consolidates the role of the minimal sentence in modern German prose; Pound exploits the possibilities in a diffuse poetic spacing initially explored by Mallarmé; Williams examines the potentials of the ultra-short line.[6] These technical innovations, which dramatize radical concepts of force (e.g., vorticism), are nevertheless accompanied by retrospective nostalgias for maternal presence and unconditional, totalized affection. Bloom's tormented curiosity about Molly's various dealings with Blazes Boylan pursues him throughout the length and breadth of *Ulysses*. The moment when the sympathetic court usher's wife is spirited away by the law student in Chapter 3 of Kafka's *Trial* is a particularly horrendous one in Joseph K.'s bizarre experience. *The Cantos of Ezra Pound* make us accessories to some of the paradigmatic instances of adultery and sexual violence and cannibalism in Western culture. In addition to the posturing and uneasy war between poisons that embellish Odysseus' bedding down with Circe, we observe the many possible outcomes of the troubadours' sexual crusades. Not only is an unsuspecting lord occasionally overturned. Sexual interloping is a threatening pastime in the *Cantos*. Its practitioners, male and female, undergo a variety of unpleasant fates, including dismemberment by animals and sexual cannibalism.

Oedipal fascination and concern are, then, the chief psychoanalytical manifestations of the misgivings with which the century announces its deviation from the past and the unprecedented technical forces of which it disposes. This interest is by no means in sole possession of the predominant male modernists, as the works of Virginia Woolf and Gertrude Stein amply attest. It is Freud, however, who furnishes the conceptual matrix in which the literature of maternal reassurance emerges.

Ironically, Freud saves his wider pronouncements on the inevitability of the Oedipal situation for the latter and retrospective phases of his work. The Oedipus complex does not establish its own indispensability in explaining certain facets of sexual object-choice and repression until such works from the middle period as *Totem and Taboo* (1912-13), and *Introductory Lectures on Psycho-Analysis* (1915-17). From these works on, the term functions as an insignia for the anomalies resulting from a certain biological precocity that leaves an ineradicable mark on human life. Human beings experience sexual desire before they are either biologically or psychologically capable of assimilating or accommodating it. One paradoxical result of this sexual prematurity is an alienation from, a need to repress, the very paradigmatic models of our psycho-sexual experience. Before Freud elaborates the Oedipus complex's literary necessity, then, he inscribes it within the nineteenth-century machinery of evolution and regression, manifestation and repression, with which he characterizes the operations of human subjectivity. "In our opinion," writes Freud in the 1919 " 'A Child is Being Beaten,' " "the Oedipus complex is the actual nucleus of neuroses, and the infantile sexuality which culminates this complex is the true determinant of neuroses" (*S.E.*, XVII, 193).[7] The essay goes on to characterize the (optimal) substitutions for the initial object-choice, those giving rise to healthy development, and, as well, the indirections and mix-ups whose end-results are the perversions.

> It will help to make matters clear if at this point I enumerate the other similarities and differences between beating-phantasies in the two sexes. In the case of the girl the unconscious masochistic phantasy starts from the normal Oedipus attitude; in that of the boy it starts from the inverted attitude, in which the father is taken as the object of love. . . . In the case of the girl what was originally a masochistic (passive) situation is transformed into a sadistic one by means of repression, and its sexual quality is almost effaced. In the case of the boy the

situation remains masochistic. . . . The boy evades his homo-sexuality by re-pressing and remodeling his unconscious phantasy: and the remarkable thing about his later conscious phantasy is that it has for its content a feminine atti-tude without a homosexual object-choice. By the same process, on the other hand, the girl escapes from the demands of the erotic side of her life altogether. She turns herself in phantasy into a man, without herself becoming active in a masculine way. . . .

We are justified in assuming that no great change is effected by the *repres-sions* of the original unconscious phantasy. (*S.E.*, XVII, 198-99)

Particularly striking in this passage is the fashion in which human sexual precocity, on both sides of the divide between the genders, produces imagin-ary sexual scenarios which supplement the limits of possibility. The imaginary can be known by the existential situation out of which it arises. The sexual fantasy of childhood is a thinkable alternative to the unthinkable. Yet even this conceptual supplement outlives its usefulness. Freud's account of object-choice and perversion describes a treacherous obstacle-course that the instinct must negotiate on the way toward its completion. The supplemental fantasy lives only in the moment between its *need* and its manifestation as threat. Freud installs conventional sociological gender expectations into the scenario that describes the declaration and repudiation of the supplemental fantasy. Passivity is more natural to girls: hence they evade one repressive loop that boys undergo. Passivity is unnatural in boys. When the sadistic father places boys in a picture of "feminine" passivity, homosexual fantasies arise, whose fate is either erasure or to become the beginning of a line of deviant behav-ior. Girls and women, by virtue of their naturalized passivity, are spared certain threats of perversion and certain convolutions, yet both models of gendrification exist in an electric field of alternating sexual charges; they transpire between an imaginary gratification and its denial and repression.

The Freudian scenario of impossible early object choices later replaced by acceptable or perverted alternatives of a more enduring nature—this theatrics or this physics occurs in a setting of intense sexual competition, in which the infant's fixation on a parental figure is not only disastrous in its own right, but risks serious reprisals by other individuals crucial to the family support system. Although an innocent and natural desire, the kiss for which "Marcel" yearns at the outset of *Swann's Way*, whose absence sets the tone for so much modern literature, acquires a double-strength. Merging with the mother not only satisfies a desire and reaffirms a nurturing; it serves a protective func-tion against sexual jealousy and aggression from outside the privileged mother-child bond. Inscribed within the Oedipal scene is a revenge for attaining the maternal care which is such a basic need. This punishment unfolds with the deliberate but inexorable certainty with which death decides a Greek tragedy.

When Freud reconstructs his Oedipal theater in "An Outline of Psycho-Analysis" (1938), he not only assembles the sequence of pictures extending from desire to aggression, from solicitation to recrimination: he returns to a primal scene of modern literature and elaborates its psycho-social conditions.

> A child's first erotic object is the mother's breast that nourishes it; love has its origin in attachment to the satisfied need for nourishment. There is no doubt that, to begin with, the child does not distinguish between the breast and its own body; when the breast has to be separated from the body and shifted to the *"outside"* because the child so often finds it absent, it carries with it as an *"object"* a part of the original narcissistic libidinal cathexis. This first object is later completed into the person of the child's mother, who not only nourishes it but also looks after it and thus arouses in it a number of other physical sensations, pleasurable and unpleasurable. By her care of the child's body she becomes its first seducer. In these two relations lies the root of a mother's importance, unique, without parallel, established unalterably for a whole lifetime as the first and strongest love-object and as the prototype of all later love-relations—for both sexes. . . .
>
> When a boy (from the age of two or three) has entered the phallic phase of his libidinal development, is feeling pleasurable sensations in his sexual organ and has learnt to procure these at will by manual stimulation, he becomes his mother's lover. He wishes to possess her physically in such ways as he has divined from his observations and intuitions about sexual life, and he tries to seduce her by showing her the male organ which he is proud to own. In a word, his early awakened masculinity seeks to take his father's place with her; his father has hitherto in any case been an envied model to the boy, owing to the physical strength he perceives in him and the authority with which he finds him clothed. His father now becomes a rival who stands in his way and whom he would like to get rid of. If while his father is away he is allowed to share his mother's bed and if when his father returns he is once more banished from it, his satisfaction when his father disappears and his disappointment when he emerges again are deeply felt experiences. This is the subject of the Oedipus complex, which the Greek legend translated from the world of a child's phantasy into pretended reality. Under the conditions of our civilization it is invariably doomed to a frightening end. (*S.E.*, XXIII, 188-89)

In perhaps no other Freudian passage do the breast's allure, the mother's seductive power, and the menace posed by the father emerge with such clarity. The evocations of the family romance triangle that Freud saves for the end of his works are among the best. So natural is the breast as an object of desire that the newly born psychoanalytical subject cannot distinguish it from him or herself. The mother is nature, but through a shift of roles characteristic of the Freudian uncanny, she is also a seducer, an autonomous agent of questionable loyalties. With the boy-subject the father shares analogous traits and natural features. Yet the father's desires are on a collision course with those of the son. Freud's explicit literary context for the events that he examines in the lives of subjects and families may be the Oedipus myth as rendered in tragedies and other ancient sources. Yet his specific descriptions of the movements in and out of the mother's bed surrounding the father's travel schedule correspond more closely to the perspective of Telemachus in Homer's *Odyssey* than to Oedipus' posture in Sophocles' *Oedipus Rex*. A substitution of Odysseus' experiences for those of Oedipus, a grafting of the Oedipal melodrama upon the Homeric quest, a displacement that we accept in the literary sources of modernism—has also taken place in the Freudian system. By the end of his writings, then, Freud has explicitly joined ranks with those authors, most notably Joyce and Pound, whose exploration of mythical narratives and structure coincides with Oedipal thematization and anxiety. For Freud as well as these authors, the quest-battle motifs and the nostalgia for sources are phases of one drama rooted in impossible desires and unavoidable separations.

Twentieth-century literature thus commemorates, by means of its not altogether haphazard appropriation of sources, the anxieties and promises of its own leave-takings, its own settings out. *The Cantos of Ezra Pound* are framed by Odysseus' encounter with the spirit of Elpenor in Book XI of the *Odyssey*.[8] Elpenor, an otherwise unmemorable crewman, had died accidentally by falling off the roof of one of Circe's buildings. The spirit of Elpenor demands a proper burial and memorial for the human subject whose body it has left. This encounter is emblematic of Odysseus', and hence Pound's relation to the materials, memories, and lingustic vestiges of the past. The figure of Elpenor in turn marks the decisiveness of Odysseus' sexual encounter with Circe to the events and narrative structure of the *Odyssey* and the *Cantos*. This coupling issues from a sequence of extreme sexual checks, feints, and aggressions on both sides. Circe's bestialization of Odysseus' crew is merely one instance of the sexual threat that she, as an aggressive female, poses. Hermes supplies Odysseus with a charm, moly, which enables him to ward off the effects of her magic potions. Circe relents, but only after Odysseus has, at the advice of Hermes, "rush[ed] forward against Circe, as if you were raging to kill her" (*Odyssey* X, 294-95). The mythic sources of psychoanalysis, Pound's *Cantos*, and Joyce's *Ulysses* thus trace a somewhat troubled sexual argosy. Homer's Circe bears striking affinities to the adored but seductive mother in "An Outline of Psycho-Analysis," as does Molly Bloom.

The domestic point of departure for the mythical adventures with which modernism announces its momentousness is thus invariably fraught with anxiety and a sense of the uncanny. The latter part of *Ulysses* celebrates the interpersonal solidarity which may be taken as an antidote to the imponderables of the domestic scene. Joyce's updated reunion between Odysseus and Telemachus, Bloom and Stephen, gives Bloom the heart to storm his own castle, or at least to place an order for a substantial breakfast with his wife. But even this return, this culmination of the mythical quest motif, cannot undo the structural if not actual impact of Boylan's presence within the household. The bond between father and son which the novel presents as the only escape-route from Oedipal uncertainty is also a partnership in that very blindness, an affirmation of its power over the seminal works of modern literature and theory.

It may be said of twentieth-century culture that it admitted unprecedented materials for use in conceptual work and esthetic composition—waste matter instead of rare commodities, fragmentary pieces rather than entire forms. Such major poets as Pound, T. S. Eliot, William Carlos Williams, and Wallace Stevens are driven to dumps and other waste sites as sources for raw materials as well as inspiration. The rise of the collage and statues fashioned out of odds and ends is a phenomenon in the visual and plastic arts coinciding with what Freud might describe as a regression to unrealized materials and designs.

The twentieth century may be said to begin and end with a realization of the primacy of language in the structuration of reality and science. Kafka, Proust, and for that matter Freud inaugurated the century with the strong sense that the dynamics of experience, sexuality, and thought derives from language. The theoretical overviews with which the century is ending, by such thinkers as de Man and Derrida, shift the scene of this apprehension from fictively constituted worlds to a critique of the history and prevalent trends of philosophy and organized knowledge. In widely divergent historical and geographical scenes, Derrida, for example, traces the suppression of the indeterminate results of language at the hands of systematic ideologies and procedures. There remains a peculiar affinity between the theory with which the century ends and the literature that inaugurated it.

Freud pursues the rise and composition of dreams from scraps of recent perception and memory, longer-standing traumas, and the immediate circumstances of the dreamer. In this sense, he is, to use a phrase coined by Claude Lévi-Strauss at mid-century, a *bricoleur*, a jack-of-all-trades who improvises solutions to problems as much through masterful combinations of materials at hand as in accordance with efficacious theory.[9] As a *bricoleur* of interpretation, Freud joins other modernists whose work-site was the repository of fragments surviving from past languages, cultures, collective dreams, and science: Charles Ives, Léger, and Picasso, as well as the poets mentioned above.

In *The Savage Mind* and other works, Lévi-Strauss renders legible the improvisations by which "primitive" peoples explain nature, crystallize social order, and produce art by discerning the structural analogies linking often widely divergent elements or logical assumptions. Where orderly construction gives way to kaleidoscopic collage, where materials of noble lineage are replaced by unidentified fragments and scraps, structure emerges as the new basis of coherence. The twentieth century is framed by the literary announcement and then the theoretical recapitulation of the pivotal role of language in organized human activity. Coinciding with these poles and continually between them occurs the structuralist moment, a moment of translation when the inherited assumptions and etiquettes of science are refitted to the structuring role that language played in their very possibility. If Lévi-Strauss discerns the symmetries and asymmetries at the basis of totemic classification and "primitive" face and body decoration, Freud begins the century as a structuralist, marshalling repetitive patterns in response to the seemingly impenetrable alogic prevalent within the construction of such phenomena as the dream-work and the joke. Myths are for Lévi-Strauss laboratories of structural repetition and variance. Their appeal as frameworks of coherence to authors bent upon twisting if not smashing conventional literary forms— including Joyce, Pound, and Proust—is quite understandable.

Nineteenth-century thought, as exemplified by the Hegelian system, suffers no shortage of structures, if by them we mean patterns or configurations that may be reiterated from one setting to the next.[10] Structures in Hegelian thought play a subsidiary role, facilitating the completion of a predetermined history, destiny, or intellectual realization. At a certain moment in twentieth-century thought, however, structure becomes the final product of intellectual deliberation itself. If we cannot ultimately explain the "whys" of life and history, we can discern the structures by which the stages of complex processes and interactions are connected. The attention to structure diverts attention away from the origin, substance, or results of intellectual and social processes and shifts it toward the questions of composition, style, and syntax.

There is no more striking instance of the structuralist milieu in which the Freudian enterprise partially unfolded than Walter Benjamin's 1939 essay, "On Some Motifs in Baudelaire."[11] One might well argue that this major statement includes among its objectives a dramatization as well as a formulation of the shock that epitomizes modern experience. For Benjamin, shock is the explosion of the structure lending experience its seeming legibility and coherence. Benjamin cites such factors as the jumbling of space in the modern city, the sexuality of cruising and fleeting encounters, the abolition of the ritual calendar in secular society, and the mechanization and meaninglessness of industry in explaining the traumatic quality of experience in advanced Western societies. Among Benjamin's most striking images for this jarring pace and quality of life are the spontaneous afterimage that both repeats and effaces a perception; the roulette wheel, which introjects the sudden mechanical gesture of the assembly line into the metaphysics of the wish; the sudden freezing of the momentary into art in photography; and the loss of "aura," the near-tangible trace of involvement and care that pervades handiwork.

In order to account for and dramatize this obliteration of structure, Benjamin's essay must incorporate its full measure of structural coherence and analogy. One could well argue that the Baudelaire essay is uniquely structured by structure. In this regard, it is a classic of structuralist interpretation.

The groundwork that the essay lays for its account of the degradation of experience in modern life largely consists in the isolation of a structure for shock. Better put, Benjamin begins the essay by superimposing four distinct contexts whose diversity is belied by the prevalence of a common structure within them. What modern historiography (Dilthey's *Experience and Poetry*), phenomenology (Bergsonian *durée*), literature (Proust's *mémoire involuntaire*), and, not insignificantly, Freudian and Reikian psychoanalysis have in common is nothing more substantial than a common structure; yet this structure not only locates a coherence between otherwise divergent modern intellectual enterprises; it accounts for the violence that penetrates each of these fields.

The structure of shock, wherever Benjamin discerns its operation, is characterized by an untoward paradox: the agent of activity, whether described as an organism, an individual or collective subject, or a cognitive function, is predicated by and dependent on what it resists and bypasses as much as on what it asserts and incorporates. Well being and efficiency are as much a function of negative relations as positive ones. Dysfunctions and diseases mark not so much the invasion of an external agent as the breakdown of an already installed system of defense. A formulation that Benjamin borrows from Freud's *Beyond the Pleasure Principle* (1919) applies as well to all the intellectual settings that he yokes in tandem by structural superimposition: "For a living organism, protection against is an almost more important function than the reception of stimuli; the protective shield is equipped with its own store of energy and must above all strive to preserve the special forms of conversion of energy operating in it against the effects of the excessive energies at work in the external world, effects which tend toward an equalization of potential and hence toward destruction" (*Illuminations*, p. 161; after *S.E.*, XVIII, 27). In this passage, Freud introduces the trauma as the subjective memory piercing the psychic shield that would, under optimal conditions, deflect it. Yet the tension between opposed energy fields, and the violence erupting not from without but from within—then structural components or vectors of force go beyond the psychoanalytical subject to the operation of memory in modern literature and phenomenology, and toward the modern historiography that would disclose the violence at the roots of narrative cohesion and continuity.

The activity that Benjamin's essay incorporates is, then, complex and dialectically interesting. Benjamin initially seeks and crystallizes a structure that will account for modern shock. He then unleashes, in an instance of negative dialectics, the abruptness of modern experience, in the form of the assembly line, the crowd, the camera, the roulette wheel, against his own structuring structure. His account of modern experience thus depends and founders on the structure. His organization of his subject-matter around an explosive and self-destructive structure brings his mediations to the threshold of postmodernism.

The structure is decisive to the realization and limitation of the Freudian unconscious as well. From early on in Freud's work, in the *Studies on Hysteria* (1893-95), the unconscious functions as a mental repository in which the incommensurate, the inconsistent, and the alogical prevail. Lending coherence to the disorderly mass of associations and tracing the origins of a trauma at least partially involve an interpretative quest for structure.

> The psychical material in such cases of hysteria presents itself as a structure in several dimensions which is stratified in at least three different ways. (I hope I shall presently be able to justify this pictorial mode of expression.) To begin with there is a nucleus consisting in memories of events or trains of thought in which the traumatic factor has culminated or the pathogenic idea has found its purest manifestation. Round this nucleus we find what is often an incredibly profuse amount of other mnemic material which has to be worked through in the analysis and which is, as we have said, arranged in a threefold order.
>
> In the first place there is an unmistakable linear chronological order which obtains within each separate theme. . . .
>
> I have described such groupings of similar memories into collections arranged in linear sequences (like a file of documents, a packet, etc.) as constituting "themes." These themes exhibit a second kind of arrangement. Each of them is—I cannot express it in any other way—stratified concentrically around the pathogenic nucleus. It is not hard to say what produces this stratification, what diminishing or increasing magnitude is the basis of this arrangement. The contents of each particular stratum are characterized by an equal degree of resistance, and that degree increases in proportion as the strata are nearer to the nucleus. Thus there are zones within which there is an equal degree of modification of consciousness, and the different themes extend across these zones. The most peripheral strata contain the memories (or files), which, belonging to different themes, are easily remembered and have always been clearly conscious. The deeper we go the more difficult it becomes for the emerging memories to be recognized, till near the nucleus we come upon memories which the patient disavows even in reproducing them. . . .
>
> For there is some justification for speaking of the "defile" of consciousness. The term gains meaning and liveliness for a physician who carries out an analysis like this. Only a single memory at a time can enter ego-consciousness. A patient who is occupied in working through such a memory sees nothing of what is pushing after it and forgets what has already pushed its way through. If there are difficulties in the way of mastering this single pathogenic memory—as, for instance, if the patient does not relax his resistance against it, if he tries to repress or mutilate it—then the defile is, so to speak, blocked. The work is at a standstill, nothing more can appear, and the single memory which is in process of breaking through remains in front of the patient until he has taken it up into the breadth of his ego. The whole spatially-extended mass of psychogenic material is in this way drawn through a narrow cleft and thus arrives in consciousness cut up, as it were, into pieces or strips. It is the psychotherapist's business to put these together once more into the organization which he presumes to have existed. Anyone who has a craving for further similes may think at this point of a Chinese puzzle. (*S.E.*, II, 288-91)

These statements frame a decisive passage in Freud's work, one never for-gotten despite its earliness in the corpus. The passage represents the complex organization of the mind, or, more specifically, the unconscious. Among the many striking qualities of this depiction must be counted the sheer num-bers of structures and types of associative movement for which the mental apparatus provides. The mind is a conglomerate of thematic seeds or nuggets around which additional psychic material arranges itself several ways: concen-trically, tangentially, and vertically. Within the concentric arrangement, "the most peripheral strata" of mnemonics (which Freud already calls "files") are the most accessible, while "the deeper we go the more difficult it becomes for the emerging memories to be recognized" (*S.E.*, II, 289). The different "pathogenic" nuclei, however, reverberate off of each other. Thus, pene-trating to the core of one concentrically organized cluster may require "an irregular and twisting path" leaping in an unpredictable manner back and forth between strata of accessibility and thematic arenas (*S.E.*, II, 289).

The types of organization which are for Freud pre-installed in the mind are, then, concentric, vertical, and linear. Freud characterizes the psycho-analytical process as the retroactive provision of the thread touching on the jarringly remote themes, associations, and moments of life that are impli-cated by genuine, defense-penetrating traumas. In this regard, Freud inscribes psychoanalysis in the myth of the labyrinth, where Theseus' return is assured by Ariadne's thread. In Freud's own language, psychoanalysis narrows the scope of memory; it forces the panoply of memories and associations through a "narrow cleft" (*S.E.*, II, 291). The "pieces or strips" produced by this lathing process become the raw materials for the metamorphosis effected by transference, for narrative and social reconstruction.

The mind emerges from this complex and innovative description as a field of forces and force transfers. If Freud organizes the heterogeneous psychic *material* by strata, zones, and (discontinuous) lines, it is so that the struc-ture(s) of the mind can sustain abrupt and sometimes self-contradictory *shifts of force*. In this respect, Freud's enterprise is not as remote from Pound's as it might seem. The mental associations whose organization Freud is trying to articulate are surely a far cry from Pound's cultural bric-a-brac. In both cases, however, Freud's psychic topology and Pound's Vorticism, structure emerges as the principle of legibility when the field of inquiry becomes het-erogeneous, when it embraces the fragmentary, the consumed, and what has fallen out of context.

Both in the materials that it admits and in its approach to them, Freudian psychoanalysis is thus a modernist undertaking. It not only legitimizes hitherto inadmissable themes, subjects, and forms of evidence; it joins the ongoing structuralist project of the century. It isolates the structures emerging, like paths in a cloud-chamber, when the linguistic dynamics underlying science come to the fore, when science suspends the conceptual stasis by which it made itself possible.

The discourse of psychoanalysis—like the truly seminal authors of the twentieth century—provides for its own leap into post-modernism. While in different ways, Kafka, Joyce, and Beckett straddle both sides of a stylistic and, in Foucault's sense, archaeological divide, psychoanalysis' post-modernity is implicit within the founding Freudian biases of the system. In a paradoxical sense, psychoanalysis' post-modern emanation was stimulated rather than hampered by the blatancy and persistence with which those biases were pronounced.

While a decidedly modernist Kafka writes a self-effacing version of the Prometheus myth based on the variants structurally (in Lévi-Strauss's sense) implicit within the myth, the post-modern Kafka records seemingly interminable interior monologues of unidentified burrowing rodents. As a novel that systematically, in scale if not execution, explores its mythic literary sources and the stylistic, cognitive, and experiential modes that make it possible, Joyce's *Ulysses* may well be the most fully realized modern novel. *Ulysses* examines a bewildering range of the socio-political conditions under which it is written. It would account both for the disjunctive meanderings of its own signs (and of itself as a mega-sign) and, through the artform of music, for the resolution of its internal tensions and its innovations as a synthetic artform. Like Kafka's "The Burrow," however, the unbounded, in some senses inarticulate, statement with which the novel ends crosses a threshold into an alien esthetic. "Molly Bloom's" monologue is characterized by a dearth of grammatical signposts, uncertainties as to where and whether thoughts begin and end, and an indifference to progression and resolution. "Molly's" discourse may represent a terminus for *Ulysses*, but it is the taking off point for *Finnegans Wake*. In the works of Samual Beckett, a climate of release and a frenzy of structural configuration with which the century begins quickly shift into a milieu of studied, relentless indifference, a depression to counteract a long celebration of anxiety's affects.

How can the notions of modernism and post-modernism be productively applied to a sea-change that "takes place" nowhere specific, but which still tempers our century, a shift in mood implicating psychoanalytical as well as literary texts? As dangerous as it may be to risk formulating a closed matrix of "modern" and "post-modern" traits, the temptation to address this question, however provisionally, is irresistible. In the fortunate absence of a comprehensive response, psychoanalysis, at least, would allow us an incomplete list of "associated" factors, a compendium analogous to Borges's Chinese encyclopaedia.

What happens when we cross over into the terrain demarcated by *Finnegans Wake*, Beckett's plays and all but his first stories and novels, and the fictive and discursive prose of Antonin Artaud, Georges Bataille, and Maurice Blanchot? Above all, there has been a loss, or relinquishing of, a certain nostalgia, a weaning from the desire for total intimacy and possession.

The angel of history, in the post-modern climate, no longer longingly faces the past. Separations, divergences, and splits do not represent tragic shatterings of various unities, but are merely facts of life. "Marcel" nods his head when he hears that his mother won't be visiting him that night and turns to his magic lantern. The affective accompaniment to the major transitions along the program of existential development has been *turned down* if not completely off. Some of the implications of this separation without sorrow, this esthetic of indifference, as Rodlphe Gasché and others recently invoke the term,[12] are as follows: Sex is not the proving ground of Being, the crucible of identity, but one activity among others, something that people do. They *do sex* for a variety of reasons and with a number of different results. Sex *means* inherently nothing in its own right; its variants are devoid of any implicit moral, political, or esthetic value.

The past is no longer an origin, a time more authentic than others because a greater degree of intimacy once prevailed there. The past, rather, is a relative position along an indifferent continuum, one might say tedium, of time.

The role of surrogation diminishes in the conception of literary characters, in favor of functionality. Characters do not so much "represent" subjects, real or imagined, as *express* functions, within language, politics, economics, and sexuality.

Literary form diminishes in its fidelity within the representation of events. Not only must "events" no longer be brought to fruition or culmination: there is no compulsion for them even to "occur." Plot, no longer an organizing schema whose internal necessities shape the narrative work of art, acquires a figural, at times even ironic function. What applies to events applies to coherence. In a post-modern setting, no dominant outcome or result need emerge. The literary text neither emulates nor instruments actions. By the same token, there is no longer a necessity for the emergence of *structure*, the coherence that announces itself within a heterogeneous setting, in the absence of any substantial resolution.

How can such developments, or perhaps better put, such non-events taking place in artifacts as incongruous as literary texts, be registered within the discourse of psychoanalysis? Within the constraints of the present essay, this question can be best answered stylistically, not systematically. Yet one way of characterizing the compendium of approaches and interventions known as "Lacan" would be to say that one decisive effect, if not aim, of this body of work has been to bring the discourse of psychoanalysis out of its modernist and into its post-modern phase. One would immediately have to add, however, that not only the Lacanian counterpoint, but a variety of neo-analytical approaches, have a distinctly post-modern flavor. In the remainder of this essay, we will devote our attention to a number of passages, by Jacques Lacan and Otto Kernberg, setting the post-modern emanation of psychoanalytical discourse in relief.

Even the Freudian passages cited above are indicative of the tendencies and structures that beg to be addressed by a Lacanian critique, if one of its major thrusts is a reorientation of psychoanalysis to the linguistic dynamics of mental and interpersonal life. "The gods may still speak through dreams," writes Lacan in "Of the Network of Signifiers."[13] "Personally, I don't mind either way. What concerns us is the tissue that envelops these messages, the network in which, on occasion, something is caught" (*FFC*, 45). Lacan's work will repeatedly stress the importance of what transpires along the chain of signifiers, within the mind and communication, at the expense of definitive results or proofs, whether of a theory's efficacy, an analyst's mastery, or a patient's cure.

As brief and widely separated as they are, then, the Freudian passages cited above are replete with the points of closure, the too-tight upholstery-buttons that a language-oriented, Lacanian critique will undo. The heavy mechanics of opposition and alternation; the coordination of linear, circular, and vertical movement, segmenting development into sequential, discrete phases; the strict division of labor between the genders; and the knowable outcome of transference, predicated by the therapist's mastery and guidance—these comprise distinctive traits of Freudian thought and major points of departure from which the Lacanian critique will set out. It is not insignificant that Lacan, when he selects visual images or insignias for the operation of the psyche, bypasses those that would enforce the closed circuitry of the machine and gravitates toward the "impossible figure," such as anamorphosis (*FFC*, 85-87), the "interior 8" (*FFC*, 156), and the gordian knot (*FFC*, 130-31)—examples leading to the heart of impenetrability, not out of the labyrinth. Stylistically, the Lacanian discourse has entered an esthetic of pronounced indirection, whose asides hopelessly confuse (and possibly "castrate") the "train" or "thread" of thought. With Lacan, psychoanalytic discourse cools to—becomes indifferent to—its prior overarching schemes, plans, and objectives.

Among the most stunning innovations of the Lacanian revision of Freudian psychoanalysis must be the Otherness of the unconscious. According to Lacan, the unconscious corresponds neither to a prior nor a logically primitive emanation of our own consciousness. The unconscious truly is Other. It does not belong to us. If it corresponds to anything, it is the linguistic network into which we were born, a network that was in place before we were. Oedipus, according to this adjustment, does not belatedly learn of his rage at his father and desire for his mother; Oedipus, like the rest of us, is a congenitally belated and confused reader of a Law that he can never fully know and is therefore fated to violate.

The unconscious is the voice of the Other; it is the linguistic nature of the system of signification that is our culture. It is also the voice of the Others that we cannot assimilate, whose heeding would be tantamount to a constitutional crisis. There are thus ancestral, social, sexual, and political equivalents to this Other: the gender we may perhaps never experience from the inside; the class identification that has been effaced in us. In certain senses, then, the feminine can function as the unconscious of the masculine; the awareness of the working class as the unconscious of the ruling class. The Lacanian unconscious is free to emerge wherever ineradicable schisms have been drawn.

We do not own our unconscious. We do not control it. It is not a prior or inferior emanation of ourselves that we can somehow school or train. This major adjustment to the Freudian system suspends certain aims, purposes, and values that Freud took over from Western philosophy. Psychoanalysis is no longer a psychomachy between our good and not so good natures because the element that we would earmark for discipline does not belong to us, is not of our own making. Instead of learning, knowing, dominating, or controlling our subliminal facet, we make a pact with it. It is there too. We best live with it.

Through his insistence on the Otherness of the unconscious, Lacan advocates an accommodation of what will be otherwise experienced as alien, hostile, primitive, as "the imp of the perverse." The form of this productive working relationship with the unconscious as Otherness will be that of exegesis, of patient, amused, and somewhat detached reading. In its new-found distance from spiritual unfolding—a patrimony from many sources but above all from Hegel—Lacanian psychoanalysis is free to challenge certain of the imperatives—in terms of psycho-sexual evolution and clinical protocol—that the Freudian system assumed. Lacan somehow manages to preserve the uncanniness of the apprehension that all reality we experience is mediated through language at the same time that he pushes psychoanalytical theory toward a productive accommodation of our irreducible Otherness to ourselves. His insistence on the linguistic nature of mental processes moves in a deconstructive direction, but his revisions of psychoanalytical theory preserve more freshly than deconstruction the strangeness of this realization, an uncanniness in no way retracting its inevitability.

If structure—or a structuralist purview—emerged as the classification that would hold the heterogeneous permissiveness of the Freudian unconscious in abeyance, the Lacanian unconscious remains another matter. At play within it is all the discontinuity that Freud would entertain, but few of the machine-fittings that would connect various fitful and disparate motions.

> Freud's unconscious is not at all the romantic unconscious of imaginative creation. It is not the locus of the divinities of night. This locus is no doubt not entirely unrelated to the locus towards which Freud turns his gaze. . . .
>   Impediment, failure, split. In a spoken or written sentence something stumbles. Freud is attracted by these phenomena, and it is there that he seeks the unconscious. There, something other demands to be realized—which appears as intentional, of course, but of a strange temporality. What occurs, what is

produced, in this gap, is presented as *the discovery*. It is in this way that the Freudian exploration first encounters what occurs in the unconscious.

Now, as soon as it is presented, this discovery becomes a rediscovery and, furthermore, it is always ready to steal away again, thus establishing the dimension of loss.

To resort to a metaphor, drawn from mythology, we have, in Eurydice twice lost, the most potent image we can find of the relation between Orpheus the analyst and the unconscious.

In this respect, if you will allow me to add a touch of irony, the unconscious finds itself, strictly speaking, on the opposite side to love, which, as everyone knows, is always unique; the expression "one lost, ten to be found again" finds its best application here.

Discontinuity, then, is the essential form in which the unconscious first appears to us a phenomenon—discontinuity, in which something is manifested as a vacillation. Now, if this discontinuity has this absolute, inaugural character, in the development of Freud's discovery, must we place it—as was later the tendency with analysts—against the background of a totality? (*FFC*, 24-25)

Not even in its predictable complexity will Lacan afford the Freudian unconscious any simplicity. The unconscious is too tricky, has too much of volition on its own to fall simply into the night or playground that Western thought reserves for its controllable negativity. Lacan professes his "adhesion to the Hegelian dialectic" (*FFC*, 221), yet the dialectics that he really deploys, and marshals against classical psychoanalysis is the negative dialectics of the Frankfurt school[14]—dialectics as the ground for sudden, inexplicable reversal, emerging with the violence of the gesture on the Chinese stage. It is Freudian psychoanalysis, with its oppositional structures and progress, that may more properly be called Hegelian.

The Freudian drive (*Trieb*) undergoes a parallel revision of its vicissitudes at the hands of Lacan.

At the other end of the chain, Freud refers to *Befriedigung*, satisfaction, which he writes out in full, but in inverted commas. What does he mean by satisfaction of the drive? *Well, that's simple enough*, you'll say. *The satisfaction of the drive is reaching one's* Ziel, *one's aim*. The wild animal emerges from its hole *querens quem devoret*, and when he has found what he has to eat, he is satisfied, he digests it. The very fact that a similar image may be invoked shows that one allows it to resonate in harmony with mythology, with, strictly speaking, the drive. (*FFC*, 165)

Let me say that if there is anything resembling a drive it is a *montage*.

It is not a *montage* conceived in a perspective referring to finality. This perspective is the one that is established in modern theories of instinct, in which the presentation of an image derived from *montage* is quite striking. Such a *montage*, for example, is the specific form that will make the hen in the farmyard run to ground if you place within a few yards of her the cardboard outline of a falcon, that is to say, something that sets off a more or less appropriate reaction, and where the trick is to show us that it is not necessarily an appropriate one. I am not speaking of this sort of *montage*.

The *montage* of the drive is a *montage* which, first, is presented as having neither head nor tail—in the sense in which one speaks of *montage* in a surrealist collage. If we bring together the paradoxes that we just defined at the level of *Drang*, at that of the object, at that of the aim of the drive, I think that the resulting image would show the working of a dynamo connected up to a gas-tap, a peacock's feather emerges, and tickles the belly of a pretty woman, who is just lying there looking beautiful. Indeed, the thing begins to become interesting from this very fact, that the drive defines, according to Freud, all the forms of which one may reverse such a mechanism. This does not mean that one turns the dynamo upside-down—one unrolls its wires, it is they that become the peacock's feather, the gas-tap goes into the lady's mouth, and the bird's rump emerges in the middle. (*FFC*, 169)

No longer is the drive an ineluctible force undergoing mechanical divisions and alternations on its way to statutory satisfaction or completion. It is instead a configuration whose process—its middle—outweighs and devours its beginning and its end. Lacan's writing in this passage becomes a veritable barnyard of unforeseen events and slapstick outcomes. Subject to fluctuations, the Lacanian drive goes precisely nowhere. Whatever action there is, is situated at the middle of something. Lacan's esthetic instances of the drive emanate from surrealism, post-modern art. The drive parallels a Rube Goldberg invention, in which hilariously inappropriate components are connected— with only the most unpredictable results. Lacan's pictoral representation of the drive's trajectory is the shape of a phallus, whose sharp rise in aim is suddenly reversed as it veers beneath the "rim" of its goal (*FFC*, 178). In the above passage, Lacan insists that the aim of his intervention is not to invent a dynamo—one could insert Hegelian or Freudian dialectics—but rather to remain in the midst of the process and work out its complex transfers. "The unconscious is structured like a language" (*FFC*, 20).

Among the casualties of such an inconsequential, non-dialectical, one is tempted to say impotent, Lacanian drive is the particularly belabored Freudian gendrification. In classical psychoanalysis, this division of labor accounts for a large number of psychological manifestations and relates the masculine and feminine by means of a troubled symmetry.

This representation of the Other is lacking, specifically, between the two opposed worlds that sexuality designates for us in the masculine and the feminine. Carrying things as far as they will go, one might even say that the masculine ideal and the feminine ideal are represented in the psyche by something other than this activity/passivity opposition of which I spoke earlier. Strictly speaking, they spring from a term that I have not introduced, but of which one female psycho-analyst has pin-pointed the feminine sexual attitude—the term *masquerade*. (*FFC*, 193)

Who would not accept this function on the biological plane? What I am saying, following Freud, who provides abundant evidence of it, is that this function is not represented as such in the psyche. In the psyche, there is nothing by which the subject may situate himself as a male or female being.

In his psyche, the subject situates only equivalents of the function of reproduction—activity and passivity, which by no means represent it in an exhaustive way. Freud even adds a touch of irony to this by stressing that this representation is not as constricting or as exhaustive as that—*durchgreifend ausschließlich*—the polarity of the male and the female being is represented only by the polarity of activity, which is manifested through the *Triebe*, and of passivity, which is passivity only in relation to the exterior, *gegen die äusseren Reize*.

Only this division—and it is here that I left off last time—makes necessary what was first revealed by analytic experience, namely, that the ways of what one must do as man or as woman are entirely abandoned to the drama, to the scenario, which is placed in the field of the Other—which, strictly speaking, is the Oedipus complex. (*FFC*, 204)

In post-modern psychoanalysis, however, gender does not lend itself so easily to schemes and the type of *explanation* that results from them. While for Freud, gender has a material impact on object-choice and on subsequent sexual alternatives, including the perversions, for Lacan gender is illustrative, above all, of symbolic functions in the imaginary. Lacan may, as a host of writers before him, no doubt including Freud, delight in the eternal slapstick of the battle between the sexes. For Lacan, however, this engagement is merely part of a much broader encounter, with the Other. The battle of the sexes is an attenuated, protean affair. The Other may be an interlocutor, but not one whose identity or response is determined in any dialectical way. Masculinity and femininity, then, are not predetermined. They are not givens. "In the psyche, there is nothing by which the subject may situate himself as a male or female being." Nor does gender predicate specific behaviors in any simple way. Its ambisexual impact may be discerned only through complex symbolical relations specific to the "subject" and the particular intra- or intersubjective rapport involved.

From this perspective, sexuality loses some of its drama and certain of the affinities to literary forms—among them tragedy, comedy, and lyricism—that have made it such a pervasive literary subject. Sexual acts comprise merely one activity we perform within the symbolic stock-exchange of language. The eternally mystifying encounter between males and females is a subcategory of the discourse of the Other. So too does the transference, which in the Freudian system comprises the very motor and hope of psychoanalysis, illustrate this open-ended confrontation with otherness.

> In analytic practice, there are many ways of conceiving the transference. They are not necessarily mutually exclusive. They may be defined at different levels. For example, although the conceptions of the relation of the subject to one or other of those agencies which, in the second stage of his *Topography*, Freud was able to define as the ego-ideal or the super-ego, are partial, this is often simply to give a lateralized view of what is essentially the relation with the capital Other.

> I can do no more than suggest here the reversion involved in this schema in relation to the model one has of it in one's head. I say somewhere that *the unconscious is the discourse of the Other*. Now, the discourse of the Other that is to be realized, that of the unconscious, is not beyond the closure, it is *outside*. It is this discourse, which, through the mouth of the analyst, calls for the reopening of the shutter. (*FFC*, 130-31)
>
> That is why we can say what is there, behind the love known as transference, is the affirmation of the link between the desire of the analyst and the desire of the patient. This is what Freud expressed in a kind of rapid sleight of hand when he said—*after all, it is only the desire of the patient*—this should reassure one's colleagues. It is the patient's desire, yes, but in its meeting with the analyst's desire.
>
> I will not say that I have not yet named the analyst's desire, for how can one name a desire? One circumscribes a desire. There are many things in history that provide us with tracks and traces here. (*FFC*, 254)

The analyst, situated within a topography of enormous complexity, is no longer the guide and master who sees and speaks from a perspective of impersonality, incorruptibility, and sublimity. The analyst is a partner in the discourse with the Other. She or he interposes desire. Analysis may allow for a certain externalization, a certain *expression* of the unconscious, but once this transition is made, the game is up for grabs; it is anyone's game. The analyst stands as much to lose—or win—as the analysand. When nip comes to tuck, in fact, when Lacan feels compelled to place the "low" voice of reason either in the mouth of the Socratic master of slave, he associates the psychoanalytical discourse with the perspective of the slave. "It is in the direction of some kind of kinship that we should turn our eyes to the slave, when it is a question of mapping what the analyst's desire is" (*FFC*, 255).

With all due respect to psychoanalysis' clinical dimensions and etiquettes, its leap into a post-modern phase runs strikingly parallel to the literary developments that have taken place in our century. Even at the beginning of Beckett's work, his literary characters are not quite aware of where they are going or what they might do next. As psychoanalysis moves beyond Freud, above all as it is interrogated by Lacan, the pace and intensity of its self-critique and of its exploration of its (above all linguistic) conditions increase dramatically. At the same time, the predictable results of its "plot" become increasingly unlikely; the roles of its principle "characters" blur; sexuality loses much of its definition, pathos, and mystique within the field of its inquiry. The middle of its language-oriented process absorbs the attention and importance once attached to psychoanalytical cosmology and teleology. *Psychoanalysis enters the stage of its productive indifference.*

The post-modernization of the psychoanalytical discourse is a phenomenon illustrative of the strategic role that literary developments play in cultural articulation. Yet it would be unfortunate were this phenomenon localized to the so-called Lacanian "school," and hence identified with the dissident role into which this approach has sometimes been thrust. I close with an extract from a more clinically oriented psychoanalytic discourse, this time from the

American school. I would argue that this language, by Otto Kernberg on the borderline personality, has been tempered no less by a post-modern esthetic than have been the Lacanian passages cited above.

> All these characteristics of internalized object relationships are reflected in typical characterological traits of the borderline personality organization. These patients have little capacity for a realistic evaluation of others and for realistic empathy with others; they experience other people as distant objects, to whom they adapt "realistically" only as long as there is no emotional involvement with them. Any situation which would normally develop into a deeper interpersonal relationship reveals the incapacity of these patients to really feel or empathize with another person, the unrealistic distortion of other people, and the protective shallowness of their emotional relationships. This protective shallowness has many sources. First, it reflects the emotional shallowness due to the lack of fusion between libidinal and aggressive drive derivatives, and the concomitant narrowness, rigidity, and primitiveness of their affect dispositions. The shallowness of the emotional reaction of the patients we are considering is also more directly connected with the incapacity to experience guilt, concern, and the related deepening of their awareness of and interest in others. An additional reason for their emotional shallowness is the defensive effort to withdraw from too close an emotional involvement, which would bring about the danger of activation of their primitive defensive operations, especially projective identification and the arousal of fears of attack by the object which is becoming important to them. Emotional shallowness also defends them from primitive idealization of the object and the related need to submit to and merge with such idealized objects, as well as from the potential rage over frustration of the pregenital, especially orally demanding needs that are activated in the relationship with the idealized object. The lack of superego development, and therefore the further lack of ego integration and maturation of feelings, aims, and interests, also keeps them in ignorance of the higher, more mature and differentiated aspects of other people's personalities.[15]

What is perhaps most striking about this passage from Kernberg's *Borderline Conditions and Pathological Narcissism* is its relentless descriptiveness. Kernberg is very precisely observing a dysfunction that is not qute exactly a disease, if by the latter we mean a malady traceable to specific causes. A character disorder is, precisely, a condition, or a set of conditions, rather than a pathology. Hence, description—neutral, exhaustive, perspectival, situational—is decisive not only to the diagnosis of the disorder but to its treatment as well. One might argue that in the borderline personality we have a new order of mental disease, one whose treatment largely entails impeccable description and the efficient transfer of descriptive material to the patient. Treatment is less a matter than before of masterful diagnosis, prescription, and delivery of a specific therapy.

The world from which the borderline patient hails might not be all that recognizable to the founders of psychoanalysis. No longer is the borderline patient the product of a stifling environment, thick with familial relations and dramas, suffused with unrelenting and multifaceted surveillance, pervaded by ubiquitous guilt. Repression is not the ultimate stumbling block that prohibits the borderline "subject" from fulfilling his or her desire, aggression, or rage. The borderline personality is, rather, native to a world of proliferating absences: absentee parents, dissolved families, in both the extended and nuclear dimensions; she or he has become habituated to superficial and whimsical relationships. While surely in many arenas the psychosexual conditions that the founders of psychoanalysis confronted in their patients persist, the notions of borderline states and pathological narcissism may well respond to a modified breed of subject, one indeed constituted through absence, neglect, and the effacement of social and educational structure. The *subject* of borderline states and pathological narcissism may well be at home in the worlds represented in the literature of post-modernity. In this sense, the development of this therapeutic field comprises an evolutionary adaptation on the part of psychoanalysis: a response to an emergent patient and a revised set of psychosexual conditions essential to its survival as a clinical therapy and a model of thought.

Conspicuously absent from Kernberg's citation above is any sense of the analyst's mission, his motives, or his views on the subject. All of Kernberg's attention is riveted upon the conditions and dynamics of the condition. Psychoanalysis does not evaluate, judge, or even, in the strict sense, intervene. It observes, and its talismanic, curative powers are concentrated in the attentiveness of its observation. It is not accidental that Lacan pays so much attention to the problematic of the gaze.

Kernberg's relentless description recalls the endless monologues in the writings of Kafka, Joyce, and, more recently, Thomas Bernhard.[16] Psychoanalysis and literature have made peace with their place; they inhabit their topology. The wider concerns of origin, generation, territoriality, and destiny have been neutralized. Post-modern literature and psychoanalysis have elected to stay in place, to work out the problems installed in their medium, language, and their setting.

10
Psychoanalysis and Deconstruction and Woman
Ruth Salvaggio

Beginning his essay *Spurs*, Derrida writes: "The title of this lecture was to have been *the question of style*. However—it is woman who will be my subject. Still, one might wonder whether that doesn't really amount to the same thing—or is it to the other."[1]

The title of my own essay here was to have been, and remains, "Psychoanalysis and Deconstruction." However, it is woman who will also be my subject. And I might also wonder whether that really doesn't amount to the same thing, or to the question of the "other"—as if "woman" were "other" to the academic discourses of psychoanalysis and deconstruction, as if she were that elusive object of their quests and their questions.

I could begin by writing not about woman, but about two men-—Jacques Lacan and Jacques Derrida—who are among the first names to come to mind whenever the subjects of psychoanalysis and deconstruction are mentioned, and who seem to me, despite their many differences, to share a quest: the quest for woman. They are, in fact, among the most notable generators of a postmodern discourse that articulates itself in terms of a reaching out for something which cannot be known, theorized, dominated, answered. They are men who do not so much pose a question about woman as take woman as their question, as the very term of their quest. They are men caught up in the dynamics of what Derrida called a "feminine operation," a "sort of scheme for how to seduce without being seduced."[2]

What I am most interested in, however, is not so much the nature of their operation—which I nonetheless want to explore as I consider these two men and their related discourses of deconstruction and psychoanalysis. What ultimately concerns me is the way in which this feminine operation, as it plays itself out in deconstruction and psychoanalysis, effects the discourse of women who are now speaking both as subjects fashioned by their own discourse and as breaking loose from a quest for woman. My subject, then, is a split notion of woman: woman as the subject of man's postmodern discourse, and woman as a speaking subject. And my quest, as one who has already internalized aspects of both notions of woman in my own writing, is to come to terms with a feminine operation that functions both as a passive "subject of" and as a more assertive "speaking subject"—that is, as both object and subject at once.

I could, then, simply take Lacan and Derrida as my own subject. But I want to do this by speaking through the terms of a woman who has written about their own undertakings, Barbara Johnson. In her essay "The Frame of Reference," Johnson discusses the attempt of Lacan and Derrida to analyze a text by producing a reading which finally amounts to a "subversion of any possibility of a position of analytical mastery. . . ."[3] Mastery over what? Over the text, we might say, or the meaning of the text, or the message that is endlessly deferred in the particular text under analysis—which, in this case, happens to be Edgar Allen Poe's "The Purloined Letter," a text which itself eludes its fictive investigators. Johnson's own "frame of reference" in writing her essay, as she explains, "is precisely, to a very large extent, the writings of Lacan and Derrida."[4] As I read what she says, however, I find myself establishing a different "frame of reference" in which to discuss these two men and their attempts to subvert the possibility of analytical mastery. For me, the question "mastery over what" can be rephrased as "mastery over woman." I believe that their attempts to subvert analytical mastery are attempts to subvert the possibility of mastering woman, since it is woman who conceptually underlies the elusive object of a quest to be endlessly deferred.

Johnson relies on terms that I find useful to describe the sexual dimensions of this continually deferred quest, the process of ceaselessly questing, that many of us now recognize as the "postmodern condition." Describing the "rivalry over something neither man will credit the other with possessing," Johnson wonders: "What kind of logic is it that thus seems to turn one-upmanship into inevitable one-downmanship?"[5] I myself wonder if it is this very sense of "downmanship"—this stepping down from the assertion and quest for a certitude associated with the masculine position—that makes Lacanian psychoanalysis and Derridean deconstruction into discourses which want to seduce the woman without themselves being seduced, that is, without themselves coming to any sexual or analytical conclusions. With this possibility in mind, I find myself shifting positions as I take Lacan and Derrida as my subject. For since my own sexual identity—female—is the very figuration of their ceaseless quest, I begin to regard myself, my subjectivity, in terms of their elusive object. I find myself reading through their discourse toward myself. Am I like them in wanting not to master it? How do women write (about) deconstruction and psychoanalysis?

In his lecture "The Freudian Thing," Lacan describes "woman" as the desired object of Freudian psychoanalysis, but also as an object that always eludes Freud's grasp. At one point in the lecture, Lacan's voice becomes the voice of this "thing" speaking of herself, uttering an almost scolding declaration: " 'So for you I am the enigma of her who vanishes as soon as she appears, men who try so hard to hide me under the tawdry finery of your proprieties! . . . Men, listen, I am giving you the secret. I, truth, will speak.' " [6] And so she proceeds, but if listeners expect to hear some well-defined articulation of truth, they will be disappointed. Her truth turns out to be more like error—not the fixed idea which we might grasp, but the elusive quality, the teasing thought. Man's attempt to imprison her truth, she says, is doomed to failure since she will always escape his dungeons and " 'wander about in what you regard as being the least true in essence . . . in chance, not in its law, but in its contingence. . . .' " Her final remarks on this matter pay homage to that disruptive feminine figure who has tormented centuries of readers: " 'I never do more to change the face of the world than when I give it the profile of Cleopatra's nose.' " [7]

This "truth" who speaks, whoever she is, is certainly not the truth of the systematic analyst who seeks answers to questions. She is, however—Lacan tells us—Freud's truth, because she represents the thing which psychoanalysis pursues—not the subject or object of analysis, but the never-ending and always exchanging process of analysis itself. As "woman," she becomes the elusive "Freudian Thing." Lacan figures her as the goddess Diana who keeps slipping Actaeon (Freud) who is not killed because of his pursuit, but who goes on living through his very quest for the goddess. [8] Woman, in this way, becomes associated in Lacan's thought with the process of desire, notably a linguistic desire which seeks meaning and wholeness through substitutions and displacement—or, as Ellie Ragland-Sullivan explains, a "drama" in which "the Symbolic Name-of-the-Father never stands on its own apart from the idea of woman." [9] In the present "symbolic order," woman may well be considered a wandering, linguistic agent who evades the fixity of meaning— she may be the seductive other, deep in the forest, who keeps desire in play and who keeps the quest alive.

In this sense, she would resemble that elusive interval of deferral that ceaselessly generates differences within writing, preventing it from being fixed or closed in meaning. She occupies, as Gayatri Spivak says, "the place" in which deconstruction takes place. [10] Derrida, like Lacan, associates "woman" with a kind of wandering discourse—but he calls her "untruth," for she cannot be inscribed, imprinted, fixed. He suggests that style—the stylus, the quill, the pen, the rapier, the spur—allows us to make a "vicious attack against what philosophy appeals to in the name of matter or matrix," an attack which both leaves its imprint on "and thereby protects the presence, the content, the thing itself, meaning, truth. . . ." Or, as he later explains, "It could be said that if style were a man (much as the penis, according to Freud, is the <normal prototype of fetishes>), then writing would be a woman."[11] We might say, then, that if this "spur" has the effect of preserving truth, and if "woman" is an elusive kind of "untruth," then the woman evades stylistic control whenever she is written and at the very same time keeps writing in process. Woman as object, in other words, is always in the process of deconstructing the order of language, always preventing the cohesion that would make conclusion and analytical mastery possible. And that is why the man-writer needs her. How could he pursue his quest without that elusive woman leading him on, insuring that he will always have something to write *about* and *toward*.

To begin to understand "writing" in terms of a sexual quest is to begin to understand how post-structural discourse writes itself within a certain "frame of reference" whose dynamics are kept in play through sexual exchange. This is not simply to say that post-structural writers define their quest in terms of a man reaching out for an object which he calls woman. If this were the case, we might then simply label his quest as traditionally sexist, and neatly place it alongside a variety of discursive traditions which have attempted to appropriate and control a variety of disturbing feminine forces. What makes Lacan and Derrida different, it seems to me, is that they finally do not want to capture and control this feminine agent. Far from it, they seem to have redefined the terms of the sexual quest. They have named woman as the very process that disrupts closure in both its sexual and discursive sense. Their naming of woman as this process explains to me, at least, why so much of the male academic establishment feels threatened by Lacanian psychoanalysis and Derridean deconstruction. I have always suspected that fear of deconstructing is a sexual fear—that is threatens to emasculate the otherwise happy humanist who pursues the truth of the system. What's more, it is setting woman loose within discourse, dislodging her from her place as "subject of" man's sexual and linguistic appropriation. If the processes of deconstruction and psychoanalysis involve the endless exchange of subject and object, and if woman is the agent of an exchange that will not "come" to conclusion and closure, then we might well regard all three "subjects" of this essay—psychoanalysis, deconstruction, and woman—as threats to the conventional (and academic) desire for a fused sexual and linguistic satisfaction.

Enough about these two men for now. I have said that woman is the real "subject" of my own writing here—not as an object of some linguistic quest, but as a "speaking subject," as the womanly thing who has become object and agent of analytical subversion. If there is a quest which might explain my own writing in this essay, it would be the quest-ion of the relationship between this speaking woman and the woman-as-subject of Lacanian and Derridean discourse. To put the issue in its largest "frame of reference," we might say that I'm addressing the relationship between post-structuralism and feminism, a topic that has already served as an elusive "subject" in the writings of so many analysts who would capture this "thing."¹² But to put the issue in my own "frame of reference," I would say that my specific concern is the question of how woman—the agent of displacement in Lacanian psychoanalysis and Derridean deconstruction—can in turn become a speaking subject who writes both about and through these very postmodern discourses. Is woman, now as a speaking and writing subject, reaching out for an object of her own discourse, desiring—like the post-structural man— to seduce without being seduced? Is woman, in other words, the subject *of* deconstruction and psychoanalysis, the subject which *seduces* psychoanalysis and deconstruction, the subject which *unhinges* the very process of subject seducing object?

I ask this question of myself, now, writing.

Much of what goes under the title of "feminist theory," both in the United States and abroad, has been caught up in the actual event of woman speaking—even as this theory addresses, in more objective fashion, the subject of this speaking woman's discourse. I have in mind several theories generating from the United States and from abroad, notably France, because the different ways in which such "feminist theory" treats and speaks the subject of woman seems strongly implicated in at least two very different understandings of what is meant by the name "woman." The somewhat infamous French/ American split on this question—perhaps now less related to actual national differences and more to different opinions that are associated with these national demarcations—has resulted in what Alice Jardine calls a problematizing of the very notion of woman. We are necessarily involved, she says, in "thinking through the apparent contradictions between that French and American thinking characterized by the conflict between *woman as process* and *woman as sexual identity*." The effect of such a distinction, Jardine explains, is that "women as thinking, writing subjects are placed in the position of constantly wondering whether it is a question of women or woman."¹³ Jardine's "frame of reference" is "woman as process," the feminine effect she describes as having "come to signify those *processes* that disrupt symbolic structures in the West."¹⁴ Yet in taking this "woman" as her subject, she has herself engaged in a process typical of post-structural feminists: she has made post-structural man the "subject" of her own discourse as a speaking woman. She has, in writing about Lacan and Derrida, taken them as a kind of "woman," and read their discourse in terms of what she calls "gynesis"—"the putting into discourse of 'woman'."¹⁵ Let me suggest that one way of "framing" Jardine's writing is to see her twisting the terms of the seductive quest: she is a speaking woman reaching out for the discourse of man, and yet she names that discourse of man the "becoming" of woman.

We might wonder: can woman, as a speaking subject, write about postmodern discourse without making the man's theories into an object of her seduction? In *The Daughter's Seduction*, Jane Gallop makes much of the process of seduction to account for the connections between feminism and psychoanalysis. In one sense, she explains, feminism has been seduced by psychoanalysis (the father) and is forced to confront the issue of sexuality. In another sense, psychoanalysis has been seduced by feminism (the daughter) and is forced to confront its own delusions of mastery. Yet ultimately, Gallop hopes, these seductions will move both "out of the familial roles of father and daughter so that they will no longer be locked into their vicious circle."[16] What I sense here is a reaching not for yet another "object," but for a new and different "circle." Jardine signals a similar search in her own quest for an understanding of man's discourse as a "subject" which puts "woman" into effect: "Whatever the risks of this project, I hope that . . . it will open new spaces for women to write in."[17]

In this apparent whirlwind of quests and questions, let us see if we can figure out exactly who is reaching for the unreachable whom. Lacan and Derrida have named woman the object of their quest for the "thing" always in process. Jardine and Gallop are naming Lacan and Derrida the object of their quest to move into new spaces. Gallop has called Lacan the "Ladies' Man" and claims that he is "with the women."[18] Jardine has described both Lacan and Derrida as engaged in a discourse which puts woman into effect. Both Gallop and Jardine, we might say, are seeking woman *through* postmodern man's womanly quest. Perhaps this is a form of seduction, but if it is, then the "subject" and the "object" have twisted their roles in such a way that "man" and "woman" can no longer be neatly aligned in a system in which male pursurer (writer) seeks female pursued (written). Instead, man as a speaking subject has become like woman as the object of discourse, while woman as a speaking subject is writing through the discourse of a womanly man in order to find new spaces.

It is toward these spaces that psychoanalysis, deconstruction, and woman lean. And yet at the same time, all three discourses seem to be keeping their space, their distance, from each other. I began this essay by wondering if the subject of "psychoanalysis and deconstruction" might after all be the same as the subject of "woman." If this is so, then I would suggest that it is because all three "subjects" have taken the other as their "object"—not an object to be captured, but a means through which each might "effect," to use Jardine's term, its own process. This would explain the uneasy yet firm connections in contemporary theoretical discourse among writers who are speaking about and through the discourses of psychoanalysis, deconstruction, and "feminism,"[19] discourses which seem desperately in search of connections which they nonetheless find suspect—as if each must maintain some distance lest it be engulfed in some other's territory. It is this very attempt to maintain distance that makes me suspect that each finds in the other its "woman"—what Derrida described as that "feminine operation" from which one must keep some distance. "Distance from," however, soon becomes for

Derrida "distance itself": "Perhaps woman is not some thing which announces itself from a distance, at a distance from some other thing. . . . Perhaps woman, a non-identity, a non-figure, a simulacrum—is distance's very chasm, the out-distancing of distance, the interval's cadence, distance itself, if we could say such a thing, distance *itself*."[20]

With this concept of woman-as-distance, we can locate not only the connections linking psychoanalysis, deconstruction, and woman, but also the ways in which Lacanian psychoanalysis and Derridean deconstruction form their non-identity as woman. Using Barbara Johnson's terminology, I have suggested that their mutual attempts at "one-downmanship" account for their engaging in a discourse that subverts analytical mastery. The object of their quests, seen from this perspective, is to become more like the subject of their quests—like the woman who is herself the distance that always defers the conventional quest for mastery. They become, in other words, woman to each other's man—the very distance between them constituting the space of otherness. Such a notion is especially descriptive of the relations between these two discourses when we keep in mind Ellie Ragland-Sullivan's description of the Lacanian "subject" as that which "undertakes all its quests (sexual, intellectual, or material) in relation to its Otherness to itself."[21] Why would Derrida want to differentiate his own quest for difference from the Lacanian subject's quest which continually defines and redefines itself in relation to otherness to itself? Could it be that Derrida saw in Lacan the very feminine operation that he wanted to claim, and therefore felt it necessary to argue that his own ceaseless deferrals were not simply engaged with otherness, but with the essence of woman herself—woman as distance? In this game of "one-downmanship," is it necessary not only for Derrida to "effect" more of the woman, but to claim woman as *the* deconstructive effect?

In a game where the object is to subvert mastery, everyone wants to be the woman. Yet the space that she occupies seems to differ according to the peculiar womanly processes effected by different writers. For Derrida, she may be "distance itself," a constant process of deferral which Jardine describes as Derrida's " 'feminine operation' that can and does subvert the history of . . . metaphysics . . . —that which disturbs the Subject, Dialectic, and Truth is feminine in its essence."[22] For Lacan, she may be the Lacanian "subject" itself, which Ragland-Sullivan describes as "an unbridgeable gap between a person's perceptions and alienation in relation to an external *Gestalt*, an internal discourse, and Desire"—an "I" that is always an "other."[23] These are spaces that disturb and distance, that constitute gaps preventing the kind of cohesion that might shape the "object" of deconstruction or psychoanalysis into a meaningful text or a unified identity.

But what are these spaces to the women who are describing them in the discourse of these womanly men? What is the expanding and shifting "frame of reference" described by Barbara Johnson, the "new spaces" sought by Alice Jardine, the space "beyond the closed circle of the family" and of seduction that Gallop seeks? I suggested earlier that woman as a speaking subject, that is, as a subject who speaks about psychoanalysis and deconstruction, seems to be speaking through the agency of a womanly man (Lacan, Derrida) to reach her own woman, a woman that she defines in terms of a new and different space. Is she, too, ultimately seeking the feminine spaces sought by these men? Has she already entered into a different space?

The women I have been citing throughout this essay, women who write about and through the discourse of Lacan and/or Derrida, all share a common grounding: they are all associated with the American academic community, and if they are not to be defined as "feminist," we might at least say that they somehow or another have addressed feminist issues. I have in fact chosen them deliberately, when I might profitably have cited other women as well, both because of the particular "frame of reference" they share, and the particular context in which they might be viewed as "speaking subjects." I have also cited them because they have much in common with another group of "speaking subjects": those women writing in France—Cixous, Irigaray, Kristeva, Montrelay—who are themselves part of the French sense of writing in which Lacanian psychoanalysis and Derridean deconstruction figure prominently. In their own search for new spaces where woman can write and become a speaking subject, these French women have moved in more radical directions—often away from a discourse confined by academic structures and into the very dynamic writing of de-centered, un-mastered expression. "I am trying," Irigaray says, "to go back through the masculine imaginary, to interpret the way it has reduced us to silence, to muteness or mimicry, and I am attempting, from that starting-point and at the same time, to (re)discover a possible space for the feminine imaginary."[24] Through the masculine to the feminine—in search of a new space. And what is it that happens when woman speaks in that space? Irigaray would respond: "the issue is not one of elaborating a new theory of which woman would be the *subject* or the *object*, but of jamming the theoretical machinery itself*, of suspending its pretension to the production of a truth and of a meaning that are excessively univocal."[25]

We might well turn to the writing of Irigaray and Cixous to see this dismantling of the subject and object in process. For them, the question of style is very much the question of woman, but not because she beckons from a distance or is the essence of "distance itself." Instead, this woman as speaking subject is writing what it means to have been distanced, alienated, reached for, appropriated. Cixous, for instance, believes that woman has been distanced from man only to ensure the workings of his desire—so that he can reach out and "appropriate" her. She tries to imagine—perhaps placing herself in the space which Irigaray seeks for the feminine imaginary—"a type of exchange in which each would keep the *other* alive and different,"[26] without one (male subject) establishing power over the other (female object). Her way out of dichotomies in which subject appropriates object is to have woman "write her body," that is, to have women write as speaking subjects who strive to break loose from their figuration as objects in male discourse. Woman emerges not as a subject who will overtake the object, but as one who will split the dichotomy, jam the theoretical machinery, and open discourse to a vibrant "bisexuality." What Cixous wants is not a melting or merging of a sexually defined subject and object, but a multiplication of effects "which does not annihilate differences, but cheers them on, pursues them, adds more."[27]

I find the beginnings of this bisexual, multiplicitous space emerging in the very exchanges among psychoanalysis, deconstruction, and woman. In one sense this is because those who generate these discourses are speaking through an "other" sex—Lacan and Derrida putting woman into "effect" in their writing; Johnson, Gallop, Jardine, Ragland-Sullivan putting Lacan and Derrida into "effect" in their writing. But what may be more important is the "effect" of these exchanges, their mapping of what Cixous would call "ways out" of a sexually fixed discourse in which a man-writer-subject desires to appropriate a woman-written-object. In the exchanges between Lacan and Derrida and what Johnson describes as their game of "one-downmanship," an elusive "woman" functioned as the object of exchange: my quest is for the unattainable woman, one would say; my quest is even more unattainable, the other would say; my quest for woman is the essence of that which cannot be attained, and so on. It is precisely at this point—at this crucial historical moment—that woman as speaking subject enters the scene of the quest, and brings into question the dynamics of this exchange. If in the postmodern discourse of Lacan and Derrida, as Jardine says, "woman" has emerged as "a new rhetorical space,"[28] then we might say that psychoanalysis and deconstruction not only had to make space for this "woman" (that elusive object which defines the "effect" of their quests), but also for the "woman" as speaking subject—the woman whose writing seeks "ways out" of those discourses in which woman, and the desire to be woman, is exchanged between men.

It is only when women emerge as speaking subjects that new spaces—bisexual, multiplicitous, expansive—can themselves emerge on the scene of the particular fields of writing that we know as psychoanalysis and deconstruction. And that may be why I find it impossible to write about "Psychoanalysis and Deconstruction" without adding the third term "Woman." It is not that all three terms constitute, after all, the same thing or even the other thing—despite their speaking to each other, despite their attempts to put the other into effect, despite even their desire to break loose from the dichotomy of same and other. Woman has, in a sense, been the hinge connecting psychoanalysis and deconstruction—and if we continue to speak of her as that hinge, then she will continue to occupy a fixed place in the discourse of men.

Perhaps the most important term to consider here is not "Deconstruction," or "Psychoanalysis," or even "Woman"—but the conjunction that links them—"and." Writing about "Literature and Psychoanalysis," Shoshana Felman suggests that we need "to reinvent the 'and' " so that it does not link two terms as subject to object, master to slave, one to other in subordinate fashion. Instead, we need to "disrupt altogether" this kind of hierarchical conjunctive positioning.[29] When we talk about such linked topics as "Psychoanalysis and . . . ," as this book does, we need to keep in mind the reinvention of the "and." But isn't this transformation the effect of woman after all? Isn't woman herself, as she enters the scene of postmodern writing, the disruptive third term? Anne McLeod uses the notion of "unhinging" to describe the effects of woman for feminism itself—the troping of the "antithetical relations between the parts in such a way that the ontological framework within which they have been thought becomes unhinged."[30]

Woman's effect as a speaking subject—as a subject who speaks about these two discourses, and as a subject who puts their own feminine operation into effect—is not her ability to act as a hinge holding psychoanalysis and deconstruction together, but instead to unhinge them, to "effect" the process of the woman in them. The door is dislodged from the frame, the very "frame of reference" itself cannot hold even in the game of "one-downmanship," and something that was inside finds a way out. We add a third term—"Psychoanalysis and Deconstruction and Woman"—because there has always been a third element inside any coupled discourse. Jessica Benjamin, herself a practicing psychoanalyst, describes women's experience in subject-object dynamics as "intersubjective." Woman's desire, she explains, is neither to be totally autonomous—as with the controlling subject of discourse, nor totally connected—as the controlled object in discourse: "It seems to me that what is experientially female is the association of desire with a space. . . . This space is in turn connected to the space between self and other. . . . This relationship can be grasped in terms of intersubjective reality, where subject meets subject."[31] In saying this, Benjamin has reinvented the "and." The space between self *and* other is that third space, the effect of what is "experientially female." To enter this space is to unhinge dualities—one and other, writer and written, subject and object.

The dynamics of comparison, of relationship, change and interchange. There is not a subject continually reaching for an object, not the one eternally in quest of the other. Instead, women write the unhinging of this dangerous pivot. Subject meets subject not at a closed door, but at the frame where the door opens. Women enter discourse. They are not the objects in it, but the subjects who transform it. Felman's remarks are entitled "To Open the Question," and that is exactly what happens when women pose questions about such matters as deconstruction and psychoanalysis. They create intersubjective space. They reinvent the "and."

Psychoanalysis and Literary Criticism

11

The Bostonians and the
Figure of the Speaking Woman
Claire Kahane

In "Medusa's Head: Male Hysteria under Political Pressure," [*Representations*, 4, (1983), 27-53] Neil Hertz discusses what he calls "a recurrent turn of mind: the representation of what would seem to be a political threat as if it were a sexual threat." Hertz introduces his discussion with reference to a dramatic scene of Freud's in which Freud simulates the terror of the little boy discovering his mother has no penis, and then adds, "In later life grown men may experience a similar panic, perhaps when the cry goes up that throne and altar are in danger" (27). *The Bostonians*, a novel about nineteenth-century feminism, is James's representation of that panic. Like his conservative hero, James evinces an intense repugnance toward, and apprehension of the social changes demanded by those feminists who were shaking up the institutions of male privilege that formed James's world. At the same time, identifying with certain feminine characteristics, and with the function, as he represented it, of the feminine conservatorship of cultural values, James was sufficiently ambivalent about the future as envisioned by the feminists to create a fiction which has all the features of that other nineteenth-century phenomenon of ambivalence, hysteria.

Hysteria reached epidemic proportion in the second half of the nineteenth century, and James knew of its effects firsthand, for not only Alice James suffered from it, but hysterical symptoms surfaced in Henry and William as

---

Parts of this reading appear in condensed form in "Hysteria, Feminism and the Case of *The Bostonians*," published in *Feminism and Psychoanalysis*, ed. Richard Feldstein, Judith Roof (Ithaca: Cornell U.P., forthcoming).

well.[1] And hysteria was very much linked both to the rise of the feminist movement and its consequent disturbance of categories of gender, and to changes in representational forms that such disturbance generated. Indeed, hysteria, Freud theorized, was a malady through representation; repressed fantasies which were unacceptable to consciousness, fantasies thus of a desire as well as its repudiation, were written across the body as symptoms rather than articulated in language. Affecting more women than men, these symptoms typically involved loss of voice and local paralysis. Ultimately, as Freud concluded, hysterical symptoms expressed a conflict involving sexual difference. As that conflict has been reinterpreted recently, hysteria represents an apprehension over the feminine position—the position of castration and submission—in heterosexuality.[2]

If in hysteria the body spoke what the voice could not, conversely, the nineteenth-century women's movement was engaged in giving women voice, not only metaphorically through suffrage but literally in the pervasive speechifying by women on platforms around the world. In America especially, women orators were increasingly common in the decades following the Civil War. Having learned to speak effectively in the cause of abolition, the "herd of vociferating women" as James's protoganist calls the feminists in *The Bostonians*, transferred their newly developed oratorical skills to the cause of women's rights. By the turn of the century, their voices were heard on the Continent as well.

The tradition of oratory, classically a male tradition, had been revived on the nineteenth-century American political scene, in great part through the expansive rhetoric of Jacksonian discourse—optimistic, hyperbolic, and incredibly egoistic in its taking of the measure of the world by the self. But the appropriation of that ego by a woman, speaking with a female voice of political rights and equality, of suppression by a male establishment, was experienced as a particularly radical gesture, and not only by James. In the histories of the feminist movement, the item always mentioned first to illustrate its revolutionary impact is the appearance of the woman speaker before a mixed audience.[3] Certainly the woman orator appropriated a male province— the voice of the father as law. Exhibiting her body and speaking with the voice of authority, the figure of the woman on the platform seems to have been a particularly horrifying one to male consciousness, judging from the heap of ridicule she elicited. If language is predicated upon maternal absence, the woman with a voice represented the power of the maternal body as a figure of presence as well as the power of the father's language. In this fantasmatic sense an avatar of the Medusa and a threat to male privilege, the speaking woman provoked in the male listener fears of his own passivity, and more often than not he responded by stiffening his neck against her insinuations.

The figure of the speaking woman haunts *The Bostonians*, both fascinating and repelling James, and arousing his own hysterical responses. Indeed, with its shifting identifications, its digressions and contradictions, James's text manifests in symptoms an anxiety about gender that it cannot speak directly. Ostensibly, *The Bostonians* is about the struggle between Olive Chancellor, a New England feminist silenced by an hysterical inability to speak in public, and her Southern cousin, the conservative masculinist Basil Ransom, for the love and possession of Verena Tarrant, a young ingenue gifted with inspired speech. Verena assumes no agency for her speech; rather, she is a vessel, a medium inspired by her father's laying on of hands to speak a text that passes through her from elsewhere, in a voice that captivates her audience. Thus James constitutes her at her entrance as an object rather than a subject of speaking, though in whose service has not yet been determined. Olive would possess Verena and her voice for the public cause of women's rights; Basil desires Verena for his own private pleasure. James represents their conflict as the ultimate civil war, the battle between male and female for authority over the future of difference, represented by Verena, who is as yet uninscribed in the conventional oedipal narrative of culture. Through this quasi-allegorical psychodrama, the novel enacts a hysterical conflict over the meaning of sexual difference in patriarchy, and exhibits in discursive symptoms its own discomfort with both the feminine position of silence and passivity and its antithesis, the fearsome power of a threatening and powerful voice.

James described *The Bostonians* as an episode connected with the "*so called 'woman's movement'* " (italics mine); wanting to write "a very American tale . . . characteristic of our social conditions," he noted that the most salient and peculiar point in social life was "the situation of women, the decline of the sentiment of sex, the agitation on their behalf."[4] Framing "the decline in the sentiment of sex" by feminist agitation and the situation of women, James's language suggests a relation between that decline and the feminist assault on difference. For James, the loss of difference, a consequence of women's "agitation" for equality, seems to threaten sexual desire itself.

The subject of difference—of clearly demarcated boundaries of sex, class, function—pervades the novel; North and South, freedom and slavery, speech and writing, the tongue and the touch, public and private—these oppositions are linked in the novel to the difference between masculine and feminine, a difference recurrently subverted by the narrator, who flirts with its collapse. But at those moments when difference does seem to collapse, the flow of discourse is hysterically disrupted. Listen for a moment to the sound of this oratorical passage in which Basil Ransom reveals his desire to save his own sex, and when asked "To save it from what" replies:

> From the most damnable feminization! I am so far from thinking, as you set
> forth the other night, that there is not enough woman in our general life, that it
> has long been pressed home to me that there is a great deal too much. The whole
> generation is womanized; the masculine tone is passing out of the world; it's a

feminine, a nervous, hysterical, chattering, canting age, an age of hollow phrases
and false delicacy and exaggerated solicitudes and coddled sensibilities, which if
we don't soon look out, will usher in the reign of mediocrity of the feeblest and
flattest and the most pretentious that has ever been. The masculine character,
the ability to dare and endure, to know and yet not fear reality, to look the world
in the face and take it for what it is—a very queer and partly very base mixture—
that is what I want to preserve, or rather as I may say, to recover; and I must
tell you that I don't the least care what becomes of you ladies while I make the
attempt! (318)

Note the exclamation points, the syntax of disruption, of breathless, pause-
less sentences which accumulate their signifiers of anger: like a hysterical
harangue, this utterance is just on the edge of control. While this is arguably
the most hysterical eruption by a character in the narrative, James's narrator tells us that "the poor fellow delivered himself of these narrow notions
with low, soft earnestness . . . that it was articulated in (a) calm, severe
way, in which no allowance was to be made for hyperbole." This disjunction
between the textual effect of Ransom's voice and the narrative commentary
on it points to the narrator's own hysterical sympathy with Ransom. Indeed, although at various points in the novel James's narrator intervenes to
dissociate his opinions from Ransom's, as when he alludes to the brutal impulses underlying Ransom's male code of chivalry and his sadistically toned
relation to women, at times those very interventions indicate the textual
confusion between Ransom and James's narrator. More often than not,
James identifies with Ransom's elitist pronouncements. Indeed, that Ransom's point of view is predominant in the novel itself sets him apart from
the more consistently ridiculed characters. James seems to think Ransom
extremely prepossessing, for only Olive Chancellor actively dislikes Ransom, and that dislike is represented as hysterical, that is, as a consequence
of her fear of men and her desire to possess Verena.

The most blatant coincidence between Ransom and James's narrator is
in their use of ridicule. It is striking that in the Jamesian canon, *The Bostonians* is the only novel that is considered satire. Just as Ransom in the novel is
made to laugh whenever he is confronted with a challenge to his concept of
sexual difference, so the narrator ridicules and satirizes the feminists, primarily by representing female authority as absurd or self-serving. Interestingly, the figure subject to the greatest ridicule is also the figure which elicits
the only other blatantly hysterical rupture in the narrative surface, but this
time spoken by the narrator rather than by Ransom; Miss Birdseye, the pathet-
ically ineffectual feminist who so much resembled Elizabeth Peabody that
William James cautioned his brother about causing embarrassment by his
ridicule of her, seems to antagonize the narrator unduly. James first deni-
grates her by analogizing her with her house:

Number 756 was the common residence of several persons among whom there
prevailed much vagueness of boundary . . . many of them went about with

satchels and reticules, for which they were always looking for places of deposit. What completed the character of this interior was Miss Birdseye's own apartment, in which her guests presently made their way, and where they were joined by various other members of the good lady's circle. Indeed, it completed Miss Birdseye herself, if anything could be said to render that office to this essentially formless old woman, who had no more outline than a bundle of hay. But the bareness of her long, loose, empty parlor (it was shaped exactly like Miss Chancellor's) told that she had never had any needs but moral needs. (27-28)

The house with its vague boundaries, the satchels and reticules which are out of their place, seem excessively irritating to the narrator. Like the description of Miss Birdseye's apartment with its bare, "long, loose, empty parlor . . . shaped exactly like Miss Chancellor's," these objects figure a body disturbing in its formlessness and its bareness. This representation of the world as a body—a rhetorical figure characteristic of hysterical discourse that recurs in the novel—is preceded by a digressive interpolation comparable in its rage only to Basil Ransom's outburst, an interpolation apparently triggered by Miss Birdseye's short skirt and the freedom of action it is supposed to represent. Having remarked on Miss Birdseye's belonging to the Short Skirts League, the narrator suddenly erupts venomously:

This did not prevent her being a confused, entangled, inconsequent, discursive old woman whose charity began at home and ended nowhere, whose credulity kept pace with it, and who knew less about her fellow-creatures, if possible, after fifty years of humanitarian zeal, than on the day she had gone into the field to testify against the iniquity of most arrangements. (26)

Why this surprising narrative intrusion? Aside from her short skirt, or perhaps because of it, Miss Birdseye seems most irksome to the narrator because of her endless generosity which has made her a dupe. No powerful mother she, her vulnerability infuriates James at the same time that he ridicules it. Her optimism, her refusal to acknowledge negativity, sex, death, aggression—and her generalized beneficence tie her to the generation of transcendentalist thinkers of whom James was contemptuous. Indeed, as Neil Schmitz pointed out recently, the fathers of the previous generation—including his own father—held for James no patrimony.[5] Miss Birdseye, whose name is James's snide commentary on her feminist vision, stands as a female representative of that parental generation—both men and women—whose naivete is marked as feminine, an inappropriate innocence which James felt as a threatening and unstable legacy. Described as totally lacking in knowledge of the real by both Olive and Ransom, Miss Birdseye is represented as a living repudiation of the phallic values the novel seems to privilege, albeit ambivalently.

Most problematic in this regard is her "openness": Miss Birdseye opens her house to everyone—gives succor indiscriminately "to negroes and refugees"—and James fumes, as in this shrill and at times incoherent passage that continues at some length:

> She talked continually, in a voice of which the spring seemed broken, like that
> of an over-worked bell-wire; and when Miss Chancellor explained that she had
> brought Mr. Ransom because he was so anxious to meet Mrs. Farrinder, she
> gave the young man a delicate, dirty, democratic little hand, looking at him
> kindly, as she could not help doing, but without the smallest discrimination as
> against others who might not have the good fortune (which involved, possibly,
> an injustice) to be present on such an interesting occasion. (26)

Delicate, dirty, democratic—this little insidious trio of signifiers not only
marks the underside of James's moral sensibility as an anglophilic writer of
privilege, but it shows him a precursor to those xenophobic modernists such
as Eliot and Pound who seemed especially to fear contamination by the im-
migrant hordes. On the psychological level, it marks again the novel's concern with the transgression of boundaries, with a violation that comes from
being open to an external threat. Through such images as her short skirt and
delicate, dirty, democratic hand, James transforms a political threat into a
physical and sexual one in the kind of hysterical slippage that pervades the
novel.

Significantly, it is the feminist Olive Chancellor who introduces Ransom
as the "real" man—although James's discourse contradicts such hard and
fast categories. Speaking of her feminist project, Olive tells Verena: "there
are men who pretend to care for it, but they are not really men. . . . any
man that one would look at . . . with him it is war upon us to the knife"
(130). Basil Ransom is James's "real man"; the narrator designates him as
"the most important personage in my narrative," important because he is
"a representative of his sex" (4), a representative of the masculine. (Appropriately, the Merchant-Ivory film version of *The Bostonians* cast the Super-
man of Christopher Reeve as James's hero!) Thus at the very beginning of
the novel, the narrator presents Basil in flagrantly phallic terms:

> He was very long . . . and even looked a little hard and discouraging, like a col-
> umn of figures . . . a head to be seen above the level of a crowd on some judicial
> bench or political platform . . . his forehead was high and broad, and his thick
> black hair perfectly straight and glossy, and *without any division*, rolled back
> from it in a leonine manner. (4)

And yet, James tells us, after having presented this accumulation of unmis-
takable masculine signifiers, so that Ransom—grim and hard—is an image
of the Law, the One ("without any division," the text asserts), James remarks
that "if we are readers who like a complete image, who read with the senses
as well as with the reason"—and senses and reason are coded as feminine
and masculine—then we are entreated not to forget the feminine components
of this phallic being—that Ransom

> prolonged his consonants and swallowed his vowels, that he was *guilty* of eli-
> sions and interpolations which were equally unexpected, and that his discourse
> was pervaded by something sultry and vast, something almost African in its

rich, basking tone, something that suggested the teeming expanse of the cotton field. (5)

Playing on the same geopsychological dichotomy that Tocqueville introduced and Henry Adams exploits in the *Education*—the South, warm, earthly, sensual, represents the feminine principle, while the North, judicial and cold, is masculine—James paradoxically makes Basil the Southerner into the judicial principle but yet marks him through the voice as sensual and feminine, noting the "curious feminine softness with which Southern gentlemen enunciate." Indeed, James makes Ransom a Southerner so that he can use the drawl—the *voice* of an already violated South—to subvert the grim and hard signifiers of masculinity, and identify the erotic component of privilege. The Law is not separate from Desire; the circle of privilege rests on both.

Just as Basil's feminine qualities are marked by a relation to speech, so is the feminization of all the male characters in the novel. Mrs. Tarrant, Verena's mother, descended from a line of public speakers, is humiliated by her husband's inability to speak, and although he has proved his "eloquence of the hand," her family "had never set much store on manual activity; they believed in the influence of the lips" (70). Matthew Pardon, the unctuous and ambitious journalist, is marked by "sentences imperfectly formed," his speech replete with exclamations such as "Goodness gracious" (116), "mercy on us," and other effete ejaculations. Language for James is the mark of potency, and as James both criticizes the increasing flatulence of language and associates that style with feminization, it seems clear that James is concerned with his own potency as a writer, a concern which might have been exacerbated by the fact that his own style had been characterized as feminine.

It is Olive, the feminist reformer about whose morbid psychology James was most curious, who has the most neurotic relation to speech. Articulate in private but voiceless in public, Olive is obsessed with the unhappiness of women:

> The voice of their silent suffering was always in her ears, the ocean of tears that they had shed from the beginning of time seemed to pour through her own eyes . . . uncounted millions had lived only to be tortured, to be crucified . . . the just revolution . . . must triumph, it must sweep everything before it; it must exact from the other, the brutal, bloodstained, ravening race, the last particle of expiation. (35-36)

In this sadomasochistic double-identification, Olive desires to be both victim and revenger, a martyr-savior in the tradition of Christ. But James makes this desire suspect:

> I want to give myself up to others; I want to know everything that lies beneath and out of sight . . . I want to enter into the lives of women who are lonely, who are piteous. I want to be near to them—to help them. (34)

By his use of a sentimentalizing diction, James undermines the legitimacy of Olive's relation to feminism. His representation of her longing for martyrdom, for an erotic merger with women victims, her flirtation with the romance of suffering, and above all, her inability to give voice to her desire, put her in the position of the hysteric, a position which obviously fascinated James. Thus early in the novel, the narrator, designating Olive's morbidity both as typical and as the key to her character, comments:

> It proved nothing of any importance with regard to Miss Chancellor, to say that she was morbid; any sufficient account of her would lie very much to the rear of that. Why was she morbid, and why was her morbidness typical? Ransom might have exulted if he had gone back far enough to explain that mystery. (11)

In a sense the novel is James's exploration of that mystery, his sufficient account. But why might Ransom have exulted? And how far back would Ransom have to go to explain that mystery? How far back does James go? Does he too exult?

James's image of morbidity is a woman crying, a figure which repeatedly ruptures the surface of the narrative and serves to bind together all three central characters. It appears not only in Olive's obsessive vision of an ocean of women's tears to which she would give voice, but also in "the desire of Ransom's heart" to protect the South, figured as a violated woman, by holding his tongue.

> To be quiet about the Southern land, not to touch her with vulgar hands, to leave her alone with her wounds and her memories, . . . waiting as a man would wait, for the slow process . . . of time, this was the desire of Ransom's heart. (48)

It most strikingly occurs as an image to Verena on her first meeting with Olive: "she looked as if she had been crying (Verena recognized that look quickly, she had seen it so much)" (73). What does this parenthesis signify? Where has she seen it so much? While the text tells us nothing directly, it leads us to speculate that this parenthesis refers to her mother, the primary woman in her life (who remains in parenthesis through the course of the novel) by insinuating that Mrs. Tarrant has had to accommodate to her husband's adulterous affairs.

Unlike the conventional patriarch, Selah Tarrant has broken the rules upon which traditional patriarchal privilege is maintained. James associates Selah with the Oneida community of free love, "a community of long-haired men and short-haired women" who have confused the forms of gender and have broken the laws of marriage and the family on which they depend, by giving the Father free access to all the women, by therefore symbolically instituting incest. Just as the boundaries of the upper class are threatened by this interloper, so James writes him as sexually suspect for his violation of the social rituals which preserve boundaries. Indeed, the rhetoric surrounding Selah is often outrageously eroticized to make that point. Dr. Prance, remarking that if Selah "were a little more dry, it might be better for him" doesn't "want him to be laying his hands on any of her folk; it was all done with the hands, what wasn't done with the tongue" (42). And even the syncophantic Matthew Pardon, who has Selah's permission to "handle" his daughter, wants Verena "to 'shed' her father altogether; she didn't want him pawing round her that way before she began." In this context, if Mrs. Tarrant is the crying woman of Verena's experience, her tears are textually related to this Father's transgression, in his yielding of paternal authority and its law. Unfortunately, as the novel shows, the laws of marriage and family serve the woman no better; there is a crying woman in Verena's future as well; for it is this prophetic image of a woman crying with which the novel ends, we recall, as Verena in tears is abducted by Ransom, at which point the narrator draws the curtain on them with the concluding sentence: "It is to be feared that with the union, so far from brilliant into which she was about to enter, these were not the last she was destined to shed."

These tears that are her future derive from Ransom's appropriation of her as wife, of her assumption of the secular vows of silence and submission to lawful phallic authority. Earlier, when Verena seductively speaks her vision of an enlightened society different from the "brute force" which she claims exists now, Basil obliterates her words as signifiers, hearing only the music of her voice, the erotics of the voice, the voice of the nightingale. Thinking that "she speechifies as a bird sings" (216), "I don't listen to your ideas," he tells her, "I listen to your voice." If like Philomela by the end of the novel she has been abducted and silenced, is there not also a verbal pun implicit in her "abduction"? Indeed, I would suggest that the figure of morbidity which James is exploring, the crying woman, derives from an imagined scene of feminine violation which crops up repeatedly in the imagery of the novel, a primal scene in which the narrator ambivalently identifies with the feminine figure—a hysterical identification shared by the protagonists and experienced as a silencing and a rape.

Once one begins to listen to the speaking body of the text, one hears the figure of rape repeatedly: listen to James's description of Tarrant's relation to the newspaper offices and vestibules of hotels, the centers of worldly power:

> He . . . had a general sense that such places were national nerve-centres, and that the more one looked in, the more one was 'on the spot'. The *penetralia* of the daily press, were however, still more fascinating, and the fact that they were less accessible, that here he found barriers in his path, only added to the zest of forcing an entrance. . . . He was always trying to find out what was "going in"; he would have liked to go in himself, bodily, and failing in this, he hoped to get advertisements inserted gratis. . . . He expected his revenge for this the day after Verena should have burth forth; he saw the attitude in which he should receive the emissaries who would come after his daughter. (99)

Without the power of the voice that his daughter has, Selah has no claim to the authority of the word that Ransom is given at the end.

Yet even Ransom—the real man—is shown as potentially subject to hysterical loss and violation, most revealingly in his response to Selah's handling of Verena: Ransom resents "Tarrant's grotesque manipulations . . . as much as if he himself had felt their touch, and which seemed a dishonor to the passive maiden. . . . They made him nervous, they made him angry" (57). Here Ransom's identification with Verena as the object of manipulation implicates him as well in the threatening feminine position to which the South has been subject. In this momentary unveiling of Ransom's own hysterical potential, the text flirts with the prohibited pleasure as well as the fear of the feminine position, being handled, being manipulated, losing subjecthood. But this gap is quickly covered over. As if Nature herself demands only the oedipal plot, requires the ransom of heterosexuality to maintain human culture, the narrative moves inexorably to take Verena from the woman and give her to the man by reversing in a series of confrontations the place and proprietorship of the speaking voice.

Indeed, Nature enters the plot as Ransom's agent, as in this scene when Olive wanders around Washington Square comtemplating Verena's future:

> The trees and grass-plats had begun to bud and sprout, the fountains plashed in the sunshine, the children of the quarter, both the dingier types from the south side, who played games that required much chalking of the paved walks, and much sprawling and crouching there, under the feet of passers, and the little curled and feathered people who drove their hoops under the eyes of French nursemaids—all the infant population filled the vernal air with small sounds which had a crude, tender quality, like the leaves and the thin herbage. (300)

This representation of the sounds of the air—crude, tender—made by the infant population is meant to signify the voice of Nature, a Nature which like the Law requires Verena's complicity in her abduction. And it is meant to be a sharp contrast to the topography of the southern cape, the feminist enclave to which Olive takes Verena in an effort to elude Ransom:

> The ripeness of summer lay upon the land, and yet there was nothing in the country Basil Ransom traversed that seemed susceptible of maturity; nothing but the apples in the little tough, dense orchards, which gave a suggestion of sour fruition here and there, and the tall, bright goldenrod at the bottom of the bare stone dykes. (329)

In the midst of this highly allusive suggestion of "sour fruition" and "bare stone dykes" at Marmion, Ransom, authorized to be legitimate hero by having had a piece of *writing* accepted for publication—writing that signifies the masculine form of representation—confronts Verena and proposes their marriage and her silence. Although he tells her, "It's not to make you suffer . . . I don't want to say anything that will hurt you," as she entreats him "to spare her"—to allow her to continue speaking for women,

> a quick sense of elation and success began to throb in his heart, for it told him . . . that she was afraid of him, that she had ceased to trust herself, that the way

he had read her nature was the right way (she was tremendously open to attack, she was meant for love, she was meant for him). (349)

Ransom's words of attack and suffering, of martyrdom and vocation, echo Olive's earlier prophetic warnings, but turn out to be more potent:

> The words he had spoken to her . . . about her genuine vocation, as distinguished from the hollow and factitious ideal with which her family and her association with Olive Chancellor had saddled her—these words the most effective and penetrating he had uttered, had sunk into her soul and worked and fermented there. . . . the truth had changed sides; the radiant image began to look at her from Basil Ransom's expressive eyes: it was always passion, but now the object was other. (365)

From this point to the climax of the novel, Ransom's actual abduction of Verena, Ransom's words are supported by the narrator's blatant but often confused manipulations of plot. In a sequence which becomes increasingly incoherent, the narrator redefines her relation to Olive and feminism as "a desire to please others" and her relation to Ransom as "a push to please herself." But this masculine constitution of feminine desire is precisely what James shows Verena's fate is NOT to be. Rather, he shows Verena increasingly becoming Ransom's possession, and both she and Olive experience, in the words of the text "a kind of shame" at her capitulation.

At the novel's end, the hysterical scenario that has haunted the novel, the primal scene from the distant past that has caused the unhappiness of women, erupts in a climax surreal in its representation of contradictions and fluid interchanges. The howling and thumping of the mob waiting in the auditorium to hear Verena (but in the novel's wings)—that fearsome mob anxiously reproduced in countless fictional scenes of revolution—sound as a counterpoint to the offstage scene, "behind the scenes of the world" which is at the novel's center stage. Verena wants to soothe the mob with her voice, but she has lost it, and her power. As Verena shrieks for Olive, Ransom wrenches her away "by muscular force"—that brute force against which she had earlier spoken, and although she says afterward "Ah, I am glad," James totally undermines the prospective happy marriage of conventional domestic narratives and confirms Olive's morbid vision of the inevitable unhappiness of women in his unsettling last line, a line worth repeating: "It is to be feared that with the union, so far from brilliant into which she was about to enter, these were not the last she was destined to shed."

Inevitable unhappiness within the structure of male privilege, that is to say. For the ambiguous position of Olive at the climax of the novel—out of sight but within voice range—suggests an alternative ending, or at least an open one, through which James's own political ambivalence could be given play. James likens Olive to "a feminine firebrand of Paris revolutions, erect on a barricade, or even the sacrificial figure of Hypatia, whirled through the furious mob of Alexandria . . . offering herself to be trampled to death and torn to pieces'' (425). But although Olive goes on stage to be hooted and insulted, ''seeing fierce expiation in exposure to the mob,'' a repetition of her ''morbid'' desire for martyrdom, interestingly, James denies her that destiny, for the crowd falls silent. We are left wondering if she will be able to speak, if she can voice herself and the women whose silence she represents into the circle of privilege. That question is not mute.

12
Faulkner's Dispossession of Personae Non Gratae
Richard Feldstein

In an article on feminist discourse in *Yale French Studies*, Alice Jardine discusses the dialogical subject and stream-of-consciousness fiction. While examining Kristeva's semiological theories in relation to Virginia Woolf's experimental novels, Jardine claims that "fiction of the interior voice" is "the last rationalization of a culture hooked on transcendence" (230). Alternately known as stream-of-consciousness fiction, interior monologue was used innovatively by such novelists as Joyce, Faulkner, and Woolf as a means of depicting the decentered subject of modernity, whose discourse reveals aesthetic representations of Freudian shifts, ellipses, breaks, of unconscious displacements and condensations. Their experimentation with stream-of-consciousness fiction that they used to illustrate examples of classical psychoanalytic theory may appear outdated today, especially if we consider current developments in post-structuralist, psychoanalytic, and feminist criticism or recent narrative representations of liminal consciousness by post-modern writers like Donald Barthelme or Kathy Acker. But in the 1920s and 1930s, when Faulkner wrote *The Sound and the Fury* and *As I Lay Dying*, he borrowed freely from Freudian theory a description of the fragmentary, dissociated condition of modern consciousness which the novelist saw against a presupposed "anterior unity" (and this is Jardine's critique of modernism) rather than in relation to a "multiplicity of the subject in process/in question [which] presupposes continuing polyvalence" (230).

It should not go unnoticed that the term "interior monologue" reinstitutes the classical dichotomy that divides the subject conceived intrapsychically from the world which is separate yet exerts influence on it. In an essay on binary representation, the third term, and feminism, Jacqueline Rose analyzes whether psychoanalysis has been complicitous in ignoring the issue of sexual violence by relegating it to the theory of the death drive, which has been discredited for attributing a species-related, intrapsychic causality to aggression. Rose argues convincingly that while psychoanalysis frequently gives an imperial wink and nod to issues of sexual violence, Freud himself worked with concepts that confound dualities like inside and outside "that follow any rigid externalisation of political space" and whose expression is an indication of the impulse towards mastery (13). Rose maintains that Freud's theory of bisexuality, which makes ambiguous the vacillating line of sexual difference, and his concept of the death drive, which she contends situates us in a sadomasochistic spiral of *indeterminate* origins, together problematize any rigid dichotomy of distinctions or geometric search for scopic surety.

Rose's argument against binary reductionism readily lends itself to the examination of terms like interior monologue which, for reasons now obvious, become suspect. Stream of consciousness, however, is an unequivalent term more appropriately judged in relation to a particular writer's understanding of the unconscious: is radical Otherness conceptualized as one pole in an inside/outside dichotomy or is it a third term resistant to such dualistic juxtapositions? One purpose of this paper is to show that in Faulkner's case there is some validity to Jardine's accusation that modernistic experimentation with fragmentary, part-object representation exists in relation to a totalizing world view that denies the fissure of a radical split upon which its basal assumptions are founded.

Faulkner, who was unable to negotiate the hyphenated uncertainty of multiple subject positions in his psycho-social fiction, divided himself from his world by identifying the unconscious as an intrapsychic construct, a dynamic internal to the subject. His representation of Otherness in stream-of-consciousness fiction attests to this topological distinction, especially in *The Sound and the Fury* where Benjy's patterns of idiot consciousness are so unconventionally idiosyncratic as to remain resistant to the attempt to historicize them. The same can be said of Vardaman and Darl Bundren in *As I Lay Dying*, but with *Absalom, Absalom!* the novelist attempted to bridge the psycho-social divide by displacing the psychoanalytic narratives of *The Sound and the Fury* and *As I Lay Dying* with a social fiction that used stream of consciousness in the service of a mythic causality its characters commented upon. It could prove interesting to examine what effect this transposition of psychoanalysis and myth had in relation to Faulkner's depiction of characters in a master-slave dialectic to which he sometimes subjected them. It is this juxtaposition of negating authorial desire and sacrificial characters that forms a focus for analysis.

Anthropopathic Characters in
The Sound and the Fury and *As I Lay Dying*

An examination of the metacommentary at the conclusion of *Flags in the Dust* shows that Faulkner recognized the need to reformulate the fictional style adopted during his apprentice years: "And if they were just glamorous enough, there would be a Sartoris in them, and then they were sure to be disastrous. Pawns. But the Player and the game He plays—who knows? He must have a name for his pawns, though, but perhaps Sartoris is the name of the game itself—a game outmoded and played with pawns shaped too late and to an old dead pattern, and of which the Player Himself is a little wearied" (369-70). Having admittedly wearied of the "old dead [narrative] pattern" and pseudo-objective stance adopted in *Soldier's Pay, Mosquitoes,* and *Flags in the Dust,* Faulkner delimited his authorial privilege while creating characters whose illusion of autonomy was belied by their symbolic function in a narrative signifying chain. To stop treating characters as "pawns"— instruments in a repetitive "game" which restitched the same "old dead pattern" used by the practitioners of American realism—Faulkner declared his distrust for the linear narrative and the omniscient narrator whose point of overview proved restrictive. This repudiation constituted a step in a sequence of narrative experiments that challenged the notion of figure and ground, an authorial two-step that traversed the improbable interface between the apprentice novel *Flags in the Dust* and *The Sound and the Fury.*

In the latter novel Faulkner displaced the realist plot with a form of psycho-narration, a variant of stream-of-consciousness fiction. Implicit in his newly adopted style was a critique of the mechanized narratives once implemented to subordinate characters to functionaries of previously learned paradigms. In his experimental novels Faulkner conflated himself with fictional personae who aired viewpoints that encouraged a "dialogic," multi-voiced discourse that "from behind its words, forms, styles, nationally characteristic and socially typical faces begin to emerge, the images of speaking human beings" (Bakhtin, 370). This type of discourse enabled the characters of *The Sound and the Fury* and *As I Lay Dying* to speak with voices that appeared to be distinct unto themselves, though Vardaman of course could not have verbalized such complex prose constructions as those attributed to him. Still, characters of this period seem unique, speak with voices that are easily distinguishable from one another, thereby presenting the illusion of individuality. To accomplish this canonical revision, Faulkner hypostatized characters with which he conflated himself, and taking them literally, confused the symbolic with the real while objectifying anthropopathic characters. Unlike the automatized literary constructions of his apprentice period, these characters became variegated others which Faulkner subjected to democratic principles; in this way he turned a rigid, programmatic fiction into one geared to provoke more immediate, less formulated responses. In his experimentation with psycho-fiction, however, Faulkner's tendency to take fictive characters literally resulted in a truth-seemingness which gave the appearance of characters standing outside the signifying system that produced them.

When Faulkner wrote *The Sound and the Fury* and *As I Lay Dying*, he devised a polyphonic psycho-fiction that blurred details by isolating fragments that remained disconnected from a readily perceptible gestalt. By radically restructuring his novels to deprioritize the omniscient interpreter who *spelled out* his version of experience, Faulkner attempted to reformulate his patriarchal relation to those like the Compsons and Bundrens. To transform cut-out characters into psychological subjects that appeared to voice their own concerns, he evolved a self-image which could withstand its own fragmentation or loss of unitary status; by losing sight of himself as himself, Faulkner better identified with others whose traits he appropriated, then imaginatively reassembled into recognizable characters that exhibited a variety of personality types.

Faulkner's literalized characters were so animated that they seemed responsible for acts they appeared to author. This strategy proved necessary because many of Faulkner's characters were societal outcasts who enacted incestuous, homoerotic, adulterous, miscegenetic, and irreligious desires. For instance, it is well documented that Benjy, Quentin, Darl, and Jewel (just to name a few) grapple with incestuous impulses in Faulkner's fiction. Quentin, Popeye, Charles Bon, and Henry Sutpen wrestle with homoerotic desires that were more problematical for the novelist. Addie Bundren and Reverend Whitfield commit adultery, as do Uncle Maury and Mrs. Patterson, while Caspey, Christmas, and Bon have miscegenetic affairs frowned upon by the majority of citizens in Yoknapatawpha County. To compound matters, sitting in judgment over such perceived "transgressions" are evangelical frauds like Shegog, Whitfield, and Hightower, who represent the fifth in a pentagonal series of forbidden desires presented textually during this period of Faulkner's work.

In an evident display of ambivalence toward a restrictive moral system and an old style historical-biographic aestheticism, Faulkner introduced stream-of-consciousness narratives and sexually coded personalities that he felt the necessity to restrain through acts of authorial intervention. So that characters would not be merely the products of a pornographic fiction, Faulkner allowed them freedom of expression only to curb their actions through the novel's narrative construction. Although refractory "dissidents" invariably veered from well-ordered behavioral pathways, their course was curbed by a sumptuary narrative that recircumscribed societal boundaries while reasserting Faulkner's conception of ethical normalcy. For example, Benjy and Darl are sent to Jackson asylum, Quentin to a watery grave, Christmas to Hightower's house before Grimm shoots and castrates him, and Bon to Sutpen's house before his brother shoots him "dead as a beef" (*Absalom, Absalom!*, 133). Anthropopathic characters grown too believable, slaves who would be masters, event-triggered repercussions, perhaps this is why Faulkner found it necessary to dispossess personae non gratae?

Doubling and The Reconstructive Narrator

Although Faulkner traded the psycho-fictive experiments of *The Sound and the Fury* and *As I Lay Dying* for a stamped-in network of narrative norms in *Sanctuary*, he continued to explore a sexology of characterological desire. While incest, homoeroticism, and adultery provided a focus for his two previous novels, *Sanctuary* features a sexual triangle in which Popeye, Temple, and Red form a *ménage à trois dangereux*. Theirs is a precedent for two other love triangles developed in succeeding novels: Henry, Judith, and Bon in *Absalom, Absalom!* and Shumann, Laverne, and Holmes in *Pylon*. Considering this proliferation of characterological desire and Faulkner's "yes, I know characters are not real but . . ." approach to the literary text, it becomes conceivable why he subsequently distanced himself from personae non gratae while exercising restitutive control over his presentation of events (Jardine, 224). By the time Faulkner penned *Sanctuary*, he felt so compromised by an all-directional expansionism that he implemented a further check on desire by anchoring the narrative in the very linear ground he had previously renounced.

Faulkner also grounded his fiction by providing a series of digressive narrative reconstructions, which, through obsessive analytical rehashing, perpetuated the illusion that he could neutralize anxiety generated by an initial narrative impetus of significant import. As in Camus's *L'Etranger*, there are a series of reconstructions of a primary narrative sequence in *Sanctuary*: Ruby Lamar recounts the details of Popeye's brutal abduction of Temple, as does the victim herself when questioned later in the novel. As in the second half of *L'Etranger*, there is a trial in which analytic reconsideration, in an absurd burlesque of justice, passes itself off as fact. This pattern of presenting an initial narrative construction doubled by various reconstructions serves as a precedent for the recapitulatory micro-narratives that form a network of lexical operations in *Light in August, Absalom, Absalom!,* and *Pylon*. Whereas *The Sound and the Fury* and *As I Lay Dying* celebrate the gap or impasse that impedes an expression of the unconscious, *Sanctuary* envisions a very different scenario for Faulkner, who once again writes a logocentric fiction that reflexively scrutinizes itself as a preemptive tactic to restrain disquieting desire.

In the novels that immediately follow *As I Lay Dying* Faulkner not only reinstated the "old [narrative] pattern" rejected at the end of *Flags in the Dust*, he also inserted himself in the text as the omniscient commentator who helped to shape and to control the interpretative process. Faulkner added this "legitimizing" overview because his novels introduced characters that in their conception were originally dissociated self-aspects. Originating from splits and schisms, dislocations and discontinuities, Faulkner patterned projected self-aspects into characterological doubles, one group of which often acted before thinking through the effects of their actions—Popeye, Joe Christmas, Thomas Sutpen, and Roger Shumann—who are studied and restudied by another group of characters who have difficulty acting on their own impetus—Horace Benbow, Gail Hightower, Miss Rosa, Mr. Compson, Quentin, Shreve, and the reporter in *Pylon*. Through this pairing of binary opposites, Faulkner sanctioned one set of doubles to act out obsessional desires that clambered for expression even as he attempted to attain analytical control over them. In each case, logos codifies desire as one set of personae, awakening from a protracted unconsciousness, mimic Faulkner's own mistaken hypostatization of characters by (mis)recognizing themselves in their narrative counterparts. Thus, such investigative intellectuals as Horace, Hightower, and the reporter of *Pylon* refind themselves in the image of their doubles in a narrative instituted for the analysis of the doppelgänger.

To understand the process of doubling in Faulkner's fiction, one need only look as far as Horace Benbow in *Sanctuary* who identifies with Popeye at the very moment that Horace confronts a perverse attraction to Temple Drake, whom the impotent Popeye raped with a corn cob, then kidnapped, and finally recruited for the *ménage à trois* between Red, Temple, and himself. After listening to Temple's story, Horace leaves Miss Reba's brothel before experiencing a delayed paroxysm of lust for the teenager that compromises his conscience. Only then do a series of displacements occur. On the way home from the whorehouse he drinks a cup of coffee that "lay in a hot ball in his stomach" for three hours; the "unassimilated" coffee is a symbolic correlate for the sexual thoughts that compromise psychic defenses previously erected to exclude them (214). During this dissociative period, sexual associations appear to consciousness along with guilty recriminations that accuse him of participating in a pattern of "Evil" that is like death itself to one who knows it. That is why "he thought of her [Temple], Popeye, the woman, the child, Goodwin, all put into a single chamber, bare, lethal, immediate and profound . . . and I, too" (214). Here Horace contemplates catastrophe-prone characters whom he considers evil but are, from another perspective, just projections of his sexual dilemma that personify interpersonally an intrapsychic conflict which Horace works through while simultaneously denying himself as the object of contemplation. Thus, he is left amputating *personified evil* to help the *world* rather than acknowledging his complicity in banishing *tabooed associations* from *consciousness*.

Because Temple's disarming sexuality leaves Horace feeling middle-aged, he develops the image of the world "approaching that moment when it must decide to turn on or to remain forever still: a motionless ball of cooling space" (215). This fiction provides Horace with the words to represent the desire of a disheveled, forty-three-year-old man seduced by adolescent girls like Temple. Once he returns home from the brothel and looks at his stepdaughter's photograph, however, Horace cannot disguise his desire. After he gazes at Little Belle's image, an unforeseeable synthesis occurs as the two displacements—the tension in his stomach and the mental projection of consciousness-as-world—cannot contain associations that converge to produce an uncanny yet computable effect: eroticized Horace focuses on Little Belle's picture until her face appears "to breathe" and "swoon in a voluptuous languor . . . [with] the voluptuous promise and secret affirmation like a scent iself" (216).

This conflation of inanimate and animate images marks the moment when the displacements give way to a convergence that precipitates a revelation for Horace, who finds that the picture of Little Belle, like that of Dorian Gray, comes alive as he recognizes his desire for Temple through the intermediary Popeye—the double he mistakes as an objectification of himself.

Like Popeye and Horace who first meet by a mirroring pool of water, Faulkner also projects an objectified image onto characters whom he confuses with himself. But the "self" he discovers is an example of the *méconnaissance* born of Lacan's mirror stage. In Lacan's theory of primary identification, the child looks into the mirror, sees an inverted image of the specular ego, and recognizes "self" in other in a psychogenetic moment of dialectical, not linear, perception. While looking in the mirror, the child experiences a pre/semiological moment when s/he colors the mirror image in the biased light of projected unity. Later, in subsequent secondary identifications, this fictional moment of constitution serves to ward off and to compensate for feelings of "self" dispersal.

With *Sanctuary*, then, Faulkner reversed priorities because at this stage in his career he sought to unify and simplify, a process that Barbara Johnson cautions will invariably present "fantasies of domination, not understanding" (170). With *Sanctuary* Faulkner attempted to unify a splintered subject masked by innumerable personae created when he wrote *The Sound and the Fury* and *As I Lay Dying* and successfully lost sight of himself as himself. Then he had animated characters who in varying degrees shared attributes with him, but later in his career Faulkner presented a visual captation of the subject in which a series of images were circumscribed for self-recognition. As Lacan put it, "just as the captation of the subject by the situation gives us the most general formula for madness, not only the madness that lies behind the walls of the asylums, but also the madness that deafens the world with its sound and fury" (*Ecrits*, 7). It is this assumption of images and restitution of alienated subjects that informs Faulkner's fiction in this next stage in his career.

The Dispossession of Personae Non Gratae

Even before *Sanctuary*, when Faulkner's characters appeared to advocate their own viewpoints, he found this paradoxical situation presented itself: with each successive novel, characters displayed societally unacceptable impulses that appeared and reappeared until the symbolic field seemed unable to contain them, so persistent was their need for expression. Although Faulkner initially rejected the linear narrative by favoring marginal aspects of a psycho-fictive gestalt, he later made canonical revisions by reinstating the structural apparatus he had declared to be outdated at the end of *Flags in the Dust*. It seems likely that because his characters' desires became predictably illicit, Faulkner wrote a compensatory fiction with *Sanctuary, Light in*

August, and *Pylon*, novels that have linear narratives and omniscient third-person narrators.

It is likely that after *As I Lay Dying* ambivalent Faulkner decided that instead of conflating himself with characters with whom he identified, he would distance himself from personae who, with each successive novel, enacted a catalogue of incestuous, homoerotic, adulterous, miscegenetic, and irreligious desires. By the time he wrote *Sanctuary*, Faulkner found himself in a trans-individual repetition of characterological desire, a perception that perhaps led to a compensatory wish to ground his fiction in a linear format, which becomes a highly ironic, if not atavistic authorial act, in light of the reintroduction of Horace, Narcissa, and Miss Jenny in *Sanctuary*—all of whom had appeared in *Flags in the Dust*.

With *Sanctuary*, then, one is tempted to conclude that Faulkner had come full circle. But just as primary and secondary narcissism should not be confused, so too should Faulkner's reuse of linearity not be misinterpreted as a literal repetition. Rather, shifting from the circle to the gyre as an analogical model, we can visualize Faulkner's reuse of the linear narrative and *Dramatis Personae* as a parallel cycling that positions him on related but not identical ground. In this way we will not be tempted to confuse *Flags in the Dust*, the apprentice novel eventually condensed into *Sartoris*, with the much acclaimed *Sanctuary*.

After *As I Lay Dying* a new pattern was established as Faulkner separated himself from characters that were previously welcomed as objectifications of desire. Instead of identifying with them and enacting their personalities dramatically, Faulkner adopted a cerebral, latinate prose style that gained ascendancy in direct proportion to the inversion of character development. Aware that his characters habitually subverted traditional moral values, Faulkner compensated for this tendency by creating a counter-impetus with attention to stylistic design. At this stage in his career, when he mediated divergent self-aspects by dichotomizing characters into doubles, the novelist peopled mythical Yoknapatawpha County with a group of recognizable regulars that appeared and reappeared from one novel to the next. Instead of generating new characters, as was his habit in previous novels, Faulkner developed functionaries that inhabited his mythic community, instrumentalities of its intricate design.

There remains one notable exception to this rule, Joe Christmas, the sine qua non of *Light in August* who revived the issue of miscegenation that had been deferred since Caspey's section in *Flags in the Dust*. In the former novel Caspey verbalized the desire to sleep with a white woman but, because he was reduced to a superfluous subaltern, young Bayard became the character that questioned the inequity of racial codes in Yoknapatawpha County. Years later when Faulker wrote *Light in August*, although he employed a patrilineal narrative and third-person narrator, he still successfully depicted Joe Christmas's quandary over his racial identity while imparting to him a dramatic quality previously reserved for characters like Quentin Compson and Darl Bundren.

Yoknapatawpha County and Mythic Self-Replication

But just as *Sanctuary* breaks little new ground by recapitulating the incestuous and homoerotic motifs introduced in the two stream-of-consciousness novels that proceed it, so too does *Absalom, Absalom!* homogenize desire by endlessly scrutinizing the Southern fascination with miscegenation that Faulkner detailed so effectively in *Light in August.* The result is that in *Absalom, Absalom!* ersatz characters are relegated to conceptual centers viewed against a complex network of socio-historical relations. In this novel of summarized styles from previous texts, Faulkner applied the vertiginous prose style of his earlier period to a reflexive social fiction that examines its place in history. In the novel's convoluted linguistic corridors Faulkner cloned characters from a body of information that, already published, now existed independently of him. With this distance from the psycho-genesis of characterization, he conceived a theoretical fiction which intellectualized characters into repositories of information, some of which were capable of distinguishing their own psycho-genesis in the Faulknerian cosmogony.

Quentin is one such character. In an example of self-questioning that lifts him past the impedimenta of personal idiosyncrasy, Quentin discovers that Shreve and Mr. Compson speak with the same voice as he—an uncanny trebling Quentin accounts for mythically when determining that they all share a mirroring consciousness whose reflexive pools visualize the interrelational nature of Faulkner's design:

> Yes. Maybe we are both Father. Maybe nothing ever happens once and is finished. Maybe happen is never once but like ripples maybe on water after the pebble sinks, the ripples moving on, spreading, the pool attached by a narrow umbilical water-cord to the next pool which the first pool feeds, has fed did feed, let this second pool contain a different molecularity of having seen, felt, remembered, reflect in a different tone the infinite unchanging sky . . . Yes, we are both Father. Or maybe Father and I are both Shreve, maybe it took Father and me both to make Shreve or Shreve and me both to make Father or maybe Thomas Sutpen to make all of us. (*Absalom*, 261-62)

Here Quentin speculates on a number of related possibilities: am I Father or Shreve or another character in this metafiction? He intuits that all of them form part of an interdependent network of personae whose "temperature of water" reflects variations of the "infinite unchanging sky." Because Quentin discovers a structural self-sameness he shares with Mr. Compson and Shreve (they relate Sutpen's story with mere tonal differences in their presentations), he accepts their copresence as interrelational extensions in a fiction that levels characterological differences to rhetorical dissimilarities.

To objectify this trans-individual realignment of character, Faulkner fashions Quentin as an assemblage of stored identifications rather than as a character with a determinable degree of autonomy: "his body was an empty hall echoing with sonorous defeated names; he was not a being, an entity, he was a commonwealth, a barracks filled with stubborn back-looking ghosts" (12). A compartmentalized barracks of multi-faced identifications, Quentin has only to don one, like a mask, to experience a particular set of emotions associated with it, which are not completely accepted as his own since many of the identifications were originally partial, split-off from consciousness, haunting it with the specter of Otherness. Such concepts as the trans-generational pool of consciousness and the identificatory commonwealth of personae helped Faulkner to transpose the psychoanalytic, stream-of-consciousness component of his early narrative experiments into the mythic element that informs novels like *Absalom, Absalom!* and *Go Down, Moses.* This transposition is important if we consider that Yoknapatawpha County is replete with recycled characters and part-traits of characters from his previous novels that comprise a mythos of self-reduplication born out of author/ character conflations whose uncanniness led to a compensatory need to distinguish the scriptor from the echolalia that lip-synced obsessional desires.

One way of differentiating the mythic characters of this period from their more lifelike correlates in *The Sound and the Fury* and *As I Lay Dying* is to examine Roland Barthes's *Mythologies.* In this text which reportedly Barthes "deplored the most" (Conley, 4), there is a distinction made between second-order metalanguage concerned with nomination and first-order language which transforms reality rather than "preserv[ing] it as an image" (Barthes, 154, 146), a distinction that Lacan dismisses when stating that "language is language and there is only one sort of language: concrete language . . . there is no metalanguage" ("Inmixing," 188). But Barthes states,

> But if I am not a woodcutter, I can no longer "speak the tree," I can only speak *about* it, *on* it. . . . Compared to the real language of the woodcutter, the language I create is a second-order language, a metalanguage in which I shall henceforth not "act the things" but "act their names," and which is to the primary language what the gesture is to the act. This second-order language is not entirely mythical, but it is the very locus where myth settles; for myth can work only on objects which have already received the mediation of a first language. (Barthes, 146)

Unlike Barthes, Lacan adroitly sidesteps binarisms like first- and second-level language systems which present such idealist conceptions as the "real language of the woodcutter." But Faulkner anticipated Barthes's *méconnaissance* on this issue by structuring characters from 1928 to 1932 with a sophisticated second-order level of linguistic elaboration, although his top priority during this period was to present first-order characters-in-process who visualized recurring memories and fantasies that colored their perception of history's narratives and (after)images. By 1936, however, characters calcified into objects resistant to transformation as the authorial emphasis on "reflexive speech" became more predominant. Considering this transformation, we should not confuse the Quentin Compson who narrates the second section of *The Sound and the Fury* with his namesake in *Absalom, Absalom!* who was conceived in relation to a prototype which proceeded it and is in turn mediated by this second-order character.

We should also refrain from equating these two characters because Quentin in *Absalom, Absalom!* is a self-reflexive spectator who mouths Faulkner's words in a common voice whose vertiginous rhythms sweep over characters and readers alike when transmitting writerly opinion as if it were his own. This hegemonic voice displaces characters whose literary prose conveys "differences not in tone or pitch but of turns of phrases and usage of words" (*Absalom*, 303). In fact, each narrator in *Absalom, Absalom!* takes a type of intellectual sustenance from reconstructing the piecemeal details of the Sutpen myth rather than focusing directly upon his or her own story. Fictional retreads, Horace, Narcissa, Shreve, and Quentin circulate from novel to novel, but other recycled characters remain patchwork reconstructions reassembled from the part-traits of those who proceed them. This is especially true of the doubles who exist for the epiphanic moment of (mis)recognition when they confuse themselves with the images of their counterparts. As we know, in *Sanctuary* Horace acknowledges the depth of his attraction to Little Belle once he learns the sordid details of Popeye's sadomasochistic relationship with Temple Drake; in *Light in August* Hightower accepts responsibility for his wife's death only after Joe Christmas, who murdered his lover, seeks sanctuary at the minister's house; and in *Pylon* the reporter gains awareness of his desire after he identifies with the fliers while recording the dissolution of their unorthodox family unit. This pattern of doubling is expanded in *Absalom, Absalom!* as a proliferation of interpreters recapitulate aspects of their counterparts' lives. Because of such multiple character splittings in the Sutpen saga, the number of reconstructers increases markedly and, as a result, the act of self-reflexive narration itself becomes a focal point of the novel.

With *Absalom, Absalom!* Faulkner circled back upon himself, again using stream-of-consciousness fiction, but now the arc itself, like a halter, became a line of demarcation that signaled an end to the expansive era which had given rise to the tortured grotesques who grappled with the question of identity and difference. In *Light in August* the vertiginous prose of the experimental period appeared in Hightower's final narrative as the wheel spun off its axis, a metaphorical representation of the minister's precarious borderline state. From the first sentence of *Absalom, Absalom!*, however, the vertiginous prose of the experimental period predominates, spinning into irruptive desire for which Faulkner compensated with a controlled, logocentric consciousness of self-reflexivity.

Although *Absalom, Absalom!* reintroduced hand-me-down characters from Faulkner's previous novels, it is highly regarded because of its experimentation with stream-of-consciousness fiction. But without this type of textual production to distinguish it, *Pylon* offers yet another set of doubles and little new in the way of characterization. *Pylon* and *The Unvanquished* signal a deterioration of Faulkner's skills as a novelist, brought about by an inability to create new characters instead of grafting them from literary constructs from previous periods. While *Pylon* offers a mere formulaic repetition of character types, *The Unvanquished* reintroduces the very Sartoris clan that Faulkner labeled as "pawns shaped too late and to an old dead pattern" in a master-slave dialectic he discredited at the end of *Flags in the Dust.*

With this reversal in mind, we can determine that *The Sound and the Fury* and *As I Lay Dying* present the flip side of Faulkner's desire to delimit his. dialogical fiction with one that is theoretical, controlled, and dogmatic in its presentation of other viewpoints. Having become a public figure, Faulkner conservatively posited a mythic unconscious while transposing characters into conceptual centers, some of which ironically recognized themselves and their counterparts as components in a depsychologized mythos of self-replication.

13

A Shattered Globe: Narcissism and Masochism in Virginia Woolf's Life-Writing

Charles Bernheimer

"The shock-receiving capacity is what makes me a writer," Virginia Woolf remarks in "A Sketch of the Past," the extraordinary memoir she wrote in 1939 and 1940, shortly before her death. Her subsequent analysis of the relation between disruptive shock and esthetic reparation reveals one of the profound sources of Woolf's appeal, which is also, I propose to argue, one of the reasons for her frequent critical misreading. The text continues as follows:

> I hazard the explanation that a shock is at once in my case followed by the desire to explain it. I feel that I have had a blow; but it is not, as I thought as a child, simply a blow from an enemy hidden behind the cotton wool of daily life; it is or will become a revelation of some order; it is a token of some real thing behind appearances; and I make it real by putting it into words. It is only by putting it into words that I make it whole; this wholeness means that it has lost its power to hurt me; it gives me, perhaps because by doing so I take away the pain, a great delight to put the severed parts together. Perhaps this is the strongest pleasure known to me. It is the rapture I get when in writing I seem to be discovering what belongs to what; making a scene come right; making a character come together.[1]

Readers of Woolf's novels will recognize in this description the efforts of protagonists such as Mrs. Ramsay, creating from the initially separate, isolated elements of her dinner party "something . . . immune from change" (TTL, 158),[2] Lily Briscoe, struggling to bring the disparate parts of her painting together so as to strike "this eternal passing and flowing . . . into stability" (TTL, 241), Bernard, seeking "among phrases and fragments something unbroken'' (W, 266), Miss La Trobe, working desperately to prevent her audience from "slipping the noose" of illusion and splitting up into "scraps and fragments" (BTA, 122). We tend to identify with these efforts, not only because they fulfill what Freud calls "the main purpose of Eros—that of uniting and binding" (SE, 19:45),[3] but also because they appear to reflect *en abyme* the esthetic goal of each novel, the creation of a harmonious whole, and to mirror the critic's own creative enterprise in demonstrating "what belongs to what." Woolf's writing generates an intense desire to repeat her reparative act and, in putting her severed textual parts together, achieve a pleasurable sublimation of reality's violent blows. Insofar as this reparation can be, and frequently has been, read psychoanalytically as the restoration of a fantasized union with a lost maternal presence, the critic in repeating Woolf's imaginary project may simultaneously fantasize him- or herself in a filial relation to Woolf's textual body. It is as if the revelation of Woolf as mother were the reader's reward for transforming the verbal shocks of her texts, their moments of potentially shattering violence, into a connected pattern of meaning.

The danger for criticism of this response is that it underestimates the value for Woolf's creative activity of the shattering force that makes her drive for unity so compelling. Attracted by Woolf's sublimating project "to make it real by putting it into words," a project easily assimilable to their own, critics have often followed her in suggesting that reality's power to hurt, to physically mutilate, was merely a negative stimulus to her writing's positive unifying function. But this is to ignore both the crucial role that Woolf attributes to shock as an agency of ontological revelation and the persistent attempt in her work to question, if not subvert, the esthetic closure her texts simultaneously strive to achieve. Viewed psychoanalytically, the prevalent tendency in Woolf criticism is to valorize her narcissistic drive to recuperate the self in the (m)other; the thesis I propose to argue here is that her works express an equally powerful masochistic impulse to fracture the self's wholeness and submit to the other's violence.

The first ten pages of "A Sketch of the Past" are particularly rewarding for the kind of analysis I want to perform since there Woolf offers a remarkably condensed account of her constitution as a female subject who writes. This account is, of course, itself an act of textualization, a fact to which Woolf draws attention by putting quotation marks around her object of inquiry, " 'the subject of this memoir' " (80), a subject that she at once creates, re-collects, and displaces in the process of what she calls her "life-writing" (80). A psychoanalytic mode of interpretation, such as I adopt here, assumes that this same subject is analogously revealed and masked in Woolf's fictional writing, and I will be referring to her novels for additional textual material productive of her subjectivity. Although a psychoanalytic method may appear to assume an object of inquiry lying somehow "behind" the text, I want to stress at the outset that my subject, like Woolf's, should be understood as produced on the text's dynamic rhetorical surface. And I would make the claim, furthermore, that this is also where Freud operated in constructing his provisional hypothesis of a pyschological subject.

Woolf's account of her first memory in the second paragraph of "A Sketch" suggests the way narrative generation and subjective creation are intertwined in her writing. She describes her originating scene of memory as not unique but dual. On the one hand, she remembers sitting on her mother's lap in a train or bus, on the other, lying in bed in her nursery at St. Ives. Although the dim light makes her think that the vehicle must actually have been on its way to London, she declares that "it is artistically more convenient to suppose that we were going to St. Ives, for that will lead to my other memory, which also seems to be my first memory" (64). Art here determines the direction life will take as a fiction. Spontaneous recollection offers a split beginning, two unconnected moments. Narrative is generated to link those moments in a temporal structure that seems to reflect the reality of experience but is actually a convenient fiction, a supposition whose plausibility is determined by conventional expectations about narrative form. Woolf thus opens the story of her life by putting the authority of memory on board a train of fiction.

Riding the same train of realistic illusion, psychoanalysis reads the content of Woolf's two first memories in terms of preoedipal object relations. The first memory could be understood psychoanalytically as "leading to" the second in much the way the biological instincts for self-preservation provide the vital basis for the creation of scenarios of satisfaction in fantasy. Woolf remembers being held on her mother's lap and seeing close up "red and purple flowers on a black ground—my mother's dress" (64). The imagery evokes a sense of organic continuity, the maternal body providing the ground for flowers to bloom and the infant herself closely identified with this natural efflorescence. The experience seems to approximate what Freud called primary identification, the original form of an infant's emotional bond with an object, in which the mother's adaptation to her child's needs is so close that the infant has the illusion that the external world will supply whatever it wants.[4]

In Woolf's second first memory, of the nursery at St. Ives, the mother is absent, but her unifying function as an agency of illusion has been transferred onto the child's environment. Thus, the rhythm of the waves breaking, one, two, one, two, to which the child listens, half asleep, half awake, seems to recreate on a cosmic scale the soothing rhythm of maternal breathing. The yellow blind behind which the waves break, heard but unseen, functions much like the screen onto which, according to Bertram Lewin, we project our dreams, and which symbolizes the mother's breast as hallucinated by the infant during the sleep which follows nursing.[5] "The globular . . .

curved shapes, showing the light through, but not giving a clear outline" (66) that Woolf tells us she would make were she to paint her first impressions are like projections onto this fantasy screen. Thus it is not surprising that she should associate her ecstatic experience with feeling "it is almost impossible that I should be here" (65). Her identity is suspended in the indefinite murmur of rhythmic repetition. Consciousness is just adequate to record the sense of its own dissolution. The result is something close to the goal Woolf set for herself in writing *The Waves*, "to saturate every atom" and "give the moment whole," the moment being defined as "a combination of thought; sensation; the voice of the sea" (WD, 136).

Another psychoanalytic analogue to Woolf's enveloping curved shapes is the protective shield against stimuli that Freud describes in *Beyond the Pleasure Principle*. He imagines this inorganic shield as "a special envelope or membrane" formed on the surface of the organism's mental apparatus in defensive response to the ceaseless impact of external excitations. The shield allows only restricted amounts of stimuli to penetrate the underlying organic layers of consciousness, thereby protecting these against "the enormous energies at work in the external world" (SE, 18:27). Such is precisely the role Woolf assigns to the semi-transparent membrane in which she pictures herself englobed. It prevents sounds from being "sharp and distinct" (66). It unifies "robust" sensations by keeping them safely at an equal distance from her receptive center: "the buzz, the croon, the smell, all seemed to press voluptuously against some membrane; not to burst it; but to hum round one . . . a complete rapture of pleasure" (66). In Woolf's life-writing, the maternal dream screen functions as a protective shield that allows her to be simultaneously in the world and out of it, conscious of sensation but immune to its sharp, potentially traumatic impact.

In the final chapter of *The Waves*, Bernard dreams of being able to sum up his life as if it were the kind of globular, semi-transparent picture Woolf evokes in "A Sketch." This is how he introduces his autobiographical narrative:

> The illusion is upon me that something adheres for a moment, has roundness, weight, depth, is completed. This, for the moment, seems to be my life. If it were possible, I would hand it to you entire. I would break it off as one breaks off a bunch of grapes. I would say, "Take it, This is my life."
>
> But unfortunately, what I see (this globe, full of figures) you do not see. You see me, sitting at a table opposite you, a rather heavy, elderly man, grey at the temples. You see me take my napkin and unfold it. You see me pour myself out a glass of wine. And you see behind me the door opening, and people passing. But in order to make you understand, to give you my life, I must tell you a story— and there are so many, and so many—stories of childhood, stories of school, love, marriage, death, and so on; and none of them are true. (W, 238)

This passage demonstrates the quasi-sacramental value of illusion for Woolf, of the illusion, caught whole in the moment, that life can be englobed, its beginning united with its end, self fused with other on the curved space of the dream screen. The figures projected on this screen, however, can be seen only from inside it. Outside the globe of illusion a subject can offer the gift of his or her life only as a narrative sequence, a collection of stories that, like Woolf's own beginning in "A Sketch," link arbitrary scenes of memory in a conventionally realistic temporal order. To the extent that psychoanalytic theory requires the fiction of such an order, it is subject to Woolf's criticism of literary realism, "this appalling narrative business of the realist: getting on from lunch to dinner" (WD, 136). Realism, the art of telling untrue stories "of school, love, marriage, death, and so on," shatters the sacramental globe and disseminates the self in a plurality of partial fictions.

But it is only through this shattering, the Woolfian life-writer now suggests, that the self becomes aware of its identity and of its difference. The agent of this awareness is the mirror, traditional metaphor for mimetic representation, here the emblem of the self's constitution as alienated, fragmented, shameful, and guilty. The mirror generates the self as a plurality of projected and introjected fictions, no one of which can recapture that nearly storyless beginning state in which everything seems to hang together in a globe. The prototype of Woolf's self-story is Biblical: the introduction of specularity into her ideal world of primary identification provokes something like a fall from Eden.

Around age six or seven, Woolf writes, she "got into the habit of looking at [her] face in the glass" (68). This was, apparently, a secretive habit in which the girl indulged only if she were sure of being alone, for "a strong feeling of guilt seemed naturally attached to it" (68). The long paragraph in which Woolf puts forward "some possible reasons" (69) for this being so, aware that there may be others and not supposing that she has gotten at the truth (given what psychoanalysis would call the overdetermination of the incident), is a remarkable exercise in self-analysis as self-construction. Woolf's first hypothesis suggests that she was ashamed to be seen examining her face in the mirror because by thus searching to confirm her femininity she was violating the "tomboy code" she shared with her sister Vanessa. Although Woolf quickly dismisses this reason as too superficial, it does serve to establish what is at stake in this analysis: the structuring of a specifically female self. Up to now gender definition had been fluid, unproblematic, a function of play and of costume. The adults called the girls tomboys; the girls themselves played, scrambled, and climbed, allowing others to give a label to their conduct, which they then accepted as a code. Only in relation to Vanessa could Virginia have felt guilt for violating that code, and she herself realizes that such a transgression of a playful bond between sisters could hardly have caused a lasting narcissistic wound.

A more likely cause, Woolf now suggests, was her parental inheritance and genealogy. The desire these factors worked against derives from Woolf's earliest fantasies of identification: the image she wants to see in the mirror is her own face suffused with resemblance to her maternal lineage. "Femininity," she writes, "was very strong in our family. We were famous for our beauty—my mother's beauty, Stella's beauty, gave me as early as I can remember, pride and pleasure" (68). The plural "our" and "we" evokes an imagined matrilineal filiation (Stella Duckworth was Woolf's half-sister by her mother's first husband). It is as if Woolf wanted the mirror to inherit the function of the dream screen, that is, to saturate her image with a fantasized maternal presence. With her identity thereby constituted as "strongly" feminine, she would be free to take narcissistic pleasure in her own physical beauty.

But it is precisely this freedom that Woolf feels to be lacking when she looks at herself in the mirror. Her text suggests two essential reasons for this profound sense of lack, one relating to her mother, the other to her father. The first evokes the conflictual dynamics crucial to English object relations theory, the second evokes the theories of specular reversal elaborated by Lacan and certain other French analysts.

There is an essential conflict in Woolf's desire to establish her identity on the ideal model of her mother's femininity: she has chosen a model whose identity is not to have one. This is suggested in the early paragraphs of "A Sketch" where the mother is a kind of rhythmical principle sustaining an ecstatic fusion of inside and outside. This exclusively positive evocation is significantly modified when Woolf later interprets the impression Julia Stephen made on her as a girl of seven or eight (approximately her age at the time of the mirror experience): "She [Woolf's mother] must have been a general presence rather than a particular person," hence "it was impossible for her to leave a very private and particular impression upon a child" (83). Woolf cannot imagine herself alone with her mother: "When I think of her spontaneously she is always in a room full of people" (83). Situated at the center of what Bernard calls "a globe, full of figures," she is "generalised, dispersed, omnipresent" (84). She is an ego without boundaries, a presence defined by its lack of definition. "I suspect," Woolf writes, "the word 'central' gets closest to the general feeling I had of living so completely in her atmosphere that one never got far enough away from her to see her as a person" (83). Or far enough to be seen *by* her as a person, an individual *Gestalt*: "she was living on such an extended surface that she had not time, nor strength, to concentrate . . . upon me, or upon anyone" (83).

Albeit indirectly, these comments reveal the frustration of Woolf's drive for individuation and differentiation and help explain why she says she was "obsessed" (80, 81) by her mother for most of her life. The individuating drive necessarily involves aggression against the (m)other. The goal of this destructiveness, as D.W. Winnicott has explained, is to place the object outside the sphere of the subject's fantasized omnipotence, thereby destroying it as a projective entity, a subjective object, and establishing its autonomous reality. The object's survival of the attack creates its quality of externality and helps define the self's independent boundaries.[6] Now, Woolf's description of the primary object of her differentiating impulse, her mother, makes it clear that placing her outside the area of fantasy projection would have been particularly difficult. Invisible as a person yet omnipresent, Julia Stephen allows no spatial separation to intervene between herself and her daughter. No distance is available for Woolf to express the violent energy of her aggressive drive. Her mother's "extended surface" seems invulnerable to attack. Hence Woolf's earliest memories, all of which have her protected underneath that surface, enveloped by it, looking out from inside as if "lying in a grape and seeing through a film of semi-transparent yellow" (65).

In the mirror experience this film becomes opaque, reflective, and a distance is created between the "I" and its specular alter ego. As Lacan has stressed, the mirror stage of the ego's constitution is characterized by aggressive tension. The ego wants to appropriate the image of its bodily wholeness apprehended in the mirror but inevitably fails in this attempt to capture the self in the other.[7] What is peculiar in Woolf's case is that the mirror is *not* entirely opaque. The mother is visible within it as a principle that contests visibility and dissolves identity.[8] She is not a model of completed selfhood, as Lacan's theory of the mirror stage would lead one to expect, but represents "the whole thing," "the panoply of life" (83), "that great Cathedral space" (81). Woolf's ego, in the narcissistic moment of its specular constitution, is lured by an ideal ego,[9] defined by its femininity, that offers not ego-syntonic jubilation but the bliss of selflessness.

According to her account in "A Sketch," Woolf was able to resist this lure only at the cost of guilt and shame. Unable to unleash her aggression against her ideal ego (an inability that extends to the text of "A Sketch" where she never criticizes her mother openly), she turns this aggression around against her self. Indeed it is precisely through this reversal that her ego initially becomes aware of its independent identity, but only as a fragmented, incomplete, unworthy being. The process is vividly illustrated by a passage toward the end of *The Waves* in which Bernard suddenly sees himself as seen by his (imaginary?) interlocutor.

> Oh, but there is your face. I catch your eye. I, who had been thinking myself so vast, a temple, a church, a whole universe, unconfined and capable of being everywhere on the verge of things and here too, am now nothing but what you see—an elderly man, rather heavy, grey above the ears, who (I see myself in the glass) leans one elbow on the table, and holds in his left hand a glass of old brandy. That is the blow you have dealt me. (W, 292)

Catching the other's eye, Bernard is himself caught, trapped, suddenly reduced from an ideal narcissism to the sordid prison of his actual body. The other's glance functions like Bernard's perception of himself in the mirror, as if the other were actually an agency of the self, shattering it with blows that reveal "disorder, sordidity and corruption" (W, 292).

Given that it painfully confirmed her negative self-image, we may well ask why Woolf as a girl made it a habit, as she tells us, of repeating her specular self-aggression. The repetition suggests that she obtained a certain pleasure in punishing herself. This pleasure can be called masochistic in the sense of Freud's conception of masochism as a turning around upon the subject's own ego of an original aggressive drive against the other (see SE, 14:126-27). Whereas that drive initially has no sexual content but aims at achieving differentiation and recognition, through specular reversal it becomes "tinged with eroticism" (SE, 21:120) in a process whereby "sensations of pain, like other unpleasurable sensations, spill over into sexuality and produce a pleasurable condition" (SE, 14:127). In Woolf's case, whatever destructiveness could not be discharged to achieve an individuating distance from the mother is introjected causing a painful split that, in fantasy, fulfills the desire to discharge aggression. The masochistic pleasure of such a fulfillment is sexual insofar as sexual excitement is produced, as Jean Laplanche and, after him, Leo Bersani have argued, by a fantasmatic shattering of the self.[10]

Let me be clear that I am *not* claiming that Woolf was a masochist in the clinical, sexological sense of the term. I am arguing that the life-writer's narrative offers a brilliant interpretation of one of Freud's most radical theses, as formulated by Laplanche, that "masochism has a privileged status in the constitution of human sexuality."[11] I want to suggest furthermore that Woolf's difficulty in establishing a coherent self-representation on the narcissistic model of her ideal ego may have made a masochistic affirmation of this coherence seem particularly attractive. I say affirmation because in masochism the shattering of the self's boundaries may serve to dramatize the existence of those boundaries and restore their fantasized cohesion, if only at the point of death. Moreover, the fact that this inverted self-assertion can occur only by repeatedly submitting the body to imaginary debasement (Woolf's shame and guilt before the mirror) sustains the ideality of the all-good, all-powerful maternal image.[12]

Woolf's story "The New Dress" illustrates the psychological dynamics I have been analyzing and serves as an extended dramatization of Woolf's statement in "A Sketch" that "Everything to do with dress—to be fitted, to come into a room wearing a new dress—still frightens me; at least makes me shy, self-conscious, uncomfortable" (68). The protagonist, Mabel, has had a new dress made in a charming old-fashioned style that she feels reflects her true self. When she first tries it on in the seamstress's workroom, the mirror gives her back her dream"—a beautiful woman . . . the core of herself, the soul of herself" (HH, 50). The seamstress, for whom Mabel feels full of love, maternally mediates a fantasy of narcissistic identification. But as soon as Mabel enters the social arena of Mrs. Dalloway's party, she goes to look at herself in a mirror, and what she sees is what she masochistically imagines others are seeing, a hideous, idiotic, grotesquely old-fashioned dress that confirms her "appalling inadequacy" (HH, 47), "her odious, weak, vacillating character" (HH, 52). Although it is clear to the reader that this crumbling self-image is just as imaginary as the blissful revelation of her core self, Mabel accepts the tortures she endures, the spears she imagines thrown at her by people's glances, as defining who she is in reality. Indeed, the reader has the impression that Mabel habitually examines herself in the mirror upon arriving at a party and *always* condemns herself through the eyes of the imagined others, as "relentlessly, remorselessly" (HH, 47) as does the subject of Woolf's memoir. Thus, the masochistic satisfaction both character and writer derive from their shame and suffering arises not only from the preservation of an ideal core self, invisible to others, but also from a reassurance, experienced as pain and humiliation, that this core is not everything, that one is indeed connected to one's own body, if only in terms of limitation and servitude, and that this bodily self is present and visible to others in the real world.[13]

In contrast, the more precarious characters in Woolf's fiction identify so exclusively with their ideally diffuse self-representations that they find any accommodation with a bounded, finite body-ego next to impossible. Septimus Smith in *Mrs. Dalloway* embraces the narcissistic vision to the point of mental collapse and depends on his wife to build up reality, and his physical place in it, from their recurrent near-dissolution. For another suicidal character, Rhoda in *The Waves*, merely to be seen by others is to be "broken into separate pieces" (W, 106), to be pierced by "a million arrows" (105). She hates to view her "real face" (44) in the mirror because "I am not here. I have no face" (43). Rhoda's sense that her true being lies elsewhere, in a dream world where identity is dissolved, her body "lets light through" (45), "All is soft and bending" (927), "The sea will drum in [her] ears" (206), and she can "float suspended" (205), corresponds precisely to the image of the ideal ego created by the writer of Woolf's memoir. To be captured by the lure of this ideal, Woolf suggests in her fiction, is not only to feel guilt and shame about one's being-in-the-world but, at the extreme, to risk madness and suicide.

According to the life-writer's memoirs, the genetic origin of her negative sense of physical identity was her father. From him, she writes, she inherited an "opposite instinct [that] checked [her] natural love for beauty" (68) and filled her with "some ancestral dread" antagonistic to the strong femininity of her maternal lineage. "Spartan, ascetic, puritanical," incapable of esthetic appreciation, her father seems to be the very embodiment of a punishing, negating superego. Although Freud attributes the superego's formation to a renunciation of oedipal wishes and a subsequent desexualized identification with the parents, Woolf's text suggests that her superego, her "opposite instinct," was established from the moment of the self's constitution. Breaking new psychoanalytic ground, Woolf's life-writing implies that her superego was created at the place of specular reversal where aggressive narcissistic libido is turned against the self.[14] Woolf's fantasy version of her father as an agent of instictual renunciation and negated desire inherits the frustrated energy of her attempted self-appropriation in the mirror. He is the name she gives to the reflexive moment in which the self is alienated from its ideal counterpart. However punitive and obdurate Leslie Stephen may have been in reality—and we know from other soruces that Woolf's description is quite true-to-life—his function as an internalized agency denying the self access to the "pride and pleasure" of femininity was prepared by the particular dynamics of her mirror stage. Elucidating this psychic division, the life-writer observes that her "ancestral dread," a specifically male legacy, ensured that the "ecstasies and raptures" nourished by her narcissistic dream of oneness would always be "disconnected with my own body" (68). That body is the object of her superego's desire to eradicate femininity and bring the body to a death-like quiescence. The situation is fraught with paradoxes. Woolf feels connected to her female body insofar as its value is negated by the "opposite instinct" that represents male otherness within her psyche. The operation of this instinct, through the agency of the superego, produces the masochistic pleasure of a self shattered and violently decomposed. However, the ultimate aim of that decomposition goes beyond sexual excitement to achieve an evacuation of desire so complete that the psyche can attain the neutrality and indifference André Green terms "narcissism of death."

Later passages in "A Sketch," to which I will turn shortly, offer insight into the final strategy in this complex psychic process. At present I want to follow the life-writer's own associations as she continues to probe the causes of her "looking-glass shame." Having suggested the role of her internalized father in shattering the self into a painful consciousness of its physicality, Woolf goes on to link the effects of this alienating inheritance to the trauma of her sexual molestation at a very young age (probably around six) by her half-brother, Gerald Duckworth. Here the origin of the aggression is external, yet it remains within the intimate family circle. Gerald Duckworth's violation of Woolf's privacy is the libidinal version of her father's "check" of her feminine pride. Indeed, if my reading of the constitution of Woolf's superego is valid (at least in terms of the life-writer's text), then Duckworth's violence may have been all the more pernicious insofar as its introjection reinforced an already established intrapsychic pattern.[15]

Woolf provides a vivid illustration of the process whereby aggression is introjected. In one of those revealing associative moves that makes her text read at times like the discourse of a patient in analysis, she offers a dream for interpretation, "for it may refer to the incident of the looking-glass" (69). In the dream the horrible face of an animal suddenly appears over her shoulder as she looks at herself in a mirror. "The other face in the glass" (69) is clearly interpretable as an element of Woolf's own psychic structure, her own face as "other," as "opposite." The split mirror image shows Woolf seeing herself as an object of male desire. Such a dream belongs with those

Freud places "beyond the pleasure principle," dreams that attempt to master the traumatic penetration of the shield against stimuli "by developing the anxiety whose omission was the cause of the tramatic neurosis" (SE, 18:32).

Reminding us once again that memory rides a train of fiction, Woolf acknowledges that she "cannot be sure whether this was a dream, or if it happened" (69). She remarks that something in the background may simply have moved and seemed alive to her. But the "real" origin is unimportant, finally, since Woolf's memory, creating her life as story, has fixed this specular monster in its fictional frame, and now the textual surface offers the dream as a plausible "reference" to the thematics of the earlier mirror experience. The subject thus constructs herself in imaginary dialogue with the self she has just written, much as the analytic patient continues to "add" material in response to the imaginary interlocutor she has projected in the analyst's place.

The patterns of reference and association in Woolf's text suggest that Duckworth's desire be interpreted as analogous to that of Woolf's superego: both seek to dominate and control her femininity. Woolf's response to Gerald's molestation, turning her anger against herself and repressing her fear and anxiety, repeats the process of her superego's formation. Like the male glance, which inherits some of its affective power, the transgressing male hand shatters Woolf's sense of her bodily integrity, convincing her that "certain parts of the body . . . must not be touched" (69).

The logic of my argument suggests, furthermore, that this shattering of her body's wholeness stimulated in Woolf a certain degree of masochistic excitement. Such a suggestion is obviously problematic and easily misunderstood. I certainly do not want to discount Woolf's memory of "resenting, disliking it" (69). The experience was no doubt traumatic, and Woolf clearly did not invite its recurrence. Moreover, one cannot argue that Woolf's apparent failure to express anger against her assailant (she only "hoped that he would stop"—69) and her failure to report him to her parents testifies to her libidinal investment in his attentions. For she must have felt that the entire patriarchal structure of her family, internalized in her superego, supported this kind of abuse against women.[16]

The stimulation I am attributing to Woolf in this instance arises from what Leo Bersani calls "the absolute 'discharge' of death."[17] In response to Gerald Duckworth's desire, Woolf, in my hypothesis, wishes to be without desire, without sexuality, invisible, untouchable, empty, dead. This wish is brought out in her text when she declares that her instinctive revulsion from Duckworth's caresses "proves that Virginia Stephen was not born on the 25th of January 1882" (69). By erasing her biological identity and her paternal inheritance, Woolf's fantasy reintegrates her into the matrilineal filiation that is her "pride and pleasure." She imagines that she "was born many thousands of years ago and had from the very first to encounter instincts already acquired by thousands of ancestresses in the past" (69). Thus she acquires, on

the basis of her self-sought death, an imaginary feminist genealogy that recaptures the lost narcissistic center of her ideal ego. By delivering herself
from all desire and taking the denial of her body under her own control,
Woolf can fantasize that she has bridged the internal split between superego
and ego, allowing her to recline once again inside the protective membrane
of the dream screen.

Having given her reader a vivid account in the first few pages of "A Sketch"
of the constitution of the subject of her memoir, Woolf subsequently describes
certain intense "moments of being" embedded in what she calls the "non-
descript cotton wool," the "non-being" (70), of her routine daily life. In my
analysis of these exceptional moments, I propose to demonstrate that Woolf
privileges them precisely because they repeat the dynamics of her psychic
constitution, confronting her consciousness with the unconscious impulses
that structure her psychic being. In particular, they offer her the masochistic
excitation of exposure to the work of her death instinct.

Such is the prestige of the Joycean epiphany that Woolf's "moments of
being" have often been assimilated to it and interpreted in terms of symbolic revelation, spiritual self-transcendence, and esthetic insight.[18] But this
analogy radically distorts Woolf's experience as she recounts it in "A Sketch."
Of five exceptional moments she explicitly describes, four leave her in a state
of paralysis and despair. Rather than esthetic form, they reveal shapeless
horror. The self in these instances is not transcended but violently aggressed.
Being emerges from non-being through the effect of "a sudden violent shock"
(71), as a function of a traumatic disruption that shatters the self and thereby
marks its reality. These marks establish certain scenes in the past, Woolf
tells us, as "representative; enduring," and they confirm her "instictive notion . . . that we are sealed vessels afloat on what it is convenient to call reality; and at some moments, the sealing matter cracks; in floods reality"
(122). This is reminiscent of my earlier comparison of Woolf's enveloping
dream screen to Freud's protective shield against stimuli. But the life-writer
no longer stresses the pleasures of being safely englobed. Rather, it is the
cracking of the seal and the implosive flooding of her mental apparatus that
she now valorizes.[19] Being is revealed to her "beyond the pleasure principle"
through her repeated submission to traumatic shocks. "Many of these exceptional moments," she observes, "brought with them a peculiar horror
and physical collapse; they seemed dominant; myself passive" (72).

The first moment of being that Woolf describes demonstrates this masochistic structure of passive submission to the other's dominance. But, as in
the case of Gerald Duckworth, the other here is simultaneously the same: he
is a close family member, Virginia's brother Thoby. The siblings were "pommeling each other with [their] fists" when Virginia suddenly asked herself
"why hurt another person?" and, dropping her hands, just stood there and

let her brother beat her. She had a feeling of "hopeless sadness" and of her own "powerlessness . . . as if [she] became aware of something terrible" (71). The meaning of this awareness remains obscure, however. The moment is opaque, yet charged with potential significance as if inviting interpretation.

The initial sibling "pommeling" is reminiscent of Virginia's tomboy conduct; it implies a playful violence in which brother and sister are equals and sexual identity is not an issue. Virginia's decision to opt out of this reciprocal violence seems to involve a sudden awareness that she intends to inflict pain. At this point, as I interpret the episode, she realizes the sexual dynamics involved in the conflict and immediately internalizes her aggression, introjecting Thoby as another male representative of her superego and repeating by her own choice the situation of powerlessness she had been in with Gerald Duckworth. Thus she responds to Thoby's beating as to an "opposite instinct" within herself. This explains why, although she tells of slinking away alone, "feeling horribly depressed" (71), the entire episode remains in her memory as a privileged moment. It offers the masochistic satisfaction of repeating her painful internal split and makes subliminally manifest her unconscious desire for death.

Woolf's third moment of being (I will return to the second) reveals the death wish overtly in the suicide of a family acquaintance, a certain Mr. Valpy. She remembers overhearing her parents' conversation about this event, then walking in the garden on the path by the apple tree and feeling that the tree "was connected with the horror of Mr. Valpy's suicide. I could not pass it," she writes. "I stood there looking at the grey-green creases of the bark—it was a moonlit night—in a trance of horror. I seemed to be dragged down, hopelessly, into some pit of absolute despair from which I could not escape. My body seemed paralysed" (71). Woolf's paralysis here, reminiscent of her submissive immobility under her brother's blows, can be explained in terms of Freud's theory of psychical trauma. Freud argues that a breach in the protective shield against stimuli summons cathartic energy from all the phychical systems to bind this influx of excitation "so that the remaining psychical functions are extensively paralysed or reduced" (SE, 18:30). This description may help answer the essential question raised by Woolf's moments of being: how can the experience of being dragged down into a pit of despair be remembered as a privileged moment of ontological discovery? There is in the first place the influx of energy, the wounding shock, the painful excitement. When the sealing matter cracks, and reality floods in, being impresses the psyche with its undisguised immediacy. But this violent influx carries with it the danger of drowning. Against this danger the psyche marshals all its forces, converting incoming energy into a quiescent state, achieving a minimum of stimulation where there had been the risk of excess. This reduction, whereby the revealing crack is sealed, is the price to be paid for the restoration of psychic wholeness. It is as if a pretended death, a paralysis, had been substituted for the threat of actual death, and this fantasy state were presented as a desirable ideal. This, I believe, is the source of Woolf's despair when she hears the news of Mr. Valpy's suicide: his fate, with which she identifies, confronts her with the operation of her own death instinct, which offers psychic wholeness in psychic quiescence, neutrality, inertia, the absence of excitation. Narcissism of death, in André Green's formulation.[20]

In the memoir writer's text, this negative narcissistic desire, the desire to suppress desire, is emblematized by the apple tree, symbol of Mr. Valpy's wish to destroy himself. Woolf had already written this episode of "death among the apple trees" (W, 24) once before, attributing the experience to Neville in *The Waves*. Interestingly, Neville deliberately attempts to *repeat* his desperate feeling of being existentially checked, as if paralyzed, by hearing the news of a violent death. He returns to the precise place where he overheard the story in order, strangely enough, to "recover" the feeling that "the ripple of [his] life was unavailing" (W, 24). Like the Woolf of "A Sketch," he associates the dead man with an apple tree, "an unintelligible obstacle" that he finds himself unable to pass beyond. "We are doomed, all of us," he reflects, "by the apple trees, by the immitigable tree which we cannot pass" (W, 24-25). Neville evidently takes pleasure in confirming the nullity of his life and of its interpretive procedures. "Implacable" in its otherness, irrecuperable by consciousness, the tree signifies the death of the signifying process (as does the puddle Woolf is unable to step across in another moment of ontological fixation—see 78). In his "summing up" Bernard uses the tree image to define "what remains outside our illusions yet cannot stay them, is changed by them for the moment, yet shows through stable, still, and with a sternness that our lives lack" (W, 251). "Unavailing" for Neville, life is "lacking" for Bernard. Stability and stillness, qualities of the outside, can be attained only at the expense of internal evacuation and the self's dissolution. "Identity failed me. We are nothing" (W, 64), reflects Rhoda as she tells her own version of being paralyzed before a "grey, cadaverous" puddle.

Rhoda experiences the loss of her identity as a shock, "sudden as the spring of a tiger [whereby] life emerges heaving its dark crest from the sea" (W, 64). The use of the word "life" here where one would expect "death" is characteristic of Woolf's descriptions of revelatory moments and a clue to their masochistic character. Death offers a glimpse of life's reality by showing that what appears to be internal to life is in reality outside its domain. Meditating later in the "Sketch" about the effect on her development of the many deaths in her family, Woolf attributes a positive value to "this mutilation of natural feelings" (117), these traumatic "cracks and gashes" (118) cut in the protective fabric of daily life. "I came to think of life as something of extreme reality," she comments. "And this, of course, increased my feeling of my own importance. Not in relation to human beings: in relation to the force which had respected me sufficiently to make me feel what was real" (118). Reality emerges for Woolf as that which shatters and mutilates the self's "natural" integrity. She turns the pain of individual loss into evidence of cosmic respect, attributing her narcissistic importance to her privileged relation to the sadistic work of death.

Death as mystical center, as empty center, center of the void, constitutes the blank flip side of the Janus figure of narcissism. On the first side is the englobed maternal center. Earlier we noted Bernard's difficulty in narrativizing his life conceived as a "globe, full of figures." He feels that any story he extracts from the globe's totality, however beautiful it may be, inevitably distorts the truth. Could he then be more successful in explaining the meaning of his life by finding a language that evokes his death? Bernard goes on to entertain precisely this possibility, as if he had simply flipped his narcissistic project onto its reverse side. He imagines himself a willing victim of the universe's indifference, "lying in a ditch on a stormy day . . . forgotten, minute" (W, 239). For such moments of "humiliation and triumph," he thinks, there can be no stories, no words, at most "some little language such as lovers use, broken words, inarticulate words, like the shuffling of feet on the pavement" (W, 238). The humiliation of the body appears to have an equivalent in the disarticulation of language and its reduction to a kind of brute semantic immediacy ("a howl, a cry" Bernard says on another occasion—W, 295). Bernard's welcome of such a violent shattering of the semantic body is analogous to the life-writer's welcome of the traumatic mutilation of her psychic wholeness. Similarly, Lily Briscoe realizes that she needs a nervous shock, of the kind that "unveils" and "intensifies," as Woolf said of the shock effect of her mother's death (93), in order to complete her painting: "Phrases came. Visions came. Beautiful pictures. Beautiful phrases. But what she wished to get hold of was that very jar on the nerves, the thing itself before it has been made anything" (TTL, 287).

The problem for esthetic expression is that a "jar on the nerves" assumes an ego capable of being shocked, and such an ego inevitably "makes" things, that is, interprets them, clothes them in phrases, puts them on a train of fiction. Moreover, the ego's existence assumes that of the superego, which constitutes the self as seen and does not allow it to be forgotten. An artistic medium adequate to render reality would have to be able to "describe the world seen without a self" and for this project, as Bernard observes,

> There are no words. Blue, red—even they distract, even they hide with thickness instead of letting the light through. How describe or say anything in articulate words again?—save that it fades, save that it undergoes a gradual transformation, becomes, even in the course of one short walk, habitual—this scene also. Blindness returns as one moves and one leaf repeats another. Loveliness returns as one looks with all its train of phantom phrases. (W, 287)

The immediacy Bernard wishes for here is the reverse counterpart of the ecstasy Woolf describes as her first memory, when she felt "I am hardly aware of myself, but only of the sensation" (67). If her first memory transports the life-writer back to a fantasized time before the birth of the self, Bernard's fantasy is premised on the self's demise. There is no maternal ground here, no soothing yellow blind, no enveloping grape, only "it," a neutral, irreducible, immitigable otherness that is distorted by the language of perception, obscured by the consolations of habit, and falsified by the appearance of repetition. Yet "it" has a "mystical" quality that feeds a Woolfian narcissistic fantasy just as powerful as that of the totalizing globe.[21] Left not with himself but with something in the universe, Bernard imagines being invulnerable to shock because removed from "the pressure of the eye, the solicitation of the body, and all need of lies and phrases" (W, 294). "How much better is silence," he reflects. "Let me sit here for ever with bare things, this coffee-cup, this knife, this fork, things in themselves, myself being myself" (W, 295). The self in this wished-for moment outside of time appropriates the world in fantasy by becoming ontologically equivalent to it, just one more "bare thing" among countless others.[22]

Confronted by temporal exigencies, Bernard cannot sustain his fantasy of an eternal, shockproof stasis and retreats to the prosaic limitations of his physical identity, which he then feels challenged to defend against the advancing army of death. Woolf performs a similar retreat from the extremity of her death narcissism. Its medium is writing. In writing Woolf flings herself, like Bernard in the final sentence of *The Waves*, "unvanquished and unyielding" (W, 297) against her own desire for death. Her defiance, like his, is simultaneously an embrace.

Woolf examines the origin of her writing impulse in relation to her moments of being in a long paragraph of "A Sketch" to which I want now to turn my attention. Her second moment of being, which I skipped over earlier, differs markedly from the others in that it leaves Woolf with a feeling of satisfaction rather than despair. Instead of causing her bodily paralysis and mental collapse, the violent shock in this case appears to be a shock of recognition. "I was looking at the flower bed by the front door," Woolf writes. " 'That is the whole,' I said. I was looking at a plant with a spread of leaves; and it suddenly seemed plain that the flower itself was a part of the earth; that a ring enclosed what was the flower; and that was the real flower; part earth; part flower. It was a thought I put away as likely to be very useful to me later" (71). Woolf calls this moment "a discovery," but to the reader it seems more like a recovery—of her first "first memory" of flowers on the black ground of her mother's dress. The mother's invisible presence provides the vital basis for the metonymic relation that rings earth and flower in one globe. What is surprising is that Woolf lists this joyful revelation of organic unity and nurturant symbiosis on a par with her depressive experiences of being beaten by her brother and of being paralyzed by the news of a suicide.

How can experiences that produce feelings as radically different as despair and satisfaction both be revelations of being? My hypothesis of Woolf's double-faced narcissism, one oriented toward fusion with her ideal ego, the other toward annihilation by her punitive superego, has attempted to answer this question. But the life-writer, as she approaches her analysis of the psychic function of writing, seems eager to minimize the role of her death drive. Thus even though she supposes that "the shock-receiving capacity is what makes me a writer" (72), she divorces the value of these shocks from any masochistic excitation they might generate and attributes it entirely to their stimulation of her Erotic impulse to bind and unify. The passage I quoted at the beginning of this article is remarkably traditional in its stress on the reparative and sublimatory functions of art. Suggesting that the reality she *writes* is a salutory displacement of the reality from which she *suffers*, Woolf shifts the originating source of the real from its threatening location behind appearances, where in other passages she associates it with death, to the writing "I," who *creates* reality by making it whole. Thereby the deathly neutrality of the "it," of the "real thing behind appearance," is brought under the sway of the pleasure principle. This sublimating denial allows Woolf to reimagine the mirror phase of the ego's constitution on the model of a simple identification with her ideal specular image. The rapture she experiences in writing seems to have precisely this origin: it is as if she were looking at herself in a mirror and, instead of becoming aware of some "opposite instinct," some animalistic "other face in the glass," felt the jubilation Lacan attributes to the child who suddenly sees how its bodily parts fit together. The text's wholeness, moreover, provides a model of limited, contained form that contrasts with the "generalised, dispersed, omnipresent" (84) centrality Woolf associated with her mother. As she discovers "what belongs to what," Woolf is constructing an ideal ego that gives her an esthetic delight closely related to the "pride and pleasure" she derives from the family tradition of feminine beauty. But she is simultaneously transforming the shape of that beauty to gain rational control over the specular lure of an ideal feminine selflessness and so reconstruct the integrity of her ego as other.

By assigning a temporal priority to the masochistic moment, Woolf excludes the "opposite instinct" within herself from any creative function in her actual scriptive process. And she ignores the threat to her narcissistic life fantasy posed by the potential conversion of inrushing energy to serve her instinctual drive toward psychic quiescence, neutrality, and death. Desire at this point in Woolf's self-writing has been dissociated from its sources in the unconscious and appears only as the desire to explain, the desire to make desire conscious "by putting it into words." Language as she here presents it does not block the way to narcissistic integration, hiding reality with its thickness, falsifying sacramental illusion with stories, but is a privileged vehicle that reveals the fundamental pattern subtending all of life. It is as if language were being conceived as a healing medium through which the psyche's severed parts could be sutured and identification with the mother accomplished in fantasy. Thus the apparently impersonal estheticism of the "philosophy" Woolf puts forward is, viewed psychoanalytically, the expression of an extremely personal wish, the wish for the esthetic experience to repeat the original englobing pattern of maternal union.

The paragraph we are analyzing concludes as follows:

> From this I reach what I might call a philosophy; at any rate it is a constant idea of mine; that behind the cotton wool is hidden a pattern; that we—I mean all human beings—are connected with this; that the whole world is a work of art; that we are parts of the work of art. *Hamlet* or a Beethoven quartet is the truth about this vast mass that we call the world. But there is no Shakespeare there is no Beethoven; certainly and emphatically there is no God; we are the words; we are the music; we are the thing itself. And I see this when I have a shock. (72)

It is easy to misinterpret this passage by forgetting that the hidden pattern behind the cotton wool is *not* the same as "the real thing behind appearances." The wholeness of the pattern is created by Woolf, though she admits at the outset of the next paragraph that her intuition of its existence "is so instinctive that it seems given to me, not made by me" (72). Her verbal making is a sublimation of the "thingness" of the real. It is, in Bernard's terms, a form of blindness whereby "loveliness returns." Indeed this seemingly universal statement of Woolf's esthetic philosophy totally ignores the question she puts in Bernard's mouth and that haunts her writing from its beginning: "How describe or say anything in articulate words again?" Language, for Bernard, violates the immitigable otherness of the real, and when he sits alone with "things in themselves" he is, precisely, *not* the words. In contrast, Woolf here becomes "the thing itself" by identifying with her words. Her fantasy fuses "the thing itself" into the ring-enclosed flower, and she recaptures the ecstatic sense of being held suspended in a grape. There is no Virgnia Woolf . . . we are her words.

In making us feel this, Woolf's writing creates an intense desire for identification, not unlike Lily's for Mrs. Ramsay, a desire to make ourselves whole as we reconstruct Woolf's sustaining pattern. Critics who repond positively to this imaginary appeal follow Woolf herself in attempting to sublimate her eroticized enjoyment of fragmentation and her attraction to "the thing itself before it has been made anything."[23] A recent critique by Jean Laplanche of Freud's concept of sublimation provides a way of understanding how Woolf's sublimated activity does not displace or repress her masochistic impulses but appropriates them for purposes of artistic production. Laplanche maintains that sublimation "involves the idea of a sort of repeated, continuous neo-creation of sexual energy, hence the continual reopening of an excitation," and he associates this reopening with a fantasmatic shattering of the body's integrity.[24] This analysis accurately describes the emergence of Woolf's sexuality in the masochistic position and suggests that its role in her literary work is not to be found, as for instance Phyllis Rose argues, in her creation of esthetic wholes, but in her "opposite instinct" to break such wholes apart and expose herself and her art to a proliferation of violent shocks.

This instinct emerges in the last sentence of the paragraph quoted above, "I see this when I have a shock," which suggests a revised temporal relation between the reception of shocks and the creation of art: they now appear to be coextensive.[25] The "I" is divided between a visionary seer and a shattered self. The writer's delight in a vision of herself as esthetic pattern coincides with her feeling the shock of being, of being other than words, in conflict with them, unnamed by them. The coincidence is brought out by a significant repetition in the life-writer's text. She considers that her "instinctive conception of a pattern hidden behind the cotton wool "proves that one's life is not confined to one's body and what one says and does" (73). This proof apparently confirms the success of Woolf's sublimating project: she feels free of any limiting physical/sexual identity. But just a few pages earlier she had expressly linked this same "disconnection with my own body" to the shattering effects of her "ancestral dread." There she attributed her capacity to feel ecstasies and raptures "without any shame or the least sense of guilt" (68) to her opposite instinct, the introjected male other that traumatizes and disrupts the self's unifying pattern. Her subsequent assertion of that pattern's coherence thus implicitly evokes its incoherence, dysfunction, fantasmatic perturbation, and the resulting sexual excitement of ontological trauma.

Recording the end of *The Waves* in her diary, Woolf, elated, notes that in this book she had "netted that fin in the waste of water which appeared to me over the marshes out of my window at Rodwell when I was coming to the end of *To the Lighthouse*" (WD, 165). In a reference to this vision written in the autumn of 1926 she associates it with her "mystical" perception that "it is not oneself but something in the universe that one's left with" (WD, 100) and with her paralysis as a child when confronted with a puddle to step over. In *The Waves* Bernard refers to the fin as "a bare visual impression unattached to any line of reason" (W, 189). The fin is the emblem of the fissure that splits the smooth surfaces of the world as work of art and of the self as patterned whole. It is the tear that Lily fears and hopes "would have rent the surface pool" allowing "something [to] emerge. A hand would be shoved up, a blade would be flashed" (TTL, 266-67). The blade severs and dismembers, but this is the welcome risk that the death impulse offers to life. The appearance of the fin, Woolf observes, is both "frightening and exciting" (WD, 100). An eloquently minimalist sign of division, difference, and death, the fin threatens to destroy the psychological and esthetic coherence of Woolf's works and their function as vehicles of rational explanation.

Woolf, I have argued, writes not in opposition to this threat but in collaboration with it. Though in a moment of creative triumph she may proclaim her success in netting the fin, she knows in that same moment that her "rounding off" is inevitably "fragmentary" (WD, 165), that the fin's severing effect is constitutive of the work's appearance of wholeness. Thus her writing is simultaneously a search for re-membered union and a means of perpetuating traumatic disunion. It is at once an attempt at maternal recuperation and an opportunity for masochistic perturbation. On the one hand it moves toward an ecstasy of esthetic impersonality, on the other toward a violent shattering of personality and illusion. If many readers feel an indefinably erotic quality in Woolf's novels, as if the sexuality that she so often renounces on the narrative level returned as an effect of her style, this is because her writing repeats and extends the traumatic constitution of her sexuality. A detailed demonstration of this thesis lies beyond the scope of this article. But I hope to have shown that Woolf's life-writing in *A Sketch of the Past* constitutes " 'the subject of this memoir' " as one of the most remarkable autobiographical texts of the twentieth century.

Notes and References

1. Psychoanalysis as an Intervention in Contemporary Theory

1. Jacques Lacan, *Ecrits: A Selection*, trans. Alan Sheridan (New York: W. W. Norton, 1977), p. 34.

2. Simon O. Lesser, *Fiction and the Unconscious* (Chicago: University of Chicago Press, 1957), p. 98.

3. Throughout this essay I have had particular people in mind in making observations about both psychoanalytic writing practices and the reception of psychoanalysis in the academy. When I presented an earlier version of this paper at the annual convention of the Modern Language Association several years ago, I left out all specific references, so I told myself, in order to fit the paper into the time limit. A number of people in the audience—and several readers later on—asked me if I had them in mind at various points in the essay. Other people asked if I had this or that well-known critic in mind at particular points. On the latter issue a number of those who talked with me guessed right. On the first issue—the question about whether I had them in mind—people were often wrong. It became clear to me, however, that the essay would in fact be more useful if this anxiety were left open for readers. Thus I have let the essay be an uncertain mirror, a fable, if you will, in which we may or may not see ourselves.

2. Psychoanalysis, Literary Criticism, and the Problem of Authority

1. Concerning the rôle of the author in Balzac's work, see my: *Unwrapping Balzac: A Study of La Peau de Chagrin*. University of Toronto Press: Toronto/Buffalo/London, 1979.

2. The Editions du Seuil have published several seminars of Lacan, and are under contract to do several more. It is also a co-plaintiff, with Miller, in the case.

3. *Ecrits: A Selection*, translated by Alan Sheridan, Norton: New York/London, 1977, pp. 310-311 (translation modified). In the original French edition (Editions du Seuil: Paris, 1966, p. 813), the text reads as follows:

Partons de la conception de l'Autre comme du lieu du
signifiant. Tout énoncé d'autorité n'y a d'autre
garantie que son énonciation même, car il est vain
qu'il le cherche dans un autre signifiant, lequel
d'aucune façon ne saurait apparaître hors de ca lieu.
Ce que nous formulons à dire qu'il n'y a pas de métalangage
qui puisse être parlé, plus aphoristiquement:
qu'il n'y a pas d'Autre de l'Autre. C'est en imposteur
que se présente pour y suppléer, le Législateur (celui
qui prétend ériger la Loi).

4. Sheridan translates, "soumission" as "subjection." Cf. *Ecrits: A Selection*, p. 304; *Ecrits* [French], p. 806.

5. Navarin, Diffusion Seuil: Paris, 1985.

6. The German translation of this essay does foreground this aspect of the term, which it renders as *Das Drängen des Buchstabens*.

7. S. Freud, *The Interpretation of Dreams*, chapter VII, A: The Forgetting of Dreams, Avon Books: New York, p. 563.

8. Cf. R. Barthes, "The Death of the Author"; M. Foucault, "What is an Author?"

3. The Sound of *O* in *Othello*

1. This paper was originally delivered at a colloquium on Lacan's *Television* (Paris: Editions du Seuil, 1974), sponsored by *October/Ornicar?*, April 9-10, 1987. The two epigraphs from *Television* appear in the translation published in *October*, no. 40, trans. Denis Hollier, Rosalind Krauss, and Annette Michelson (Spring 1987), pp. 45 and 34, respectively. All Shakespeare references are to *The Riverside Shakespeare*, ed. G. B. Evans, et al. (Boston: Houghton, Mifflin, 1974).

2. Forthcoming, University of California Press.

3. Joel Fineman, *Shakespeare's Perjured Eye: The Invention of Poetic Subjectivity in Shakespeare's Sonnets* (Berkeley: University of California Press, 1986).

4. For Shakespeare's probable Greek education, see T. W. Baldwin, *Shakspere's Small Latine and Lesse Greek*, 2 vols. (Urbana: University of Illinois Press, 1944). According to F. W. Gingrich's *Shorter Lexicon of the Greek New Testament*, rev. F. W. Danker (Chicago: University of Chicago Press, 1983), *thelō* means primarily "wish," "will," "desire," but, also, "resolve" and "purpose"; as with French *vouloir*, *thelō* also carries the sense of want as lack, for example, a *want* "to mean" or "to be," e.g., *Ac.* 2:12, "*ti thelei touto einai*," "what does this mean?"

5. Of the many plausible Greek etymologies to associate with the name Desdemona, Cinthio, in conclusion, stresses: "It appeared marvelous to everybody that such malignity could have been discovered in a human heart [here speaking of the Iago prototype]; and the fate of the unhappy Lady was lamented, with some blame for her father, who had given her a name of unlucky augury" (excerpt from *Gli Hecatommithi* [1566 edition], trans. and ed. Geoffrey Bullough, *Narrative and Dramatic Sources of Shakespeare* [New York, Columbia University Press, 1973], Vol. 7, p. 250). There are alternate speculations regarding Shakespeare's source for the name Othello, e.g., Thorello, in Ben Jonson's *Everyman in His Humour* (1598). Shakespeare often associates Venus, or Aphrodite, with Cyprus, referring directly to her mythological birthplace, e.g., the final couplet of *Venus and Adonis*: "holding their course to Paphos, where their queen/Means to immure herself, and not be seen" (1193-1194). The *Revels Accounts* records the first performance of *Othello*—before the king, on November 1, 1604—as "The Moor of Venis" by "Shaxberd" (Bullough, *Sources*, p. 193).

6. In his Introduction, Bullough reviews arguments for and against Shakespeare's knowledge of Cinthio's text (*Sources*, pp. 193-238). Cinthio's text was first published in 1565, and Shakespeare may have read this; there is also a French translation, dated 1584, by Gabriel Chappuys, which Shakespeare may also have read. The first English translation appears in 1753.

7. The prefix-marker in Greek for aorist or imperfect tenses is *e* (ε) or, under certain circumstances *ē* (ω). The first-person imperfect for *thelō* is thus *ēthelōn*, with the final *ōn* marking the first person. Hence my remarks above. Various Greek scholars with whom I have conferred are willing to hear a collation between the sound of *O* in *Othello* and the initial prefix—*ē*—but they also insist they do not hear a convincing collation between the sound of *O* and the final *ōn* of the first-person imperfect. Despite such philological objections, I continue to think Shakespeare—who had very little Greek indeed, and who regularly makes greater and far freer auditory free-associations in English—would have heard a connection between the sound of *O* and the final *ōn* of the first-person imperfect of *thelō*. However, if one does not grant this final association, then my argument above about the subjective force of the sound of *O* in *Othello* loses only one half of its two markers of the first-person imperfect, and, in either case, the argument retains its validity with regard to the subjective apprehension of the present. However, in the context of what I say later about Lacan's account of the constitution of the subject, it is significant that the two markers of the on-going first-person past (*ē* at the beginning and *ōn* at the end) are bound up together in the sound of *O* in *Othello*, for, thus conjoined, they register the durative experience of the (insistently repeated) moment of the constitution of the subject as the sustained and immediate *passing* of the present, as in my discussion above of "That's he that was Othello, here I am" (5.2.284).

8. The most immediately relevant Shakespeare Sonnets are 135 and 136. I quote them here so as to recall, first, the performative way Shakespeare exploits the fact that his name designates both male and female genitals, second, the "overplus" arithmetics of *Will* (for discussions of these sonnets, see *Shakespeare's Perjured Eye*, chapter 5):

135

Whoever hath her wish, though hast thy *Will*,
and *Will* to boot, and *Will* in overplus;
More than enough am I that vex thee still,
To thy sweet will making addition thus.
Wilt thou, whose will is large and spacious,
Not once vouchsafe to hide my will in thine?
Shall will in others seem right gracious,
And in my will no fair acceptance shine?
The sea, all water, yet receives rain still,
And in abundance addeth to his store,
So thou being rich in *Will* add to thy *Will*,
One will of mine to make thy large *Will* more.
Let no unkind, no fair beseechers kill;
Think all but one, and me in that one *Will*.

136

If they soul check thee that I come so near,
Swear to thy blind soul that I was thy *Will*,
And will, thy soul knows, is admitted there;
Thus far for love my love suit, sweet, fulfil.
Will will fulfill the treasure of thy love,
Ay fill it full with wills, and my will one.
In things of great receipt with ease we prove

> Among a number one is reckon'd none:
> Then in the number let me pass untold,
> Though in thy store's account I one must be,
> For nothing hold me, so it please thee hold
> That nothing me, a something sweet to thee.
> Make but my name thy love, and love that still,
> And then thou lovest me, for my name is *Will*.

9. Lacan accounts for the subjective experience of original sin by reference to the lack imported into the subject through His (his/her), subjectively constitutive, accession to a name through the discourse of the Other: " 'I' am in the place from which a voice is heard clamoring 'the universe is a defect in the purity of Non-Being.' And not without reason, for by protecting itself this place makes Being itself languish. This place is called *Jouissance*, and it is the absence of this that makes the universe vain. Am I responsible for it, then? Yes, probably. Is this *Jouissance*, the lack of which makes the Other insubstantial, mine, then? Experience proves that it is usually forbidden me, not only, as certain fools believe, because of a bad arrangement of society, but rather because of the fault [*faute*] of the Other if he existed: and since the Other does not exist, all that remains to me is to assume the fault upon 'I,' that is to say, to believe in that to which experience leads us all, Freud in the vanguard, namely, to original sin" ("The Subversion of the Subject and the Dialectic of Desire in the Freudian Unconscious," *Ecrits: A Selection*, trans. Alan Sheridan [New York, W. W. Norton, 1977], p. 317).

10. Jacques-Alain Miller, " 'La suture': Eléments de la logique du signifiant," *Cahiers pour l'analyse*, no. 1/2 (1966), pp. 37-49; e.g., "C'est l'énoncé décisif que *le concept de la non-identité-à-soi est assigné par le nombre z*éro qui suture le discours logique," p. 46.

11. Shakespeare probably took the anthropophagi topos from Philemon Holland's 1601 translation of Pliny's *Natural History*. Shakespeare regularly conceives eating in terms of self-consummation, as in the opening procreation sonnets to the young man or, for another example, as in *Troilus and Cressida*, "He that is proud eats up himself. Pride is his own glass, his own trumpet, his own chronicle, and whatever praises itself but in the deed, devours the deed in the praise" (2.3.154-157). Lacan remarks, apropos of Freud's dream of Irma's injection, "If there is an image that might represent for us the Freudian notion of the unconscious, it is exactly that of a headless subject, of a subject who has no more ego, who is beyond the ego, decentered in relation to the ego, who is not of the ego" ("S'il y a une image qui pourrait nous représenter la notion freudienne de l'inconscient, c'est bien celle d'un sujet acéphale, d'un sujet qui n'a plus d' *ego*, qui est extrême à l' *ego*, décentré par rapport à l'*ego*, qui n'est pas de l' *ego*") (*Le moi dans la théorie de Freud et dans la technique de la psychanalyse* [Paris: Editions du Seuil, 1978], p. 200).

12. See *Shakespeare's Perjured Eye*.

13. The relation of vision to speaking, mediated by the motif of writing—a writing which is neither the former nor the latter and yet, nevertheless, a little of both—is how the play, quite apart from its critics, explains the original motivation of Iago; this is specified quite clearly in the opening lines of the play, when Iago complains about

> One Michael Cassio, a Florentine
> (A fellow almost damn'd in a fair wife),
> That never set a squadron in the field,
> Nor the division of a battle knows
> More than a spinster—unless the bookish theoric,
> Wherein the toged consuls can propose
> As masterly as he. Mere prattle, without practice,
> Is all his soldiership.
> But he, sir, had th' election;

And I, of whom his eyes had seen the proof
At Rhodes, at Cyprus, and on other grounds
Christen'd and heathen, must be belee'd and calm'd
By debitor and creditor—this counter-caster,
He (in good time!) must his lieutenant be,
And I (God bless the mark!) his Moorship's ancient. (1.1.20-33)

What Iago here calls "bookish theoric," the preference for which explains why, according to Iago, "Preferment goes by letter and affection,/And not by old gradation, where each second/Stood heir to th' first" (1.1.36-38), can serve as both the motto and the explanation of *The Tragedy of Othello*, if we remember the etymology of "theoric," from Greek *theorein, to see*, and if we appreciate the way this "bookish theoric" stands at odds with the immediate vision of an "I" "of whom his eyes had seen the proof." This is related to the military, erotic, and semiotic issues at stake in the matter of Iago's promotion, his rise from the ranks of "Ancient," or ensign—the man who bears before the troops the flag or insignia of their collective power—to the rank of "Lieutenant," the man who, behind the troops, stands as executive *place-holder* of a power that is thus represented rather than seen; hence my first epigraph from *Othello*: Iago's "I must show out a flag and sign of love,/Which is indeed but sign" (1.1.156-157). Very roughly, I am here connecting Lacan's three knotted registers, the imaginary, the symbolic, and the real, to, respectively, Shakespeare's equally knotted concatenation of the visual, the verbal, and the written; see footnote 24, below.

14. Frank Kermode, Introduction to *Othello, The Riverside Shakespeare*, p. 1198.

15. Lacan, "The Subversion of the Subject," p. 316; subsequent references to this essay will be noted in the text within parentheses.

16. I thank Helena Schulz-Keil, first, for many helpful and instructive conversations about the work of Lacan, second, for bringing to my attention both the existence of this unpublished typescript redaction of the *Seminar on Identification* and its discussion of the *trait unaire*; on the unitary trait, see also Helene Muller, "Another Genesis of the Unconscious," *Lacan Study Notes*, 5 (Summer 1985), pp. 1-22. I will be referring to the eighteenth meeting of Lacan's Seminar, May 2, 1962; page numbers refer to the typescript's numeration.

17. *Seminar on Identification*, p. 9. I discuss this paradox in relation to proper names and Lacan in "The Significance of Literature, *The Importance of Being Earnest*," *October*, no. 15 (Winter 1980), pp. 79-90.

18. *Seminar on Identification*, p. 9. For the Shakespearean resonations—especially the materialized liquidity of ejaculate suspense: "the phenomenology of the spurt"—attaching to this image of a space both within and without itself, see my illustration and discussion of the death of Lucrece in "Shakespeare's *Will*: The Temporality of Rape," *Representations*, no. 20 (Fall 1987), pp. 25-76.

19. "En fait c'est une chose excessivement bête et simple ce point très essential que le signifiant en tant qu'il peut servir à se signifier lui-même doit se poser comme différent de lui-même" (*Seminar on Identification*, p. 10).

20. *Television, October*, p. 45 (" 'Il n'y a pas de rapport sexuel': Il est frappant que ce sens réduise au non-sens: au non-sens du rapport sexuel, lequel est patent depuis toujours dans les dits de l'amour," *Television*, p. 18).

21. Exceptionally and suggestively, Stanley Cavell stresses the interruption of Othello's honeymoon night (*The Claim of Reason* [New York: Oxford University Press, 1979], p. 487).

22. The anal and syphilitic reverberations of the "wind in this scene are significant:

> Clown: Why, masters, have your instruments been in Naples, that they speak i'
> the nose thus?

> *Musician:* How, sir, how?
> *Clown:* Are these, I pray you, wind instruments?
> *Musician:* Ay, marry, are they sir.
> *Clown:* O, thereby hangs a tail.
> *Musician:* Whereby hangs a tale, sir?
> *Clown:* Marry, sir, by many a wind instrument that I know. But, masters, here's money for you; and the general so likes your music, that he desires you for love's sake to make no more noise with it.
> *Musician:* Well, sir, we will not
> *Clown:* If you have any music that may not be heard, to't again; but (as they say) to hear music the general does not greatly care.
> *Musician:* We have none such, sir.
> *Clown:* Then put up your pipes in your bag, for I'll away. Go, vanish into air, away!
> *Exeunt Musicians* (3.1.1.20)

23. Norman Sanders, editor of *The Cambridge Othello*, notes: "This is a version of a song well-known before Shakespeare used it and often quoted in earlier plays and poems. The fullest texts of the original can be found in Percy's *Reliques of Ancient English Poetry*, 1765, 1, 199-203, and *The Roxburghe Ballads*, ed. W. Chappell, 1888, 1, 171. For his version Shakespeare changed the sex of the singer and drew mainly on stanzas 1, 2, 5, 6, 7, and 11 of the original. There are three contemporary musical settings of the song in British Library Add MS 15117 (1616 or earlier), The Lodge Book, Folger Library (early 1570s) and the Dallis Book, Trinity College, Dublin (c. 1583)" [Cambridge: Cambridge University Press, 1974], p. 190).

24. I have argued elsewhere, in "Shakespeare's *Will*: The Temporality of Rape," that Shakespearean signature effects are regularly related not only to Shakespeare's registration of his name but also to the orthographic staging of the writing of this name through the chiastic coordination of the letters *WM*, the first and last letters of Shakespeare's first name, and also Shakespeare's abbreviation of his name, at least as he signs it to the mortgage deed of Blackfriar's House, "W^M Shakspē"; this happens here, again, with the *O* of Desdemona's "Willow Song," for example, "The fresh streams ran by her, and *m*ur*m*ur'd her *m*oans,/Sing *w*il-low, *w*illow, *w*illow," or "Sing *w*illow, *w*illow, *w*illow;/If I court *m*oe *wom*en you'll couch with *m*oe *m*en"—lines, by the way, Freud cites to exemplify the logic of projective jealousy; see Sigmund Freud, "Certain Neurotic Mechanisms in Jealousy, Paranoia, and Homosexuality" (1922), in *Sexuality and the Psychology of Love*, ed. Philip Rieff (New York: Collier Books, 1970), p. 162.

It can not only be shown that this *WM* formation is related to greek omega—written as ω, but sounded as *O*—but in addition, that there is a longstanding tradition that interprets the orthography of Greek omega in thematic terms that correspond to those I am arguing are associated with the subjectivity effect of the "characteristically Shakespearean." I refer here, too briefly, to the opening of the treatise "On Apparatus and Furnaces: Authentic Commentaries on the Letter Omega," by the third-century hermetical alchemist known as Zosimos:

> Round Omega is the bipartite letter, the one that in terms of material language belongs to the seventh planetary zone, that of Kronos. For in terms of the immaterial it is something else altogether, something inexplicable, which only Nokotheos the hidden knows. In material terms Omega is what he calls "Ocean, it says, 'the birth and seed of all gods.' " as he says, "the governing principles of material language." (*Zosimos of Panopolis On the Letter Omega*, ed. and trans. Howard M. Jackson [Missoula, Mo.: University of Montana Press, 1978], p. 17).

Zosimos, though obscure, is important because he contributes to an influential tradition of hermetic and alchemical iconography that survives up through and beyond the Renaissance; there are many manuscript versions of his commentary scattered through the libraries of Europe. (There is also reason to suppose that Lacan would have been familiar with the document, either from the partial version printed in the *Corpus Hermeticum*, ed. Arthur Nock and André-Jean Festugière, Vol. 4 [Paris: Société d'éditions "les Belles Lettres," 1954], pp. 117-121, or the full version printed in Carl Jung's *Psychologie und Alchemie* [Zurich: Rascher Verlag, 1952], pp. 360-368.)

The significance of this text, in this context, is that for someone like Shakespeare, who has only a little Greek, the Greek alphabet would not have been a transparent medium of signification; on the contrary, the graphic inscription of the Greek alphabet would have been for Shakespeare something whose typographic materiality would be literally visualizable. This suggests that when Shakespeare had Greek in his mind, or when he thought the letter omega—again, written as ω, but sounded as O—he would have *seen* ω but would have *heard O*. Accordingly, it is through this slippage between the visual and the spoken, mediated by the unrepresentable phenomenality of writing, that the sound of O in *Othello* acquires its *characteristically* Shakespearean subjective properties.

What is thus *idiosyncratically* Shakespearean, however, also corresponds with what is a general, even a generic, tradition assembled around omega. Consider, in this context, the editor's note on the passage from Zosimos cited above: "The shape of the Greek letter omega (ω) suggests the descriptions of 'round' and 'bipartite.' The reason for their inclusion is not so obvious, but it is probably in anticipation of correlating the letter omega with Ocean. Ocean was conceived to be a river that encircled the world; Homer describes the shield of Hephaistos for Achilles as depicting Ocean flowing around its outer rim (*Iliad*, 18.607; cf. also Herodotus 4.8) [cf. the Mandeville or Lacan illustrations above; also the circular river of blood that surrounds the dying Lucrece]. This fact accounts for omega's being called *stroggulōn* [round]. The explanation for *dimerēs* [bipartite] is perhaps that Zosimos held ocean to be a hermaphrodite being. The alchemist Ólympiodoros (who just may be identical with the Neo-Platonic commentator of Plato) cites Zosimos as saying that the sea is *arreno-thēlus* [bisexual] (Berthelot II, iv, 32, texte grec 89.19). The background for this odd, un-Greek conception is supplied by a statement in Diodorus of Sicily (actually his source Hekataios of Abdera): the Egyptians say that 'the ancients named the moist element "Okeane," which means "Sustenance Mother"'; but by some of the Greeks it is held to be "Okeanos" (i.e., masculine)' (1.12.5). In classical Egyptian cosmogonies the primeval waters of chaos are a divine syzygy, Nwn and Nwnt. Furthermore, Diodorus (1.12.6) goes on to say that the Egyptians consider Ocean to be the Nile, and the ancient Egyptians often depicted the god Nile as a man with pendulous breasts" (p. 39).

The central practical literary question raised by the regular occurrence of the Shakespearean signature is to determine what topoi control the relation of the speaking to the writing of a name. In *Othello*, writing calls up a particularly coded erotic name, which is why Othello would rather not write: "Was this fair paper, this most goodly book,/Made to write 'whore' upon?" (4.2.71-72). Accordingly, Othello strangles Desdemona rather than scar her, for reasons Lacan articulates in the conclusion of the quotation from "The Subversion of the Subject" cited above: "For this subject who thinks he can accede to himself by designating himself in the statement, is no more than such an object. Ask the writer about the anxiety that he experiences when faced by the blank sheet of paper, and he will tell you who is the turd (*l'étron*) of his phantasy," p. 315. In Shakespeare's tragedies *l'étron*, like the "letter," always returns to its sender in inverted form:

> *Othello:*   I took by th' throat the circumcised dog,—and smote him—thus.
> *Lodovico:* O bloody period! (5.2.355-357)

4. Why Does Freud Giggle When the Women Leave the Room?

1. Freud, *Jokes and Their Relation to the Unconscious*, trans. James Strachey (New York: Norton, 1963). Page numbers will be found in the text.

2. Jeffrey Mehlman, "How to Read Freud on Jokes: The Critic as *Schadchen*," *New Literary History*, VI, no. 2 (1975): 439-61.

3. This analysis of the male homosexual economy that underlies Freud's theory as well as our supposedly heterosexual cultural institutions and that insists on the form of homology is based on the work of Luce Irigaray. See, especially, *Speculum de l'autre femme* (Paris: Minuit, 1974).

4. Freud, *Jokes*, p. 16. Quoted from Heinrich Heine, "The Baths of Lucca" in *Pictures of Travel*, trans. Charles Godfrey Leland (New York: Appleton, 1898), p. 296. Leland translates the condensed adverb as "famillionaire."

5. The Female Subject: (What) Does Woman Want?

Bernheimer, Charles and Claire Kahane, eds., *In Dora's Case: Freud-Hysteria-Feminism* (New York: Columbia University Press, 1985).

Cardinal, Marie, *Parole de Femme* (Paris: Livre de Poche, 1984).

Chasseguet-Smirgel, J., *La sexualité féminine* (Paris: PBP, 1964).

Chawaf, Chantal, "La chair linguistique," in *Nouvelles littéraires* (May, 1976). Translated in *New French Feminisms*, Marks and de Courtivron, eds.

Cixous, Hélène, "The Laugh of the Medusa," *Signs* (Summer, 1976).

Cixous, Hélène, and Catherine Clément, "La jeune née" (Paris: Union Générale d'Editions, 10/18, 1975).

Clément, Catherine, "Enclave Esclave," in *L'arc*, no. 61 (1975), excerpted in *New French Feminisms*, Marks and de Courtivron, eds.

Clément, Catherine, *Vies et légendes de Jacques Lacan* (Paris: Grasset, 1981).

Davis, Robert Con, ed. *Lacan and Narration* (Baltimore: Johns Hopkins University Press, 1985).

Flieger, Jerry Aline, "The Purloined Punchline: Joke as Textual Paradigm," in *Lacan and Narration*, Davis, ed.

Gagnon, Madeleine, "Corps I," in *La venue à l'écriture* (Paris: Union Générale d'Editions, 10/18, 1977).

Gallop, Jane, *The Daughter's Seduction: Feminism and Psychoanalysis* (Ithaca: Cornell University Press, 1982).

Garner, Shirley Nelson, Claire Kahane, and Madelon Sprengnether, eds., *The (M)Other Tongue: Essays in Psychoanalytic Interpretation* (Ithaca: Cornell University Press, 1985).

Gaudin, C., M. J. Green, L. A. Higgins, Marianne Hirsch, V. Kogan, C. Reeder, and Nancy Vickers, eds., *Feminist Readings: French Texts/American Contexts, Yale French Studies*, no. 62 (1981).

Hertz, Neil, ed., *Freud and Dora: A Fine Romance, Diacritics* (Spring, 1983).

Hirsch, Marianne, "Jocasta's Dream," paper presented at the December 1985 Modern Language Association Convention.

Horer, Suzanne, and Jeanne Socquet, *La création étouffée* (Horay, 1974), excerpted in *New French Feminisms*.

Irigaray, Luce, *Ce sexe qui n'en est pas un* (Paris: Editions de minuit, 1977). Translated by Catherine Porter as *This Sex Which is Not One* (Ithaca: Cornell University Press, 1985).

_____. *Speculum de l'autre femme* (Paris: Editions de minuit, 1974).

Jardine, Alice. "Pretexts for the Transatlantic Feminist," in *Yale French Studies*, no. 62 (1981) (cited above).

Johnson, Barbara, "The Frame of Reference," in *Literature and Psychoanalysis: The Question of Reading: Otherwise* (Baltimore: Johns Hopkins University Press, 1982).

Kahn, Coppélia, "The Hand That Rocks the Cradle: Recent Gender Theories and Their Implications," in *The (M)Other Tongue*, Garner, Kahane, and Sprengnether, eds., cited above.

Kofman, Sarah, *The Enigma of Woman* (Ithaca: Cornell University Press, 1985).

Kristeva, Julia, "La femme, ce n'est jamais ça," in *Tel Quel* (Autumn, 1974), excerpted in *New French Feminisms*.

———. *Polylogue* (Paris: Editions de minuit, 1977).

Lacan, Jacques, "Séminaire sur 'La Lettre volée,' " *Ecrits I* (Paris: Editions du Seuil, 1966).

Leclerc, Annie, *Parole de femme* (Paris: Livre de Poche, 1984).

Marks, Elaine, and Isabelle de Courtivron, eds., *New French Feminisms* (New York: Schocken Books, 1981).

Mitchell, Juliet, *Psycho-analysis and Feminism* (London: Allen Lane, 1974, and New York: Pantheon Books, 1974).

Mitchell, Juliet, and Jacqueline Rose, eds., *Feminine Sexuality: Jacques Lacan and the école freudienne* (New York: W.W. Norton and Co., 1983).

Montrelay, Michèle, *L'Ombre et le nom: sur la féminité* (Paris: Editions de minuit, 1977).

Rich, Adrienne, *Of Woman Born* (New York: W.W. Norton and Co., 1976).

Rose, Jacqueline, "Dora: Fragment of an Analysis," in *In Dora's Case*, Bernheimer and Kahane, eds. (cited above).

Ruthven, K. K., *Feminist Literary Studies: An Introduction* (Cambridge: Cambridge University Press, 1984).

Schor, Naomi, "Female Paranoia: The Case for Psychoanalytic Feminist Criticism," in *Yale French Studies*, no. 62 (1981) (cited above).

———. "*Eugénie Grandet*: Mirrors and Melancholia," in *The (M)Other Tongue*, Garner, Kahane, and Sprengnether, eds. (cited above).

Sprengnether, Madelon, "Enforcing Oedipus: Freud and Dora," in *In Dora's Case*, Bernheimer and Kahane, eds. (cited above).

Suleiman, Susan Rubin, "Writing and Motherhood," in *The (M)Other Tongue*, Garner, Kahane, and Sprengnether, eds. (cited above).

6. Lacan's Seminars on James Joyce

André, Serge. *Qui veut une femme?* Paris: Navarin, 1986.

Aramburu, J., et al. "Journal: 'Le Seminario Lacanio' de Buenos Aires." *Ornicar?* 33 (1985): 170-73.

Aubert, Jacques. "Avant Propos." *Joyce avec Lacan.* 13-18.

———. "Galeries pour un portrait." *Joyce avec Lacan.* 69-84.

———. "Le sinthome, Séminaire du 20 janvier 1976." *Joyce avec Lacan.* 49-67.

———, ed. *Joyce avec Lacan. Paris: Navarin, 1987.*

Bergeron, Danielle. "Jouer sa vie sur un semblant." Folie, Mystique et Poésie. Ed. Raymond Lemieux. Québec: Collection Noeud de GIFRIC, 1988. 161-82.

Freud, Sigmund. *Beyond the Pleasure Princple.* 1920. *The Standard Edition of the Complete Psychological Works of Sigmund Freud*, vol. 18. Ed. James Strachey. 24 vols. London: Hogarth, 1953-74.

———. *The Psychopathology of Everyday Life.* 1913. *Standard Edition*, vol. 6.

———. *Totem and Taboo*, 1913. *Standard Edition*, vol. 13, pp. 1-162.

Grigg, Russell. "The Function of the Father in Psychoanalysis." *Autralian Journal of Psychotherapy* 18 (1986): 116-26.

Grisolia, Adriana. "James Joyce y el nombre del padre." *Revista del cercle psicoanalic de Catalunya* 5 (1988): 29-31.

Guir, Jean. *Psychosomatique et cancer*. Paris: Points Hors Ligne, 1983.

Joyce, James. *Finnegans Wake*. New York: Viking, 1939.

———. *A Portrait of the Artist as a Young Man*. New York: Viking, 1964.

———. *Ulysses, the Corrected Text*. Ed. Hans Walter Gabler, et al. New York: Random House, 1986.

Kuberski, Philip. "The Joycean Gaze: Lucia and the I of the Father." *Sub-stance* 46(1985): 49-66.

Lacan, Jacques. "The agency of the letter in the unconscious or reason since Freud." *Ecrits: A Selection*. 146-78.

———. *Ecrits: A Selection*. Ed. and trans. Alan Sheridan. New York: Norton, 1977.

———. "The Freudian thing or the meaning of the return to Freud in psychoanalysis." *Ecrits: A Selection*. 114-45.

———. "The function and field of speech and language in psychoanalysis." *Ecrits: A Selection*. 30-113.

———. "Joyce le symptôme I." Aubert, *Joyce avec Lacan*. 21-29.

———. "Joyce le symptôme II." Aubert, *Joyce avec Lacan*. 31-36.

———. "Kanzer Seminar, Yale University." 24 November 1975. Unedited lecture. Written down by some of Lacan's students from stenographed notes and from tapes. Published as *Jacques Lacan: Conférences et entretiens dans des universités nord-américaines*. Later published in *Scilicet* 6/7.

———. "La psychanalyse et son enseignement." *Ecrits*. Paris: Seuil, 1966. 437-58.

———. *Le Séminaire: livre XX: Encore* (1972-73). Ed. Jacques-Alain Miller. Paris: Seuil, 1975.

———. *Le Séminaire: livre XXIII: Le Sinthome*, 1975-76. Text to be edited by Jacques-Alain Miller.

———. "Le Sinthome, Séminaire du 18 novembre 1975." Aubert, *Joyce avec Lacan*. 37-48.

———. "Le Symptôme, Columbia University." 1975. Published as *Jacques Lacan*. Later published in *Scilicet*.

———. "Subversion of the subject and dialectic of desire in the Freudian unconscious." *Ecrits: A Selection*. 292-325.

Lajonquière, Carlos, et al. "Quelques questions sur la prépsychose." *Clinique différentielle des psychoses: Fondation du champ freudien*. Ed. Lilia Mahjoub-Trobas, et al. Paris: Navarin, 1988. 11-24.

MacCabe, Colin. *James Joyce and the Revolution of the Word*. London: Macmillan, 1979.

Miller, Dominique. "Sur le signifiant du transfert: des entrées en analyse—'Les trois transferts.'" *Ornicar?* 33 (1985): 31-36.

Miller, Jacques-Alain. "A and a in Clinical Structures." *Acts of the Paris-New York Psychoanalytic Workshop*. Ed. Stuart Schneiderman. 1986. New York: Schneiderman, 1987. 14-29.

———. "Avertissement." *Cahiers pour l'Analyse* 1 (1966): 4-5.

———. "Introduction to *Television*." *Newsletter of the Freudian Field* 3 (1988): 6-16.

_____. "Préface." Aubert, *Joyce avec Lacan.* 9-12.

Millot, Catherine. "Epiphanies." Aubert, *Joyce avec Lacan.* 87-95.

O'Brien, Edna. "She was the Other Ireland." Rev. of *The Real Life of Molly Bloom,* by Brenda Maddox. *New York Times Book Review,* 19 June 1988: 33.

Ragland-Sullivan, Ellie. *Jacques Lacan and the Philosophy of Psychoanalysis.* Urbana: U of Illinois P, 1987.

_____. "La forclusion lacanienne: les origines de la psychose." *Folie, Mystique et Poésie.* Ed. Raymond Lemieux. Québec: Collection Noeud de GIFRIC, 1988. 199-227.

Rotmistrovsky, Hugo. "Joyce, el nombre." *Revista del cercle psicoanalic de Catalunya* 5 (1988): 33-39.

Schreiber, Francoise. "Sept remarques de Jacques-Alain Miller sur la création." Notes taken from Miller's Seminar on "Les psychoses et le sinthome." *La lettre mensuelle* 68 (1988): 9-13.

Zizek, Slavoj. "The Limits of a Semiotic Approach to Psychoanalysis." Chapter Seven in this volume.

_____. "The Marxist Symptom." *Lacanian Theory: A Reader.* Ed. Mark Bracher et al. Urbana: U of Illinois P, forthcoming.

_____. "Why Lacan is Not a 'Post-Structuralist.' " *Newsletter of the Freudian Field* 2 (1987): 31-39.

7. The Limits of the Semiotic Approach to Psychoanalysis

1. J. Lacan, *Le Séminaire III* (Paris: Seuil, 1981), p. 303.

2. E. Nolte, *Three Faces of Fascism* (University of Toronto Press, 1969), p. 85.

3. G. K. Chesterton, "Défense des romans policiers," in *Autopsies du roman policier* (Paris: 1983), pp. 40-41.

4. B. Pascal, *Pensées* 294.

5. I. Kant, *Die metaphysik der Sitten. Erster Teil: Metaphysische Anfangsgründe der Rechtslehre,* par. 49 and 52.

6. Cf. J. Lacan, *Ecrits* (Paris: Seuil, 1966), p. 168.

7. I. Kant, *Anthropologie,* par. 60.

8. J. Lacan, *Le Séminaire XI* (Paris: Seuil, 1973), p. 168.

9. Lacan, *Le Séminaire XI,* p. 169.

10. G. W. F. Hegel, *Grundlinien der Philosophie des Rechts,* par. 280, *Zusatz.*

11. Hegel, *Grundlinien,* par. 279, *Zusatz.*

12. Hegel, *Grundlinien.*

13. S. Kierkegaard, "Der Begriff des Auserwählten," quoted from M. Horkheimer, *Traditonnelle und kritische Theorie* (Frankfurt: 1968), p. 210.

14. J. Lacan, *Le Séminaire III,* p. 313.

15. J. Lacan, *Ecrits,* p. 821.

8. The Politics of Impossibility

1. Perry Anderson, *In the Tracks of Historical Materialism* (London: New Left Books, 1983), p. 57.

2. Martin Jay, *Marxism and Totality: The Adventures of a Concept from Lukács to Habermas* (Berkeley: University of California Press, 1984), p. 537.

3. Fredric Jameson, *The Political Unconscious: Narrative as a Socially Symbolic Act* (Ithaca: Cornell University Press, 1981), p. 70.

4. Ernesto Laclau and Chantal Mouffe, *Hegemony and Socialist Strategy: Towards a Radical Democratic Politics* (London: New Left Books, 1985).

5. For *l'une-tévue*, see "*L'insu que sait de l'une-bévue, s'aile a mourre,*" Lacan's seminar of 1976-77, a portion of which is in *Ornicar?*, 14 (Spring 1978). *Encore* (Paris: Seuil, 1975) is the seminar in which Lacan most directly addresses the concept of *pas-toute*.

6. Among feminist interpreters of Lacan, Jacqueline Rose has been most insistent and successful in pointing out the political significance of continuing to ask psychoanalytical questions about the difficulty of sexual identity. See *Sexuality in the Field of Vision* (Verso: London, 1986).

7 Sigmund Freud, *An Autobiographical Study, Standard Edition of the Complete Psychological Works*, ed. J. Strachey (London: Hogarth Press, 1955), Vol. XX, p. 74. The last page of the main text reads: "While [psychoanalysis] was originally the name of a particular therapeutic method, it has now also become the name of a science—the science of unconscious mental processes" (p. 70).

8. Freud, Letter to Schnier (July 5, 1938) quoted by Ernest Jones in *The Life and Work of Sigmund Freud* (New York: Basic Books, 1957), Vol. II, p. 301.

9. An impressive critique along these lines can be found in Samuel Weber's *The Legend of Freud* (Minneapolis: University of Minnesota Press, 1982). Weber's sense of a coherent "system" draws more upon its antecedents in metaphysics that upon any overview of the synthetic aspirations of science itself. On this general point, Freud was insistent that psychoanalysis need not publicize a world-view of its own: "it does not need one: it is a part of science and can adhere to the scientific Weltanschauung." He goes on to quote Heine's lines about the philosopher's audacious eccentricity in order to decorate his point: "with his nightcaps and the tatters of his dressing gown he patches up the gaps in the structure of the universe." *New Introductory Lectures on Psychoanalysis, Standard Edition*, Vol. XXII, p. 181 and p. 161.

10. François Roustang, *Psychoanalysis Never Lets Go*, trans. Ned Lukacher (Baltimore: Johns Hopkins University Press, 1983), p. 120.

11. Freud met head-on with such an origin-based complaint at least once, in *The Question of Lay Analysis*, and responded with a properly psychoanalytical reading of the medical claims to possession of his work:

    It is argued that psychoanalysis was after all discovered by a physician in the course of his efforts to assist his patients. But that is clearly neither here nor there. Moreover, the historical argument is double-edged. We might pursue the story and recall the unfriendliness and indeed the animosity with which the medical profession treated analysis from the very first. That would seem to imply that it can have no claims over analysis today. And although I do not accept that implication, I still feel some doubts as to whether the present wooing of psychoanalysis by the doctors is based, from the point of view of the libido theory, upon the first or the second of Abraham's substages—whether they wish to take possession of their object for the purpose of destroying or of preserving it. (*Standard Edition*, Vol. XX, p. 253)

12. Lacan, "Conferences et entretiens," Yale University, November 1975, *Scilicet*, 6/7 (1976), p. 18.

13. Jacques Lacan, "Une practique de bavardage" (Seminar, November 1977), *Ornicar?*, 19 (1979), p. 9.

14. For sundry discussions by Lacan on the question of the "impossibility" of the "group," see "Le psychanalyse de l'école," *Scilicet*, 1 (1968), p. 36, and "L'étourdit," *Scilicet*, 4 (1973), p. 31.

15. Jacques Lacan, "Lettre de dissolution," *Ornicar?*, 20/21 (1980), pp. 9-10. Over the course of the year preceding the dissolution Lacan had made ample reference to the "horde" effect. In the two months before the dissolution, he had been silent, an event which gave rise to the long predicted mass anxiety, and at the pitch of that anxiety, he played out the hitherto unvoiced assumptions about his magisterial discourse by suggesting that "if it turns out that I have to go away, tell yourselves that it is in order to be the Other at last," "L'Autre manque," *Ornicar?*, 20/21, p. 12. While Lacan was only confirming what had long been obvious to his students, the dissolution still produced all of the calamitous social effects normally reserved for a catastrophe no one had thought possible. In this way it truly was made to appear as if it were an "impossible" occurrence.

16. "La mort de Jacques Lacan—Un communiqué de l'Ecole de la Cause Freudienne," *Quarto*, 2 (September 1981), p. 4. See also the "Dossier on the Institutional Debate," trans. Jeffrey Mehlman, *October*, 40 (Spring 1987), pp. 51-133, which brings together important documents relating to Lacan's splits with various psychoanalytical institutions, from 1953 onwards.

17. In his analysis of the history of the relation of psychoanalysis to social thought, Russell Jacoby argues that the Frankfurt critique of "character" was a way of further mediating the often contradictory claims to critical attention of "social necessity" and "individual instinct." *Social Amnesia* (Boston: Beacon Press, 1975), p. 84ff.

18. François Roustang, *Dire Mastery*, trans. Ned Lukacher (Baltimore: Johns Hopkins University Press, 1983). I have dealt with Roustang's arguments and various objections to them at greater length in "Knowledge and Theory in Psychoanalysis," *The Dalhousie Review*, 64, 2 (Summer 1984), pp. 221-46.

19. Sigmund Freud, "On the History of the Psycho-Analytic Movement," *Standard Edition*, Vol. XIV, p. 45.

20. For a meticulous assault on the empirical point of view in the philosophy of science, see B. R. Cosin, G. F. Freeman, and N. H. Freeman, "Critical Empiricism Criticised: The Case of Freud," in *The Journal of the Theory of Social Behaviour*, I, 2, pp. 121-51.

9. Psychoanalysis Modern and Post-Modern

1. See Paul de Man, "Literary History and Literary Modernity," in *Blindness and Insight: Essays in the Rhetoric of Contemporary Criticism* (Minneapolis: University of Minnesota Press, 1983), 142-44, 148, 150, 152, 164-65.

2. Henry Sussman, *High Resolution: Critical Theory and the Problem of Literacy* (New York: Oxford University Press, 1988), pp. 11-15.

3. Twentieth-century literature has demonstrated its structuralist interest and form in a variety of ways: thematically, through its references to kaleidoscopes, decks of cards, and other combinatorial instruments and games; formally, through its incorporation (and disfiguration) of such formats as outlines, bibliographies, and lists. My list of favorite twentieth-century structuralist literary works would include the following: Franz Kafka, "Prometheus," "Description of a Struggle;" James Joyce, *Ulysses*; Albert Camus, *The Plague*; Jorge Luis Borges, "Tlön, Uqbar, Orbis Tertius;" Julio Cortázar, *Hopscotch*; and Italo Calvino, *If on a winter's night a traveller*.

4. See Walter Benjamin, "Theses on the Philosophy of History," in *Illuminations*, ed. and intro. Hannah Arendt (New York: Schocken, 1969), pp. 257-58.

5. See Marcel Proust, *A la recherche du temps perdu*, ed. Pierre Clarac and André Ferré (Paris: Pléiade, 1954), I, 208-11, 222-25, 344-53, 434-40, 446-51, 549-58, 834-40; III, 248-65, 995-98, 1002-03, 1013-15, 1029-48.

6. Henry Sussman, "The University of Verse," in *High Resolution*, pp. 124-31, 180, 186-89.

7. Citations of Freud in this paper refer to Sigmund Freud, *The Standard Edition of the Complete Psychological Works of Sigmund Freud* (London: Hogarth Press, 1953-74). I henceforth abbreviate this edition "*S.E.*".

8. Homer, *The Odyssey of Homer: A Modern Translation by Richmond Lattimore* (New York: Harper & Row, 1975), pp. 168-84 (Book XI in entirety).

9. See Claude Lévi-Strauss, "The Science of the Concrete," in *The Savage Mind* (Chicago: University of Chicago Press, 1966), pp. 16-22, 29-33.

10. Henry Sussman, "An American History Lesson: Hegel and the Historiography of Super-imposition," forthcoming in *Theorizing American Literature: Hegel, the Sign, and History*, ed. Bainard Cowan and Joseph Kronick (Baton Rouge: Louisiana State University Press).

11. See Benjamin, *Illuminations*, pp. 157-65, 174-76.

12. See Rodolphe Gasché, *The Tain of the Mirror: Derrida and the Philosophy of Reflection* (Cambridge: Harvard University Press, 1986), pp. 147-53, 194-205.

13. See Jacques Lacan, *The Four Fundamental Concepts of Psycho-Analysis*, ed. Jacques-Alain Miller, trans. Alan Sheridan (New York: W.W. Norton, 1978), p. 45. All citations of Lacan in the present chapter refer to this volume, which I abbreviate "*FFC*".

14. See Theodor Adorno, *Negative Dialectics*, trans. E. B. Ashton (New York: Continuum, 1973), pp. 4-7, 13, 19, 21, 27, 29, 34-40, 56-57.

15. See Otto Kernberg, *Borderline Conditions and Pathological Narcissism* (New York: Jason Aronson, 1975), pp. 36-37. This passage is an exemplary of Kernberg's writing as it is extraordinary.

16. I think in particular of the endless self-qualification to be found in Thomas Bernhard, *Correction*, trans. Sophie Wilkins (New York: Vintage, 1979).

10. Psychoanalysis and Decosntruction and Woman

1. Derrida, *Spurs: Nietzsche's Styles*, trans. Barbara Harlow (Chicago: University of Chicago Press, 1978), pp. 35-36. All subsequent references to Derrida are to this essay.

2. Derrida, *Spurs*, p. 49. Alice Jardine has recently explored the attempts of such postmodern theorists in terms of what she calls "gynesis," or a putting into discourse "a woman-in-effect that is never stable and has no identity." See *Gynesis: Configurations of Woman and Modernity* (Ithaca: Cornell University Press, 1985), p. 25. I will be elaborating some of the implications of Jardine's writing later in this essay.

3. Barbara Johnson, "The Frame of Reference: Poe, Lacan, Derrida," *The Critical Difference: Essays in the Contemporary Rhetoric of Reading* (Baltimore: Johns Hopkins University Press, 1980); rpt. in *Literature and Psychoanalysis, The Question of Reading: Otherwise*, ed. Shoshana Felman (Baltimore: Johns Hopkins University Press, 1982), p. 458. Subsequent page references are to this edition, also cited later for Felman's remarks.

4. Johnson, "Frame," p. 505.

5. Johnson, "Frame," pp. 465-67.

6. Jacques Lacan, "The Freudian Thing," *Ecrits: A Selection*, trans. Alan Sheridan (New York: Norton, 1977), p. 121. Subsequent references to Lacan are to this essay.

7. Lacan, "Freudian Thing," p. 122.

8. Lacan, "Freudian Thing," p. 124.

9. See Ragland-Sullivan's commentary on "Lacan's rewriting of Actaeon myth" in her *Jacques Lacan and the Philosophy of Psychoanalysis* (Urbana: University of Illinois Press, 1986), pp. 300-301.

10. Gayatri Chakravorty Spivak, "Love Me, Love My Ombre, Elle," *Diacritics*, 14, 4 (1984), 22.

11. Derrida, *Spurs*, pp. 38-39 and 57.

12. Consider this comment, for instance, from Gayle Greene and Coppélia Kahn in their introduction to a collection of essays on feminist literary criticism: "Feminist scholarship received its impetus from the women's movement of the late 1960s and 1970s, but it participates in the more general dethroning of authority begun by Freud, Marx and Saussure. . . ." See *Making a Difference: Feminist Literary Criticism*, ed. Greene and Kahn (London: Methuen, 1985), p. 2.

13. Jardine, *Gynesis*, pp. 37-41.

14. Jardine, *Gynesis*, p. 42.

15. Jardine, *Gynesis*, p. 25.

16. Jane Gallop, *The Daughter's Seduction: Feminism and Psychoanalysis* (Ithaca: Cornell University Press, 1982), p. xv. Though my references to Gallop are to this book, a richer appreciation of her own exchange with Lacan would also take into account her more recent book, *Reading Lacan* (Ithaca: Cornell University Press, 1986).

17. Jardine, *Gynesis*, p. 28.

18. Gallop, *The Daughter's Seduction*, p. 34.

19. See, for instance, Toril Moi's discussion of these matters in *Sexual/Textual Politics: Feminist Literary Theory* (London: Methuen, 1985), especially pp. 1-18.

20. Derrida, *Spurs*, p. 49.

21. Ragland-Sullivan, *Jacques Lacan*, p. 15.

22. Jardine, *Gynesis*, p. 183.

23. Ragland-Sullivan, *Jacques Lacan*, p. 67.

24. Irigaray, *This Sex Which Is Not One*, trans. Catherine Porter (Ithaca: Cornell University Press, 1985), p. 164.

25. Irigaray, *This Sex*, p. 78.

26. Cixous, "Sorties," in *The Newly Born Woman*, trans. Betsy Wing, Theory and History of Literature, Vol. 24 (Minneapolis: University of Minnesota Press, 1986), p. 79.

27. Cixous, "Sorties," p. 85.

28. Jardine, *Gynesis*, p. 38.

29. Felman, "To Open the Question," in *Literature and Psychoanalysis*, pp. 5-10.

30. Anne McLeod, "Gender Difference Relativity in GDR-Writing or: How to Oppose Without Really Trying," *Oxford Literary Review*, 59.

31. Jessica Benjamin, "A Desire of One's Own: Psychoanalytic Feminism and Intersubjective Space," in *Feminist Studies/Critical Studies*, ed. Teresa de Lauretis (Bloomington: Indiana University Press, 1986), pp. 97-98.

11. *The Bostonians* and the Figure of the Speaking Woman

1. See Jean Strouse's biography, *Alice James* (Boston: Houghton Mifflin, 1980) for a fascinating discussion of the symptoms of the James household.

2. On this reading of hysteria, see Juliet Mitchell, "The Question of Femininity and the Theory of Psychoanalysis" in *Women: The Longest Revolution* (New York: Pantheon, 1984). For other recent readings of the meaning of hysterical symptoms, see *In Dora's Case*, ed. Charles Bernheimer and Claire Kahane (New York: Columbia University Press, 1985).

3. In conversation with Ellen DuBois, historian. Also see Ellen DuBois, "The Radicalism of the Woman Suffrage Movement: Notes Toward the Reconstruction of Nineteenth-Century Feminism," *Feminist Studies*, vol. 3 (Fall, 1975).

4. *The Notebooks of Henry James*, ed. F. O. Matthiessen and Kenneth B. Murdock (London: Oxford University Press, 1947), pp. 46-47. cited in the appendix to *The Bostonians*, ed. Alfred Habegger (Indianapolis: Bobbs-Merrill, 1976), p. 429. All quotations from *The Bostonians* are to this edition.

5. See Neil Schmitz, "Mark Twain, Henry James, and Jacksonian Dreaming," *Criticism*, 27 (1985): pp. 155-173.

12. Faulkner's Dispossession of Personae Non Gratae

Barthes, Roland. *Mythologies*. Trans. Annette Lavers. New York: Hill and Wang, 1972.

Bakhtin, M. M. *The Dialogic Imagination*. Ed. Michael Holquist. Trans. Caryl Emerson and Michael Holquist. Austin: U Texas P, 1981.

Conley, Tom. "Reading Ordinary Viewing." *Diacritics* 15.1 (1985): 4-14.

Faulkner, William. *Absalom, Absalom!* New York: Random House, 1936.

_____. *Flags in the Dust*. New York: Random House, 1973.

_____. *Sanctuary*. New York: Random House, 1931.

_____. *The Sound and the Fury*. New York: Random House, 1956.

Jardine, Alice. "Pre-texts for the Transatlantic Feminist." *Yale French Studies* (1981): 220-236.

Johnson, Barbara. *A World of Difference*. Johns Hopkins UP, 1987.

Lacan, Jacques. *Ecrits: A Selection*. Trans. Alan Sheridan. New York: Norton, 1977.

_____. "Of Structure as an Inmixing of an Otherness Prerequisite to Any Subject Whatever." *The Structuralist Controversy*. Ed. Richard Macksey and Eugenio Donato. Baltimore: Johns Hopkins UP, 1970.

Rose, Jacqueline. " 'Where does the misery come from?': Psychoanalysis, Feminism and the Event." *Feminism and Psychoanalysis*. Ed. Richard Feldstein and Judith Roof. Ithaca: Cornell UP, 1989.

13. A Shattered Globe

1. Virginia Woolf, *Moments of Being: Unpublished Autobiographical Writings*, ed. Jeanne Schulkind (New York: Harcourt Brace, 1976). All references in my text, unless otherwise identified, are to this volume.

2. References to Virginia Woolf's works, all published in New York by Harcourt Brace, will be abbreviated in the text as follows:

> BTA *Between the Acts* (1941); HH *A Haunted House and Other Short Stories* (1941); TTL *To the Lighthouse* (1929); W *The Waves* (1931); WD *A Writer's Diary* (1954).

3. References abbreviated SE are to Sigmund Freud, *The Standard Edition of the Complete Psychological Works of Sigmund Freud*, ed. James Strachey (London: Hogarth Press, 1953-1966) by volume and page number.

4. See D. W. Winnicott, *Playing and Reality* (London: Penguin, 1971), pp. 13-14.

5. See Bertram Lewis, "Sleep, the Mouth, and the Dream Screen," *The Psychoanalytic Quarterly* XV (1946) and, by the same author, "Reconsideration of the Dream Screen," *The Psychoanalytic Quarterly* XXII (1953).

6. See Winnicott, pp. 101-11.

7. See Jacques Lacan, "The mirror stage as formative of the function of the I as revealed in psychoanalytic experience," in *Ecrits: A Selection*, trans. Alan Sheridan (New York: Norton, 1977).

8. See Winnicott, pp. 130-38.

9. Following the lead of Lacan and others, I am using the term "ideal ego" here to refer to an unconscious narcissistic formation that "involves a primary identification with another being invested with omnipotence—namely, the mother" (Daniel Lagache, as quoted by J. Laplanche and J.-B. Pontalis, *The Language of Psychoanalysis* [New York: Norton, 1973], p. 202). This concept should be distinguished from that of the "ego ideal," associated with the system of prohibitions internalized in the superego.

10. See the chapter entitled "Aggressivité et sado-masochisme" in Jean Laplanche, *Vie et mort en psychanalyse* (Paris: Flammarion, 1970), translated by Jeffrey Mehlman as *Life and Death in Psychoanalysis* (Baltimore: Johns Hopkins University Press, 1976), and Leo Bersani, *Baudelaire and Freud* (Berkeley: University of California Press, 1977).

11. Laplanche, p. 155 (my translation).

12. See Robert Stolorow, "The Narcissistic Function of Masochism (and Sadism)," *International Journal of Psychoanalysis* (1975) 56:331-38 for an illuminating overview of psychoanalytic opinion on this subject.

13. André Green observes that for the narcissist "the body is the Other that returns despite the effort to efface its trace" (*Narcissisme de vie, narcissisme de mort* [Paris: Editions de minuit, 1983], p. 191).

14. My analysis here is indebted to Leo Bersani's extremely suggestive discussion of the role of the superego in the constitution of the self in *Baudelaire and Freud*, pp. 92-93 and 113-15.

15. Writing specifically about the responses of children who have been subjected to incestuous seductions, Sándor Ferenczi observes that a frequent reaction of these abused children who feel "physically and morally helpless [in relation to] the overpowering force and authority of the adult" is to identify themselves with, or introject, the aggressor. Thereby, comments Ferenczi, the aggressor "disappears as part of the external reality, and becomes intra- instead of extra-psychic [becomes, in Woolf's case, part of an 'opposite instinct']. . . . The attack as a rigid external reality ceases to exist and in the traumatic trance the child succeeds in maintaining the previous situation of tenderness." (Sándor Ferenczi, "Confusion of Tongues Between the Adult and the Child," *International Journal of Psychoanalysis* 30 [1949], p. 228). This interpretation helps explain Woolf's silence about Gerald and her later amiability with George, Gerald's brother, who also molested her.

16. Later in *A Sketch*, Woolf describes some of the "brutal" scenes her father indulged in before women and answers her own question about why he never acted in this manner in front of men: "Partly of course because the woman was his slave—being the most typical of Victorians" (125).

17. Bersani, p. 88.

18. See, for instance, Jeanne Schulkind's introduction to her edition of *Moments of Being*, pp. 17-22.

19. Freud is explicit in defining trauma in terms precisely analogous to Woolf's: "We describe as traumatic," he writes in *Beyond the Pleasure Principle*, "any excitations from

outside which are powerful enough to break through the protective shield. . . . There is no longer any possibility of preventing the mental apparatus from being flooded with large amounts of stimulus" (SE, 18:29).

20. "The hallucinatory *negative* realization of desire has become the model governing psychic activity. It is not unpleasure that is substituted for pleasure, it is the Neutral. One should not think of depression in this context, but of aphanisis, asceticism, anorexia of living" (Green, p. 23).

21. In a diary entry of October 1923, Woolf writes of the peculiarly intense experience she had one wet, windy night when she suddenly said to herself "Now I am meeting it; now the old devil has once more got his spine through the waves. . . . Reality, so I thought, was unveiled" (*The Diary of Virginia Woolf*, Vol. II, ed. Anne Olivier Bell [New York: Harcourt Brace Jovanovich, 1978], p. 270). "It" here is an agent of revelation, causing Woolf such strong feeling that she "became physically rigid" (the paralysis that marks nearly all her moments of being, as if in these moments she identified with death). The image of a spine emerging through waves is closely related to that of a fin in a waste of water, which, as I argue later, is an emblem for Woolf of ontological rupture.

22. It is too frequently overlooked that Lily Briscoe's vision of Mrs. Ramsay occurs as a function of her effort "to be on a level with ordinary experience, to feel simply that's a chair, that's a table, and yet at the same time, it's a miracle, it's an ecstasy" (TTL, 300). Lily brings back the dead precisely at the moment when she has accepted the death of her subjective priority over bare things.

23. Martin Gliserman, for instance, sees the *To the Lighthouse* as exemplifying "a kind of female bravado" and interprets Lily's completion of her painting as "yet another statement of the powers of the female center, genital and existential, to bring together and to bring forth" ("Virginia Woolf's *To the Lighthouse*: Syntax and the Female Center," *American Imago* [Spring 1983], vol. 40, no. 1, p. 100).

24. Jean Laplanche, *Problématiques III: La Sublimation* (Paris: Presses universitaires de France, 1980), pp. 249-50.

25. This corresponds in remarkable fashion to Walter Benjamin's thesis about Baudelaire. Alluding to Freud's theory of traumatic shocks in *Beyond the Pleasure Principle*, Benjamin asserts that "Baudelaire placed the shock experience at the very center of his artistic work" (*Illuminations*, ed. Hannah Arendt [New York: Harcourt, Brace & World, 1968], p. 165).